'Dr. Nayak has undertaken the gargantuan task of describing his country's development in the broad context of globalization. From his long-time seat at the centre of Indian investing, he has a unique perspective. He persuasively argues that the caution of India's Reserve Bank paid off in avoiding the blunt effect of the Asian crisis by not following the then-popular recipe book and holding off on Rupee convertibility until its capital account was less vulnerable. With the recent growth of India's reserves to unprecedented levels, he now believes that the reward for past caution should be the use of some of these reserves on critical infrastructure needs.'

Antoine W. van Agtmael, President and Chief Investment Officer, Emerging Markets Management L.L.C., Past board member of the India Growth Fund, author of *The Emerging Markets Century* (Simon & Schuster, New York, 2007) and *Emerging Securities Markets*

'Satyendra Nayak's book provides an outstanding analysis of the evolution of the international monetary system and a penetrating evaluation of India's financial performance and economic prospects in the rapidly globalizing world of today. A must-read for anyone interested in these important topics.'

Dr. Dominick Salvatore, Distinguished Professor of Economics and Director of the Ph.D. Program, Fordham University, New York

'Satyendra Nayak's impressive analysis of India's step-by-step approach to capital-account liberalization is important reading for anyone interested in the essentials of financial globalization. He skillfully contrasts the pragmatic Indian approach to the gung-ho financial capitalism that produced the Asian financial crisis of 1997, and offers recommendations for the future.'

Dr. Alfred E. Eckes, Editor, *Global Economy Journal*, Ohio Eminent Research Scholar and Professor in Contemporary History, Ohio University, Athens, Ohio

'India's economy, long a slumbering giant, has benefited greatly from a successful policy of gradualism in reform, which has averted crises while promoting increasingly rapid growth. Full convertibility, Dr. Nayak contends, would be the last mile on the road of economic liberalization. This book should be of interest to anyone interested in the future of a country that is destined to be a major force in the world economy of the twenty-first century.'

Dr. Benjamin J. Cohen, Louis G. Lancaster Professor of International Political Economy, Department of Political Science, University of California, Santa Barbara, Santa Barbara, CA 93106-9420

Globalization and the Indian Economy

This book examines the impact of globalization on the Indian economy, exploring the trade, investment and financial aspects of globalization, and also considering its implications for the balance of payments and currency exchange rate.

The first part of the book deals with the evolution of the philosophy of globalization and its impact on exchange rates, global liquidity, currency markets, and global trade and payments. It highlights the catalytic role played by the US in driving the globalization process, and provides detailed analysis of the evolution of the international monetary system to illustrate current processes of globalization. Furthermore, a critical discussion of the Asian financial crisis of 1997 is presented as well as the lessons that have emerged from the crisis.

The Indian economic experience and its own policy of dealing with globalization is the focus of second part of the book. The author examines the genesis of economic reforms and liberalization in India. The success of the Indian policy of gradualism is discussed in the context of the Asian crisis, and the reasons as to why India averted a similar crisis are explored. Finally, the author examines whether the Indian currency, the rupee, can be made fully convertible.

This book makes a valuable contribution to the literature on globalization and development and should be of interest to academics interested in the global economy, international finance, international development and also to academics with an interest in South Asian Studies.

Satyendra S. Nayak is an independent advisor and consultant. His experience stems from 27 years of working in Commercial Banking and Mutual Fund at the Bank of Baroda and Unit Trust in India, as well as years of experience in operation, international finance, project financing, foreign exchange operations, mutual fund management, equity and debt investments and portfolio management. He received his PhD in International Economics and Finance from the University of Bombay, India. He teaches at ICFAI Business School in Mumbai in the Centre for Advanced Banking and Finance Studies.

Routledge studies in the growth economies of Asia

Globalization and the Indian Economy

Roadmap to convertible rupee

Satyendra S. Nayak

Routledge
Taylor & Francis Group

LONDON AND NEW YORK

First published 2008
by Routledge
2 Park Square, Milton Park, Abingdon, Oxon, OX14 4RN

Simultaneously published in the USA and Canada
by Routledge
270 Madison Ave, New York NY 10016

Routledge is an imprint of the Taylor & Francis Group, an informa business

Transferred to Digital Printing 2009

© 2008 Satyendra S. Nayak

Typeset in Times by Wearset Ltd, Boldon, Tyne and Wear

British Library Cataloguing in Publication Data
A catalogue record for this book is available from the British Library

Library of Congress Cataloging in Publication Data
A catalog record for this book has been requested

ISBN10: 0-415-44739-9 (hbk)
ISBN10: 0-415-54481-5 (pbk)
ISBN10: 0-203-93795-3 (ebk)

ISBN13: 978-0-415-44739-3 (hbk)
ISBN13: 978-0-415-54481-8 (pbk)
ISBN13: 978-0-203-93795-2 (ebk)

To Economics Guru, P.R. Brahmananda

Contents

Illustrations

Figures

Tables

Preface

MOT Revolution: precursor and accelerator of globalization

With all the free and not so free resources with which mother Earth and the solar system has endowed us, it is three human creations – money, organization and technology (MOT) – that have enabled civilization to progress and, more particularly, take breathtaking leaps in the twentieth century. The advances in MOT and their assiduous management in the closing century of the last millennium have been so overwhelming that they have resisted all pressures to be contained within the physical, geographical and political borders called countries. Since the dawn of civilization, money, in different forms, has facilitated and accelerated economic progress, which means more and more, and better and better products and services for consumption by every human being and other benign species that survive and prosper with us. From corn and shells to gold and silver coins, to paper currency, to plastic and digital or electronic money, money or IOUs (I Owe You) have changed shape and size, weight, content and form, and their transaction velocity. The control of money moved from private hands to Kings, and later to autonomous Central Banks. The revolution in money and its prudent management has been the key driver of the post-war sustained and rapid growth in the global economy. Imprudent and uneconomic management of money has bred hyperinflation and also economic depression.

The corporate form of organization, with limited liability, has been the harbinger of large-scale manufacturing, trading and other businesses, and the cornerstone of last century's growth. The ingenuity of this organization is that it has created, nurtured and developed the markets, stock exchanges and capital markets, which moved money flows into productive enterprises, thereby accelerating the investment and growth. Finally, technology has been of overriding importance. It has enabled the transformation of nature's bounties into everything that can satisfy human hunger, need, greed and ego. Technology has squeezed space and time beyond everyone's comprehension and expectations.

MOT abhors borders. It does not recognize political boundaries. It transcends color, caste, creed, race, sex and language. Gresham's Law has taken a U-turn. No longer is bad money driving out good, as Gresham prophesized. The good money is crossing national boundaries and driving bad money out. What is happening to money is also witnessed in organizations and technology. Good organizations are replacing bad ones, and good technology is making bad technology obsolete globally. The forces in MOT over the last two decades of the twentieth century have been so overpowering, and pressing for global access and occupation, that governments and political authorities across the world have accepted the philosophy of globalization. Globalization is no longer an alternative. It has been the natural and next phase in progressive civilization. Anything to curb, delay or control it would have been the most retrograde step. It may at best be shaped and driven to yield the best results for all partners.

The new economic philosophy in Galbraith's terms has replaced the conventional wisdom, or the old economic policy, of the regimented development of the global economy under the pressure of the new circumstances. Globalization has given true vent to the forces of MOT, to contribute further to human welfare and raise productivity to higher levels. The economic policies are the enablers, but wrong ones can be blocks or hindrances. Conventional wisdom can be a drag on progress. Conventional wisdom is often not easy to shed because of sheer inertia, vested interests, or closed minds, or egos, or confusion and inaction, and finally risk of the unknown. Some of the best minds who decide policy issues have been, and can be, the victims of conventional wisdom in economic matters, if not for above reasons then for the risk of not disturbing the established order and retaining the status quo. If not shed at the right time, conventional wisdom is swept away by the march of events.[1]

The MOT Revolution that shaped and drove the philosophy of Globalization is next in importance only to the Keynesian Revolution. From the brink of Depression, the global economy was rescued and set on the depression-proof noncyclical sustainable economic growth path by the Keynesian philosophy that took root in economic policy-making in the late 1930s. Keynesianism, with the Bretton Woods fixed exchange rates architecture (also built under Keynes' advice and influence), spun an unprecedented global economic prosperity until the early 1970s when the signs of imminent economic malaise became evident in the emergence of the malignant phenomena of stagflation and exchange rate uncertainty. The Keynesian economic machine needed an overhaul and a fine tune to be able to grapple with the new problems that beset growth and stability. The global economy had entered the post-Keynesian phase demanding a new philosophy of more equitable development.

Globalization was the next natural phase. It had to address the issues of removing the structural imperfections, natural or policy made, in the global economy, and improve efficiency and productivity levels. The post-Keynesian twenty-first century faces the challenge of raising the welfare from more efficient use of global resources. Globalization is aimed in this direction. While Adam Smith is now credited for the greater use of his *laissez-faire* philosophy of the free market, the economists, historians and policy makers need to give greater kudos to the long forgotten David Ricardo, whose principle of comparative cost of trade, forms the basis of free trade for global welfare. At no time in history has global trade occurred on a scale following Ricardo's theory, as it does now, contributing to higher efficiency and greater welfare among the trading nations. While the oil trade has been dominated by the huge rent element, the non-oil trade, under globalization, has contributed to the more efficient and equitable global growth and distribution of its gains.

The 3W Model (Washington, World Bank and Wall Street) of globalization is built around the theoretical structure of three great economists – Adam Smith, David Ricardo and John Maynard Keynes. Their theories give a logical base to the philosophy of globalization: Adam Smith's invisible hand of efficient market mechanism for optimum allocation of resources; Ricardo's comparative cost theory for cost-efficient global trade and production structures; and Keynes' principle of sustaining deficit (trade and budget) through consumption and investment spending to promote higher global growth. In this 3W Model of the trio of great economists, the MOT Revolution is the chain through which the process of globalization is brought to fruition.

In the twenty-first century, money is no longer a currency or a cheque. From paper, money has graduated to being digitized. It is plastic money, capable of giving you access for payments. It is electronic money, which can be transferred by wire or even wirelessly. Money that is managed well is gaining in strength and universal acceptability, replacing weak and bad money. The strength of good money is breaking the national barriers and political boundaries. The capital account controls aimed at stemming capital inflows or outflows which arise out of structural weaknesses of economies will not be sustainable for a long time and will have to be phased out with policies to iron out the basic inconsistencies in the financial structure and its functioning.

Like money, companies are becoming global, transcending national borders. Companies want to have a global presence to capture markets and harness resources better for capturing synergies in production and marketing by achieving far larger economies of scale.

In the shrinking world and global village, technology is replicating and spreading faster between companies and also countries. Very few technologies used for global consumption are the monopoly of a company or a country. The speed at which technology is advancing also makes it imperative to have large global markets.

The fiber-optic, wireless and internet networks have crisscrossed the globe, empowering the transfer of audio, video signals and data on a massive scale and speed to give perfect real-time access. The access to information has been scaled up exponentially in terms of time, quality and cost. The structure of Adam Smith's market and its mechanism has undergone an incredible transformation. The buyer–seller equation has been bypassing the traditional distribution channels. The time and space dimensions of the demand–supply equation have witnessed an enormous change. One of the biggest gains of technology has been the increase in competitiveness in markets, thus improving its efficiency. With the advent and advance of the digital technology, economics will never discuss the market theory as it used to. Lack of information, inadequate information, and wrong information created information asymmetries in markets that made them imperfect. Inadequate and costly access to markets between the buyers and sellers also created layers of distribution channels. The internet substantially eliminated asymmetries in information as well as in market access, and thereby shrank the time, distance and costs in markets. The markets became even more perfect and efficient. The airlines and hotel industries, which sell a service for a particular period of time, and which cannot be stored if unutilized, have witnessed flexible pricing and a direct buyer–seller interface of unimaginable proportions. The internet has made the markets truly global in the real-time sense. The lags in the market in demand-supply responses have been largely eliminated. Like exchanges (stock markets, commodity exchanges, foreign exchange markets) the internet has offered a real-time, cost-free global platform for buying-selling of goods and services. The process of globalization has been exceedingly accelerated and brought to fruition by the internet. Fortunately, the internet did not have to force its way and bring pressure for faster globalization. The philosophy of globalization was on the way long before the advent and rapid growth of the internet, so that the latter only facilitated reaping its higher productivity gains faster.

So much for the implications of technology for the transformation of market structure and functioning. But technology has not remained exclusive. It has been inclusive and permeated into the other two critical factors bringing speedier globalization. Both money and organization have been globalized by the internet and digital technology. Money is mobile globally with international credit cards and wire transfers, but only with technology. Technology has also facilitated the global listing of shares and global operations of corporations. The policy responses of nation states have respected the imperatives of technology in pursuing the path of globalization.

Money is crossing its territorial, political and national borders, like the euro, enlarging with European regional cooperation, or like the dollar, replacing weak money through the market forces. With the euro, the EU (European Union) member nations have rendered the multiple exchange rates among the European currencies redundant. By the end of 2006, in five years of its creation, the euro currency notes in circulation passed the figure of an equivalent $800 billion to surpass the US dollars in circulation. The concept of an exchange rate will soon be dead within the European Union. The nonexistence of exchange rates will make the monetary management in Europe much simpler than before. Over time, global money will make exchange rates obsolete, and a portion of economic theory and experiences about exchange rates will disappear from the texts on Monetary Economics into the annals of monetary history. When the currency is global, trade becomes regional rather than international. The labor, capital and entrepreneurship under globalization will be more mobile. The disparities in the availability of these factors across nations will narrow. This will make world trade more natural-resource based. Natural-resource endowments will dominate the trend and pattern in global trade. Bioengineering could overcome the constraint of geographically localized agriculture. Yet, current energy sources and metals will continue to be dominated by regional endowments and natural bounties. The biggest boost to the economic freedom of nations could emerge out of the emancipation from the current thick geographic concentration of energy sources and move towards more ubiquitous sources of energy. If commercial production from more ubiquitous energy sources, such as solar or hydrogen, becomes feasible, it would be truest economic emancipation and would write a new chapter in human civilization. This scenario is a little too far fetched and futuristic, but undoubtedly we are moving towards it and the pace is perhaps unknown. It could be reality soon, if the political friction in global affairs lessens, and wisdom, rationality and graciousness replace greed for power and control, and self-realization conquers fear and suspicion.

Introduction

The global economy entered the twenty-first century with a distinguished track record of a long period of economic progress and stability. Human civilization at its pinnacle has no comparable parallel or record of growth and development, accomplished on the strength of an abounding stream of technological innovations and sustained by cohesive new economic policies. In contrast, the pre-war era of the last century witnessed unprecedented instability, uncertainty and insecurity. A period of two world wars, the collapse of the gold standard, the Communist revolution and the rule of Marxism, record hyperinflation and Nazism, stock market boom and bust, the Great Depression, beggar-thy-neighbor trade policies, and fluctuating exchange rates, presented a picture of fragmentation and sharp volatility in the world economy. In contrast to this stressful period, the post-war era has been marked by cooperation in global trade, monetary and economic affairs under the auspices of GAAT, IMF and World Bank, and has witnessed stability and growth in the developed and developing world. Keynes' *The General Theory of Employment, Interest and Money*, published in 1936, offered a fresh and novel perception of the behavior of an economy and its key drivers. It revolutionized the macroeconomic management policy and paved way for the policy of counter-cyclical growth and stability. Marx had prophesized the collapse of capitalism through the depression cycle. Western capitalist nations faced their worst crisis when they all gradually slipped into the Great Depression in the 1930s. Keynes emerged as the savior of capitalism with his novel theory, giving the new economic logic for government intervention and deficit financing as the lasting cure of massive unemployment and depression. The conventional wisdom of traditional *laissez-faire* economic theorists preached a free market, government nonintervention and balanced budget. To Keynes, they were all antithetical to sustainable growth. The slow but steady acceptance of Keynes' philosophy in the late 1930s gave the capitalist world its new lease of life.

To the global economy ravaged by World War II, and the disorganized and unstable global money markets, Keynes also offered a new global monetary and financial framework at the Bretton Woods conference in 1944, compatible with his economic philosophy of government intervention and deficit financing. The conventional and anachronistic gold standard was replaced by a more flexible gold-dollar standard with fixed but adjustable exchange rates.

Keynesian economic philosophy and international monetary system sustained growth and stability in the global economy for two and half decades. That was the lease of time offered by the gold–dollar standard on the strength of the value of gold stocks of the Federal Reserve. The global monetary system was showing signs of weakness by the late 1960s. Fixed exchange rates revolved around the fixed price of gold of $35 per ounce. By 1970, the persistent upward pressure on the market price of gold, crossing the official price despite the sale of gold by the Federal Reserve and other major central banks in the open market, necessitated a systemic change to meet the growing demand for international liquidity and more responsive exchange rates. The gold-dollar standard had to be abandoned in favor of a more flexible floating exchange rates system in 1971. Gold had served its purpose as a bridge from the unstable pre-war period to post-war prosperity. The unequal distribution of gold stocks among central banks did not present gold as an ideal anchor of the global monetary system. Hence, the exchange rates arrangement was delinked from gold in 1971 and the Smithsonian Agreement of 1973 paved the way for a new regime of floating exchange rates replacing the Bretton Woods system of 1944.

Another significant development in the global monetary system in this period of the gold-dollar standard was the phenomenon of the euro-dollar market. The dramatic accumulation and growth of dollars outside the US, put international and offshore banking centers beyond the control of the central banks. The parallel euro-dollar international banking system outside the influence of the monetary authorities emerged as one of the major sources of private and public funding. Working efficiently on the thinnest of margins, the euro-dollar provided the lowest cost of intermediation. It served as the lucrative outlet for depositors and a cheaper funding source to borrowers. Thanks to the enormity of its size and the dynamism and efficiency of its management, following the oil crisis of 1974, the euro-dollar market undertook the mammoth task of recycling the petro-dollar surpluses for lending to the needy oil importing nations, and rescued the global economy from the clutches of what would have been the worst depression since the 1930s. The external debt route was, however, less diligently and cautiously used by several developing nations for government budgetary funding and also for non-project purposes having no positive impact on their balance of payments (BoP). The debt servicing ratios of these nations went beyond the cautionary limits. The second oil price hike in 1979 and the dear money policy pursued by Paul Volcker in 1980, which caused record high interest rates of 21 percent, put a crushing burden on the debt servicing by several counties Latin America, Africa and East Europe, imperiling the US banking system. The global economy was once again saved from one of the worst banking crisis by the largest rescheduling of external debt of the LDCs by the top American banks in the mid 1980s.

Disenchantment with the debt model for the Third World created a need to evolve a new model of development. Foreign direct investment has always been treated in development theory as one of most potent, effective and dynamic factors and tools to promoting growth. The 1980s also marked the maturing of several commodity industries in those developed nations facing cost constraints. The shift of the industrial base to the cheaper labor countries of Asia and Latin America became the focal point of the new model. Multinational companies were willing to relocate production capacities in low-cost emerging market economies. The developed countries also possessed large savings of institutional investors, such as pension funds, insurance companies, and mutual funds, which required a lucrative outlet for investment. A part of the institutional investors' funds could be deployed in the emerging markets. Professional investment institutions pursued Markowitz's principle of investment diversification more vigorously in practice, both domestically and internationally.

The experience of the success of the floating exchange rate by the late 1970s was a great boost to the liberal economic philosophers who resurrected Adam Smith and advocated the application of the free market mechanism to the other sectors of domestic and international economies. The oil crisis, debt crisis, the end of the Cold War, crumbling Communism in USSR and Eastern Europe, US–China détente, and China's ideological reversal to accept reforms, market economy and privatization to modernize its economy in order to push up its growth rate, all set the tone for the new model of development. The global economic environment and setting was most congenial for the new model and philosophy of economic reform comprising liberalization and privatization leading to globalization. It took shape in the US Treasury Department in Washington supported by the World Bank and Wall Street. The World Bank had the role of overseeing and monitoring the reform process. Wall Street, with its investment bankers, was to be the main catalyst in channeling both direct and portfolio investments. The Washington–World Bank–Wall Street Model (3W Model) was ready to be launched in Latin America and Asia. The model for China was substantially diluted to the Chinese dictates of adopting a 'One Country–Two Systems' ideology.

The new economic philosophy of growth, centered on the 3W Model of economic reform, deregulation and privatization, took the shape of Reaganomics in the US and Thatcherism in the UK. Communist nations had their own share of problems of low economic growth, unemployment, inflation and massive civil unrest. Behind the Iron Curtain, the winds of change began to blow. The end of the Cold War, the collapse of Berlin Wall in 1989 and unification of Germany signaled the unfolding of events in the rest of Eastern Europe and the USSR. The structure of communism was getting economically and politically weaker. Growing public resentment against economic stagnation, eroding living standards, growing unemployment, creeping inflation and persistent scarcities of essentials evoked mass movements and revolt for political change in communist countries. The Big Brother, the USSR, was finding the system economically unsustainable. The economic burden of the arms race put an enormous pressure on the system and its damaging economic effects on more productive economic systems were getting more visible and pronounced. The elaborate economic planning apparatus, devoid of signals from price and market mechanisms, was unable to adapt the giant production machine under its control to changing times. Production system became inefficient, lacked technological upgradation, and developed large unused capacities, leading to stagflation and growing unemployment. A political system that works at keeping the two economic ills, unemployment and inflation, at bay is always at less risk of destabilization. Clearly, the communist juggernaut in the USSR and East Europe was at the risk of transformation, and also ripe for adoption of the 3W Model. The leadership in the USSR was perceptive and pragmatic, and not doctrinaire and dogmatic. Gorbachev talked about Perestroika and Glasnost as the only route to save communism in the USSR from collapsing.

The political foresight in China undoubtedly needs much better acclaim. India and China, the world's oldest civilizations and cultures, enjoy a rich heritage of political and economic wisdom. Their ancient disciplines and philosophies are still widely read, discussed, researched and followed now, in modern times, for their practical wisdom in the fast-changing post-industrial technologically dominated material world. These philosophies deal with institutions and change. It seems from the global experience of the second half of the closing century of the last millennium, that these two cultures and societies have succeeded in handling the change with finesse for speedier progress without traumatic disruptions. Chanakya, also known as Kautilya, in India and Confucius in China seem to have left their genes in succeeding generations involved in political ideology, economic philosophy and administration.

After the communist rule in 1949, China did not acquire the territories of Hong Kong and Taiwan but maintained and exploited them as links for trade and investment with the capitalist world. The change of leadership from thinker-founder Mao to Deng, who was known as the reformist, did provide China with the right bridge to migrate from the conventional communist state to a modern quasi-capitalist, market oriented, pragmatic socialist state. China learnt its lesson a hard way in realizing that the modernization of its colossal economic machine needed foreign capital, technology and deregulation towards marketization. Deng spearheaded the new initiative of modernization that paved the way for a historic US–China collaboration for mutual economic advantage and growth. China transformed itself into a giant foreign capital driven export-oriented growth machine. Liberalization in China began much earlier than in other nations. The largest flows of direct investment from the US moved into China for its new experiment. Chinese liberalization was very peculiar. It did not encompass all sectors of the economy. It left foreign trade and investments free in certain provinces with other sectors still regulated. The dualistic system did give China the results it sought. By the annexation of Hong Kong in 1997, China further extended its quasi-capitalist, market-oriented economy. The dualistic model and 'One Country–Two Systems' ideology was working well for China.

In India, Rajiv Gandhi took the semi-regulated economy off in 1985, by launching its first phase of liberalization involving radical reforms in industrial, trade, taxation and financial sectors. Narasimha Rao and Manmohan Singh accelerated the process in the right sequence in a phased and gradual manner with great finesse, skill and adroitness, and the abounding success evoked global acclaim.

Globalization is a broad issue, having not only economic but also political, socio-cultural, ethnic, geological and ecological ramifications. From the economic standpoint, the subject of globalization encompasses several aspects of the global economy and sectors of domestic economies, influencing economic structure, price mechanism, market institutions, resource allocation, price levels, financial system and its efficiency, trade pattern and its growth, BoP structure, and finally, income and wealth distribution. Discussion on globalization here centers on the process of trade and financial liberalization and integration with the global capital market. This book looks at the trade, investment and financial aspects of globalization, also covering the BoP and exchange rate implications of the process for the global monetary system and the India economy. My earlier, award-winning, book *Global Monetary Experience and India* was written in 1991. Since then, a lot of water has flown down the Mississippi, Yangtze and Brahmaputra rivers. This volume attempts to grasp and characterize the more recent developments, and analyze and assess their impact on, and implications for, the global monetary system and the Indian economy.

The first part of the book deals with the evolution of the philosophy of globalization and its impact on the exchange rates, global liquidity, currency markets, and global trade and payments. It takes a broad look at the process of globalization and highlights the catalytic role played by the US therein. It also dwells on the major drivers as well as the weak spots in the course of globalization, against the backdrop of the analysis of the evolution of the international monetary system.

A historical perspective to the evolution of the global monetary system from the gold standard to the current dollar standard is given in Chapter 1. The floating exchange rates, the oil crisis of the 1970s and the commercial debt crisis in the 1980s led to the development of a new model, the 3W (Washington–World Bank–Wall Street) Model, for global development in the form of globalization and closer integration through economic reforms and liberalization. The genesis of the philosophy of globalization covering the experience of earlier development policies and theoretical development of the equity routed growth are outlined in Chapter 2. The philosophy of globalization laid an emphasis on the global reallocation of equity capital for promoting the development in the emerging market economies (a term used for the developing nations under globalization). Globalization has brought about a transformation in global trade, payments and liquidity structure. Financing globalization, its imperatives and outcome, like bulging US trade deficit and swelling forex reserves of the Asian economies, are discussed in Chapter 3. It underscores the crucial and critical role played by the floating exchange rates in this transformation. In fact, the global monetary system under the floating exchange rates mechanism forms the core around which the process of globalization is revolving. The floating exchange rates system, which opened a new era in international monetary order, ushered in globalization as the logical end of an international economic evolution.

As the major participant in the process of globalization, the US economic structure, its dynamics, economic policy responses and management have undergone a dramatic change. US balance of payments behavior, Federal Reserve monetary policy gyrations and a boom on Wall Street are inextricably linked with closer integration of the global economy. This aspect is analyzed and discussed in Chapter 4 which highlights how a buoyant US capital market helps drive the global economy. The changing behavior of the currency markets is both the cause and effect of globalization. The dynamics of the forex markets and the mechanics of currency crises under closely integrated global capital markets are the focus of Chapter 5. The biggest experiment of globalization took place in the late 1980s in the Asian Continent. However, the Asian crisis of 1997 shook the gung ho globalization advocates. The genesis of the phenomenon and lessons to be drawn there are covered in Chapter 6. The IMF has been marginalized in the phase of floating exchange rates and globalization. The role of the IMF in the new milieu needs a fresh and unconventional focus. Chapter 7 discusses the inadequacies of the IMF in dealing with the challenges of globalization and its marginalization due its resource inadequacy. It covers the reform proposal for the IMF for its more constructive role in the new global environment.

The globalization experience over the last two and half decades has given mixed results. The success in many cases is marred by the trauma of some crises. The economic reform is like changing the atomic structure of an element. It is like transforming the old, rigid and less productive atomic structure with the new one that is more refined, intricate but flexible and super efficient, running faster and giving better results. As altering the atomic structure of an element causes radiation, the reform process does bring out its deleterious side effects. Sometimes they can be small and slow, and therefore, tackled easily. But other times they could be more cataclysmic and traumatic. These are manifest in recession, hyperinflation or currency crisis. Since Keynesianism and globalization have made the economies depression and hyperinflation proof, the trauma of jet-speed globalization invariably manifests itself in currency crisis. These are the radiation effects of high-speed reforms. The failures of reform are usually reflected in the currency crises. This has something to do with the speed, sequencing and timing of the reform process. The Mexican, Asian and Russian crises offer lessons for course correction and better trajectory for softer landings in the future. The success of China and India in Gradualism in reforms, in their own different ways and in different systems, is laudable and suitable for emulation elsewhere in the world.

Globalization is not without its social costs, and they become more pronounced and have to get higher priority in the emerging market economies because of greater consideration for economic equity and social justice. The emerging markets, which have a large destitute population without a social safety net, require the programs and care for those rejected by the market mechanism. These are often not provided by the market mechanism and action, but have to emerge from proactive government measures. It is the absence or paucity of provision for a social safety net or program for rehabilitation of the poor and destitute market rejects that has been the biggest failure of globalization, in addition to currency crises. This has been the central and common theme of the attack of the 3Ss (Stiglitz, Sachs and Soros) against the 3W Model. The governments of emerging market economies are now more vigilant about filling this void caused by the rapid pace of globalization and are instituting a variety of programs to this end.

The Indian economic experience under its own philosophy of proceeding with globalization is the subject matter of second part of this book. It takes us through the genesis of economic reforms and liberalization in India to the path and sequence of measures now culminating into fuller capital account convertibility. The economic logic for policy liberalization against the backdrop of semi-regulated market economy with planning by direction is described in Chapter 8. Globalization in India has been slower but steadier in comparison to its Asian counterparts. Like China, India also would not follow the 3W Model. Its model of Gradualism in Reform was the best fit for its ideology. One can now unequivocally call the process of liberalization and reforms in India a success story and a global model to be emulated elsewhere. Due to its philosophy of Gradualism in unbundling regulations and controls, and in unleashing the forces of market mechanism, economic reforms in India have been without any traumatic after effects. There have not been any radiation effects of economic reforms in India. The Indian model of gradualism has in fact become the role model for other emerging market economies. The purpose of this study is to review the financial reforms and liberalization in the banking, capital markets, balance of payments and exchange rate fronts. Chapter 9 gives the sequence of economic gradualism encompassing several policy measures. It goes through the 1991 forex crisis, and the measures and longer term policy initiatives taken to address the crisis and put the BoP on a path of sustainable equilibrium.

The gradual liberalization of banking and the financial sector and capital market reforms have brought greater efficiency in the financial markets. Stock markets are state of the art and global in comparison, and leading in electronic transactions turnover. The banking system has been transformed from a regulated one to a liberalized, market-oriented, competitive and efficient intermediary conforming to Basel norms. These developments are dealt with in Chapter 10. From crisis to forex bounty in the 1990s, this has been a story of resounding accomplishments producing growth and stability in India. With over $200 billion in its kitty, the Reserve Bank of India is now in the big league of top seven central banks. India's exchange rate policy has played a proactive role in creating healthier trends in balance of payments and record forex reserves. Chapter 11 focuses on the effect of reforms in developing a sustainable BoP equilibrium and the role of rupee exchange rate policy. Capital account convertibility has been a debatable issue in the emerging markets opening up their external sector. India's step by step approach towards capital account convertibility has helped in skipping potholes of volatility disturbing the normal behavior of exchange rates. The policy has yielded a rich dividend and has been acclaimed globally. Controls on short-term borrowings and capital outflows by the residents have kept the BoP safe from destabilizing speculation, which causes spiraling changes in exchange rates. Financial liberalization in India has brought about a transformation in creating mature financial and capital markets contributing to growth and yielding better economic returns. Gradual global integration of the Indian financial system has produced laudable economic results skipping the trauma of change.

Full convertibility is the last mile on the road of economic liberalization and reforms leading to globalization. The developments in respect of capital account liberalization following the Capital Account Convertibility Report of 1997 and India's progress towards full convertibility are reviewed in Chapter 12. The Convertibility Report, the author's report on fuller convertibility considering alternative options towards this goal with appropriate safeguards is presented in Chapter 13. The recent developments towards Fuller Convertibility and future scenarios are discussed in Chapter 14. With gradualism in economic liberalization and reforms, India's trillion dollar economy has taken a smooth trajectory into a higher growth orbit of 9 percent and is now targeting 10 percent growth. The infrastructure sector is the new harbinger of growth in the coming decades in India. The mismatch between private and public goods is enlarging at a rapid pace under globalization driven by market forces. The failure to meet this rapid growing demand for infrastructure services can not only hamper growth rate but also create social tensions. Not only is the infrastructure needed to be given the highest priority to meet the huge private–public goods gap but also to be the new harbinger of growth for the 10 percent target. Due to the enormity of the size of investment, the infrastructure growth cannot be left to the private and foreign investors. The government has to play the role of a partner and facilitator in this huge investment program. On the one hand, India's growing forex reserves reflects the redundancy of its external resources, on the other it is still short of capital for huge investments in infrastructure. While, the RBI's monetary reserves earn low monetary returns on US T bills, economic returns on infrastructure projects is substantially higher. Hence, there is a strong case for using forex reserves for infrastructure development. In order to use the forex reserves more effectively to promote capital formation in the infrastructure sector, the economic logic for monetization of reserves is considered. This argument, with the history of development of infrastructure in the US, is presented in Chapter 15. The foregoing unconventional proposal has now been accepted by the Government. After great deliberation in the Reserve Bank of India (RBI), the Planning Commission and the Ministry of Finance, the Finance Minister, P. Chidambaram, one of the chief architects of reform and who also spearheaded the second phase of liberalization, in his Budget speech in February, 2007, announced the setting up of a Special Purpose Vehicle (SPV) of $5 billion from the forex reserves for the purpose of financing infrastructure projects.

Part I

Global monetary system

1 Gold standard to globalization

From gold standard to globalization, the international monetary system has traversed through the closing century of the last millennium fairly easily, without any major disruption in global trade, payment flows and its mechanism. For the first four and half decades, until the end of World War II, it was gold that ruled the global monetary system. Under the pre-war gold standard, money supplies and liquidity were linked to gold stocks of the central banks, and the fixed gold price retained fixed exchange rates between the currencies. The system collapsed due to its rigidity. It did not give flexibility to exchange rates, nor could it increase money supplies due to slow growth in the global gold output and the gold stocks of the central banks. During the 1930s, Keynesianism not only put an end to the *laissez-faire* economics but also built an architecture for the global monetary system based on flexible exchange rates. The economic philosophy of John Maynard Keynes, articulated in The *General Theory of Income and Employment, and Money* in 1936, paved the way for the global economy to move from the brink of depression in the 1930s to sustained economic growth for nearly three decades. The post-war economic infrastructure and institutions were built on the logic of the philosophy of Keynesianism. The conventional wisdom of Government non-interference in the dynamics of the economy had brought the global economic system to the brink of disaster under the affliction of the Great Depression. An economic architecture of policies and institutions serves a system in certain circumstances, and needs to change over time as the conditions surrounding it alter slowly or dramatically. The global monetary system erected on the platform of the gold-convertible US dollar for the central banks became shaky in 1971 when the external liabilities of the Federal Reserve overshot the value of its gold stocks. The gold-based dollar standard gave way in 1973 to floating exchange rates. With gold demonetized from the global monetary system, the US dollar reigned supreme as its major currency and reserve asset. The seeds of globalization, as a new phase in the evolution of the global economy, were sown with the emergence of floating exchange rates.

The floating exchange rates necessitated a change in the orientation of global economic policies. The new framework of more flexible exchange rates afforded greater elbow room for the central banks to follow more independent monetary policies, with the exchange rates taking care of adjustment in external imbalances. It also gave the logical option of moving towards deregulation of the financial sector to some developed nations, including Japan. The 1980s also marked the resurrection of Adam Smith's philosophy of removal of economic controls and regulations for freer play of a benevolent market mechanism, unrestricted foreign trade and investment, and downsizing of Government by privatization of public sector enterprises. With the global economy migrating into the depression-proof phase of a sustained growth trajectory, Keynesianism completed its major function of leading the global economy into the new phase. While the post-war economic growth was dominated by Keynesianism, the need for globalization became imperative in the post-Keynesian phase of global development. The future growth of the global economy and its sustainability rested on both the productivity gains and also higher utilization of global economic resources. Globalization was the most logical phase of the post-Keynesian global economy for further growth and sustainable development.

Early history

It is hard to speculate the course of human civilization if the glittering yellow metal that caught human fancy for centuries had not existed, or for that matter, too little or too much of it was available. However, for a period spanning millennia, gold did a splendid job in creating the right medium for transactions that form the basis of an economic society, its growth and prosperity. As universally accepted measure of value, it acted as a natural regulator of liquidity, and of value and prices within an economy and also between countries. As it naturally developed as money by the forces of the market, gold reined the greed of the Kings or the Central Banks to issue too much of it. Nevertheless, it was tyrannical, inequitable, discriminatory, conventional and economically unscientific. Economic logic, wisdom and policy under the compulsions of fresh economic events over the twentieth century gradually evolved the international monetary order free from the shackles of gold and its inequities. Yet, because of its past baggage, the huge stocks of gold still lying with the central banks, with its market value of $680 billion (at the price of $690 per ounce of gold), are the only effect gold now impinges on the global monetary system.

Gold dominated the economic fate of nations in the pre-war period. The metal possesses remarkable qualities to match the human needs and psychosis that govern economics. While nations and the global economy prospered under its bounty, at times it became tyrannical and the prophet of doom in the 1930s. Gold's scarcity, durability, portability, liquidity, homogeneity, stability and, most importantly, the inability to counterfeit the metal, made it the perfect matter for use as money for centuries. Under the gold standard, money supply remained governed by the exogenous forces of discovery of gold stocks and gold flows from country to country. The system was inequitable. It gave a natural bounty to gold-producing countries to the detriment of gold-importing countries for its use as money. While the sudden discoveries of new gold mines brought periods of boom, the fluctuations in the production of gold also triggered depression. Since the exchange rates between the currencies, determined by their gold content, remained fixed, countries could not control money supply to the domestic needs of desired economic growth and price stability. Economies swayed between high growth and inflation on the one hand, and recession, deflation and depression on the other. The rules of the gold standard brought automatic economic fluctuations in economies as they maintained a gold-based exchange rate parity of their currencies. Hence, Keynes termed the regime as barbaric. Chance discoveries of gold and the extent of these finds governed the global economic fate for centuries. If gold had not existed, man may have settled for silver or an other metal as money. The economic truth is that the metallic standard left the course of economies to the mercy of nature's endowments and man's discovery of these fortunes. The discoveries came at irregular intervals in time and space. Certain times were better than the others. Certain countries benefited more than others. Naturally, it was an unequal economics.

Price discovery of gold

Gold remained the anchor of the global monetary system for several centuries, although the gold standard was officially introduced by Great Britain in 1821 by the Gold Standard Act of Parliament, with Pound Sterling serving as the global currency. An outstanding feature of gold, which enabled it to emerge and survive as the center of the international monetary system for more than 700 years of recorded history, is the remarkable stability in its price until 1971. From 1257 until 1971 the gold price did not increase by more than 0.62 percent per annum.[2] Isaac Newton, in his capacity as the Supervisor of the British Mint, had officially fixed the price of gold in 1717 at Pounds 4.2 per ounce. It remained stable for nearly 200 years. Hats off to the genius and intuition of Newton! Not only did he have an uncanny ability to grasp and articulate the laws of motion of material objects before anyone else, but he also possessed an unusual sense of perceiving and anticipating the motion of gold price for nearly four generations ahead. He displayed his unique intellect and skill in unraveling nature's psyche as well as the human psyche; although the former is immutable, the latter changes with time. The subsequent gold price fixations were not as long lasting as Newton's. Newton's success was the result of the right amalgam of economic wisdom and political pragmatism. At critical times in economic history, unconventional economic wisdom was often not acceptable to the ruling political thought and power. Translation of genius of economic judgment into a policy needs political candor, objectivity and farsightedness. In 1925, not heeding the advice of Keynes, Winston Churchill, as the Chancellor of Exchequer decided to return to the gold standard at the pre-war exchange rates and gold price, and disastrously failed. In came the Great Depression.

The outbreak of World War I in 1914 marked the end of the gold standard. Major industrial nations such as Germany, France, and Austria followed Britain in 1919 in suspending the convertibility of their currencies into gold and thereby abandoning the gold standard. The US, which entered the war late in 1917, also went off the gold standard since its gold stocks doubled in three years, and money supply expansion, honoring the rules of the game of the gold standard, was causing uncontrollable price inflation. Without the anchor of gold holding the exchange rates fixed and stable, the global economy entered an era of freely fluctuating exchange rates. In 1920, the Pound sterling and French franc depreciated considerably, with rates moving from $4.87 to $3.4 per pound and from 5.45 francs per $ to 19 francs. Hyperinflation in Germany in the early 1920s took a heavy toll on the German mark. From 81 marks to the $ in 1921, the mark went to 670 to the $ in 1922 and to 30,000, then to 152,000, and in July 1923 to a record million marks to the $.[3] It was the worst hyperinflation in human history.

Disorderly and chaotic exchange rates behavior during this period necessitated a return to a more organized and orderly international monetary payments and exchange rates mechanism. The most popular, debatable and controversial talk among economists was about the return to the gold standard. Britain was the first country to initiate action on this thought, with a view to re-establishing the Pound Sterling as the major trading currency and London as the capital of the world's financial system. Winston Churchill, who was then the Chancellor of Exchequer, announced the return to the gold standard in 1925 to restore Britain's past preeminence in the global economic order and international trade. Keynes was opposed to the return to the gold standard, and more so at the pre-war gold parity and gold content of 123.27 grains of fine gold, its old exchange rate of $4.87 against the US dollar, when in 1920 the pound had fallen to as low as $3.40 in gold-based dollars.[4] At the overvalued pound, 'British coal, textiles and other manufactured goods could only become competitive at the new exchange rates if their prices were to come down by 10 percent. A very uncomfortable process'.[5] Britain had to pay a heavy price for its prestige of retaining the pre-war exchange parity. It paved an easy way for falling output, declining wages, rising unemployment, stagnation and finally depression. The gold holdings of the Bank of England also remained perilously low, requiring support from the US. In the US, an economic upsurge, which had triggered an unprecedented stock market boom, was also at its peak in the late 1920s. In October 1929, the speculative driven overheated stock market suffered the Great Crash, igniting the reversal of the economic cycle, which culminated in the Great Depression. By the end of 1933, half of US banks had disappeared, GNP was one third less than in 1929 and with 13 million unemployed, one in every three in the labor force was without job.[6] The worsening economic situation in Britain finally forced her to suspend gold convertibility under the Gold Standard Act in 1931, while the US suspended the gold standard in 1933. The US also made the private holding of gold and dealing in bullion by its citizens illegal. The beggar-thy-neighbor trade policy of retaliatory tariffs and quotas reduced the value of world trade to an unbelievable one third of the 1929 level. 'In Britain, in 1932, unemployment was worse than ever before, at a rate of 22 percent. In Germany and the US it was even higher'.[7]

In retrospect, Keynes' view that Britain's decision to return to gold standard was fraught with risks of deflationary potential was shared and supported by several economists. 'The 1925 return to gold standard was perhaps the most decisively damaging action involving money in modern times'.[8] The most recent study by Ben Bernanke on the causes of the Great Depression reinforces the earlier views about the erroneous policy approach on the return to the gold standard despite Keynes' sane advice. His analysis, covering 24 countries, considering the relationship between the decision to adhere to the gold standard and some key macroeconomic variables, such as wholesale prices, money supply, industrial production and real wages, establishes the evidence of a strong link between the adherence to the gold standard and the severity of deflation and depression. The cross-country data clearly showed that the severity of depression was substantially less in those countries that were not on the gold standard and the ones that abandoned the gold standard early rather than in the others, such as the US, France, and Italy, that went off the gold standard late.[9]

If the gold standard had not returned after World War I in its crude and original form with rigid rules of the game of strictly varying money supply with the gold flows from abroad and gold stocks in vaults of central banks, the course of global economic development would have been different. The global economy may have skipped the worst deflationary cycle of the 1930s. In that case, Keynes may have been deprived of the chance to pursue his obsessive desire to untangle the mystery of cyclical depression faced by the capitalist economies and weave the novel General Theory. But as it transpired, the onset of depression and its miseries were too heavy a price for humanity to gain from Keynes the theory that discovered a policy prescription to eliminate its recurrence. Since then, the malady of economic depression, like polio has been eradicated from the planet. The great discoveries have always occurred under the pressure of compelling demands of adverse circumstances and calamities. One is reminded of the old adage, 'Necessity is the mother of invention'.

History is replete with instances of the most critical decisions on economic matters, at times following the conventional wisdom, disregarding fresh, novel, and unorthodox ideas and views. Even after the Wall Street Great Crash of October, 1929, which spread to other stock markets of the world and engulfed the global economy with a great depressive spell, Keynes advocated public works and deficit financing to cure global economic depression. His philosophy of deficit financing was against the conventional theory and policy of balanced budgets, and Keynes was active in propagating it even before he published the *General Theory*, wherein he wove a comprehensive theoretical and logical framework and basis underlying his policy.

Writing to George Bernard Shaw on New Year's Day, 1935, Keynes said: 'To understand my state of mind, you have to know that I believe myself to be writing a book on economic theory which will largely revolutionize – not, I suppose, at once but in the course of next ten years – the way the world thinks about economic problems'. Never was such apparent arrogance so amply justified.[10]

The General Theory was published in 1936. So much was the antipathy in Britain towards deficit financing for its supposedly inflationary potential, even in the midst of the worst depression and double-digit unemployment, that the British economists even criticized President Roosevelt for adopting the Keynesian prescription in the US much ahead of Britain.[11] The experience of the US, in fact, has been much better and luckier in adoption of unconventional thought. New economic ideas and philosophy received quicker and better political acceptability in the US. Roosevelt gave the New Deal in the US, the first but mammoth Keynesian avatar, to surmount the Great Depression.

War, hyperinflation, the collapse of the gold standard, stock market boom and bust, and depression, all offered a great challenge to economists and policy makers of the day to forge new models of growth, stability and monetary order. Gold was tyrannical in its rigid form of the gold standard but could not be dispensed with, due to the baggage it had accumulated over centuries. A monetary institution is built and functions on the foundation of faith and trust. Money is an IOU (I owe you) issued by the central banks. The central banks are owned by governments in some countries and are private and autonomous in others. The governments and central banks are the custodians of the wealth of nations. The value of wealth and the process of wealth creation and destruction is partly determined by the number of IOUs in circulation and their price. Gold evolved over centuries and millennia as the basis of public trust, both within and across nations as the most acceptable means of trade and financial settlements. Although, by 1914, the currency convertibility into gold lost relevance nationally and was no longer a necessity to run the monetary system, it continued to remain as the anchor of the international monetary system to establish the gold-based structure of exchange rates.

Gold dollar standard à la Bretton Woods

The post-war period marked a new era into a relatively gold free global monetary system. Gold was not totally abandoned, but its influence on the economic behavior of economies was considerably moderated. Gold stocks continued to be the core source of international liquidity and reserve assets of the central banks, and exchange rates were determined by the gold content of currencies. Nevertheless, the domestic monetary policies were divorced from the gold flows and were dictated by domestic economic considerations and not the balance of payments situation. John Maynard Keynes, whose philosophy formed the main architectural base for economic policies in the post-war period, played a major role in moving towards a gold-free global monetary system. The success of the Keynesian philosophy in lifting the depression-ridden economies from their economic morass also made the gold standard anachronistic.

Keynes was instrumental in building the post-war monetary system that led to the abandonment of the gold standard and the formation of a new international monetary system, with the gold-based dollar centric flexible exchange rated system of fixed but adjustable exchange rates. Although Keynes had proposed to have the new international monetary system totally divorced from gold, with an international currency without the gold base named 'Bancor', it was probably thought not pragmatic and expedient to dislodge gold entirely from the monetary system, especially in the light of large gold stocks held by the Federal Reserve and other European central banks.

The new international monetary system was formed in 1944 at Bretton Woods, New Hampshire in the US, after the negotiations between Keynes representing Europe, Harry White from the US, and other member nations of the UN. The center of the new monetary order shifted from gold to the US dollar. Gold price was fixed at $35 per ounce of gold and all countries had to declare the gold content of currencies in order to arrive at their exchange rates with the dollar. In 1944, the US Federal Reserve was the largest holder of gold stock, of 697 million ounces (21,678 tonnes) valued at $24 billion then ($480 billion at the gold price of $690 an ounce in April, 2007), compared with the second largest holding of 35 million ounces, valued at $1.6 billion by the Bank of England. But the supply of international liquidity under the new system shifted from chance discoveries of gold mines to the US Federal Reserve, which supplied dollars to the rest of the world. The economic advantage or *seigniorage*, which was accruing to the gold mining and exporting countries under the gold standard, was enjoyed by the US, which met the global liquidity requirements through dollar deficits in its balance of payments.

The money in an economic system is an IOU. Its existence, survival, and sustainability are confidence. The gold standard met with several characteristics of ideal money and because of the metal's scarcity in terms of its overall stock as well as incremental supplies and demand, the gold standard and gold survived in the monetary system for centuries. It became an anachronism, with Keynesian economic philosophy, emanating from his *General Theory*, of managing macroeconomic aggregates like economic growth and employment with proactive and unconventional fiscal and monetary policies. Consequently, there was a collective global desire to have non-cyclic sustainable economic growth, free from the levels of gold stocks and gold flows. In addition to the holdings of large gold stocks, a factor that helped the US to continue a more refined, flexible and Keynesian version of gold standard was its legislation forbidding US citizens from holding gold. This aspect of US gold policy and its underlying logic and significance has not been adequately highlighted and analyzed well by economists, policy makers and critics.

The US ban on private gold holding pre-empted a large portion of global private demand for gold. Such a measure of depriving its residents from their freedom to hold gold by a country championing the cause of free trade, free enterprise and right to property, was in fact not consistent with US economic and political philosophy. But it was not only imperative but also expedient in the larger global interest of maintaining the free market price of gold stable at $35 for a longer period. Private demand and holdings in gold in the US would have put an enormous pressure on the market price of gold much earlier than in 1971, when despite the sale of gold by the major central banks, they could not succeed in containing the gold price rise, which finally led to snapping of the gold–dollar link. The gold–dollar standard, which sustained the lease of 25 years before collapsing and under which the US enjoyed the benefits of *seigniorage* by supplying liquidity to the rest of the world, would have closed much earlier under the pressure of rising market gold price, had US citizens been allowed to hold gold. The US had to deprive its citizens from accumulating gold in their asset portfolios and benefiting from the capital appreciation emanating from rising gold prices after gold was demonetized in 1971. The *seigniorage* enjoyed by the US government was the bounty for the sacrifice of loss of freedom for the US households to gain from the collapse of the gold– dollar standard. The US government gained free access to global resources by dollar deficit financing, but US citizens lost the opportunity to realize monetary capital gains by holding gold when the gold price started moving up after 1971. Economists would also argue that the ban on gold holding was actually a blessing in disguise, since the absence of private demand for gold in the US released enormous financial and economic resources for more productive use and helped in the growth of its banking and financial system, stock market, and contributed to real capital formation in the US for 25 long years. The US policy was pragmatic, rationalist, and truly economic to its core. India also tried to control private use and holdings of gold by the Gold Control Act of 1962, which banned the holding of primary, or bar gold except by authorized dealers and goldsmiths, and sought to limit the gold jewellery holdings of families. However, the situation was different in India. Gold plays a more important role in Indian households because of a long tradition and custom of using it as jewellery as well as a quasi-financial asset. Further, at that time, India had one of the largest private holdings of gold. The gold control could not succeed due to the large demand for consumption of gold in India for jewellery arising from the continuing fascination for gold in jewellery, the use of the metal and jewellery as a store of value and quasi-money, and large domestic holdings of gold jewellery. Further, the jewellery business comprises a large number of small-scale enterprises spread throughout India giving employment to artisans and traders. The Act was soon relaxed to repeal the ban on holding and was finally abolished in 1992, allowing free import of gold subject to import duty.

The gold–dollar standard would have been a short-lived phenomenon had US households enjoyed the holding of gold for jewellery in their asset portfolio. Despite its handicaps on personal freedom, which the US economy so espouses, this was the matter of economic strategy and policy that gave a comfortable bridge for the global economy to traverse from the ravages of depression, war and exchange rate volatility and disorder to the climate of economic stability and sustained growth. Gold did serve its economic and social link and purpose in providing a systemic potential for pursuing the Keynesian Revolution and enabling Technology to realize its full potential for rapid economic progress and global development, bypassing the longer and treacherous traditional cyclical route.

Gold–money rift

The Bretton Woods system was not as rigid as the gold standard, but the currency values were expressed in terms of gold content, and the US dollar gold price of \$35 (compared to \$20.67 in 1933) per ounce of gold formed the basis for the structure of exchange rates of all currencies. The switchover to the dollar standard necessitated global confidence in the dollar. And the confidence in the dollar stemmed primarily from the US gold stocks, its ability to maintain an open market gold price to the gold–dollar parity, and the economic and balance of payments strength of the US. Looking to the size of US gold stocks and the requirements of global liquidity in 1944, the system had the sustainability to run efficiently for about two decades. Under Bretton Woods, the US bought a lease for 25 years to enjoy the *seigniorage*. It was natural that Bretton Woods was only a bridge in the long process of evolution of a gold-free global monetary system and would have to give way to the new evolving system.

In 1944, the predominance of US gold stocks of 21,678 tonnes (now valued at \$480 billion), which accounted for 80 percent of the value of monetary gold of all central banks weighed in favor of the US positioning the dollar as the international currency and major reserve asset. It was still a formidable force in the global monetary and economic system, looking to the scarcity value of gold and popular attachment to the metal worldwide and its use by the central banks as a reserve asset. By retaining gold at the center of the system, the US could capitalize on its strength for another two and half decades. The US pursued the policy of '*benign neglect*' in respect of its BoP management and the role of the US dollar in the international monetary system. Under this philosophy, the US pursued its monetary and fiscal policies exclusively to meet the demands of growth, employment and price stability. It refrained from imposing any restrictions on trade and capital movements. And also kept the value of the dollar in terms of gold fixed and let other countries change their exchange rates.[12] The policy of '*benign neglect*' remained effective under the gold-based dollar standard to enable the global economic system to have stable economic growth during the 1950s and 1960s. By the late 1960s the signs of structural disequilibrium in the system were evident. In 1971, the gold stocks of the US dwindled to \$10.2 billion compared with \$24.4 billion in 1948, and liquid liabilities of US to foreigners bulged to \$40 billion. The '*gold–money rift*' that developed in the late 1960s lifted the market price of gold above \$35 an ounce, at which the US guaranteed conversion of its liabilities to foreign central banks into gold.[13]

Gold was ready and ripe for demonetization from the international monetary system under the pressure of market forces. A monetary system survives, lives, runs and prospers on confidence. Historically, gold shaped the monetary world, guided the economic behavior of many economies and the global economy for centuries. The system was inequitable. It gave bonanza to the gold producing nations and worked against those countries not producing gold. That is what economics is all about: to analyze the inequalities arising from tnatural phenomena and to devise measures to evolve systems that would be more equitable. What is with gold is also with oil. Each natural resource has its time frame to play its role in economic development. Gold could not meet the pressure of demands from global economic development and had to give way to a new system.

Since Bretton Woods worked under fixed but adjustable exchange rates, the time was ripe for the move to a more flexible exchange rate mechanism for many reasons. Although Bretton Woods was not as rigid as the gold standard, the economies did not have the choice of independence in monetary policies. Monetary policies used to be harmonious. Alternatively, the central banks had to either permit changes in the level of forex reserves or alter the exchange rate parity. With the experience of inflexibility of exchange rates and the desire for greater independence in monetary policy, the stage was set for a switchover to the floating rates mechanism.

The Bretton Woods exchange rates system, which pursued managed flexibility, continued for nearly two and half decades before showing signs of cracking under the pressure of an increasing build up of an overhang of the US dollar liabilities to other central banks on the one hand, and a failure to keep the gold price in the free market from going above $35, owing to relatively higher imbalance in private demand for gold and the supply of gold from the central banks' holdings in the free market, on the other. The system benefited three nations immensely. The USA incurred deficits on the capital account, which were financed through US Treasury Bills holdings by the foreign central banks. It could loan or invest dollars abroad when warranted by its trade surpluses, and still finance it without pressure on the dollar exchange rate through its Treasury Bills. Japan and Germany, rebuilt from the ravages of war, emerged as export-led growth economies and models in the development experience, only with prolonged undervaluation of their currencies. Any revaluation of the D-Mark or the Yen during the 1960s would have thrown their growth model awry and invariably slowed their speed to prosperity. Revaluation of the D-Mark and the Yen would also have meant devaluation of the US dollar, although it could have been achieved by Japan and Germany by increasing the gold content of their currencies. It would not have meant a generalized devaluation of the US dollar. However, this would have substantially curtailed exports and the economic growth of Germany and Japan.

By late 1960s, the confidence in the gold–dollar standard was shaken by the gold–money rift, i.e. excessive accumulation of US external liabilities to the foreign central banks far surpassing the value of gold stocks at Fort Knox. This overhang of overseas dollar liquid liabilities brought upward pressure on the market price of gold, necessitating central banks releasing supplies of their gold in the free market to keep it at the level of $35 an ounce. Threatened by the sustained loss of gold reserves of the central banks to the free gold market, President Nixon, in a historic decision in August, 1971, abandoned gold from the international monetary system. The US dollar became non-convertible into gold and was untied from gold. The currencies became free to float in the exchange market for exchange rate determination. The regime of floating exchange rates began operating in 1973.

Euro-currency market and commercial debt crisis

During the late 1960s, accumulation of dollar deposits outside the US and the growth of offshore banking centers developed the euro-dollar market, a parallel money market for the US dollar outside the US. The market assumed a new dimension in the aftermath of the oil crisis in 1974. The oil price hike brought a structural transformation in the composition and direction of international payments. The balance of international payments swung in favor of OPEC. And these surpluses found a way into the lucrative euro dollar market. The other side of the surpluses was the huge deficits faced by the oil importing nations. The massive disequilibria in the balance of international payments were required to be both financed and adjusted. Macroeconomic and exchange rate adjustments were both inadequate and undesirable for global economic welfare. There was an imperative need for financing this massive deficit faced by the oil importing nations. The constitutional rigidities as well as inadequate capital and resource base did not permit the World Bank and IMF to provide adequate financial assistance. These institutions made a limited effort in mitigating the payments problem of the oil importing nations. They could not undertake the massive petrodollar surplus recycling operation, which was imperative. At this juncture, the euro currency market operated by the international banks came to the rescue of the global economy by working as an efficient recycling mechanism, meeting the foreign currency requirements of developing nations. The global economy survived another depression, which may have engulfed it but for the dynamism of the euro-dollar market run by major multinational commercial banks. The market phenomenon and institutions, rather than joint government action, rescued the global economy from the clutches of the first most serious recessionary threat in post-war history. The euro currency market recycled the petrodollars and avoided a major international financial catastrophe.

Oil importing LDCs made heavy borrowings in the euro-dollar market and some countries went to the extent of making them a budgetary funding source. Debt servicing ratios of many countries went beyond the prudential limits. High interest rates sparked by the dear money policy of the Federal Reserve in 1980 put a crushing burden of debt servicing on several borrowing nations. This led to several nations of Latin America, Africa and East Europe making payments defaults, and triggering the debt crisis in 1982 which required write offs and extensive rescheduling of loans by the banks.

Globalization under the 3W Model (Washington–World Bank–Wall Street model)

The post-war development experience of the less developed world, for more than three decades, showed the fulfillments remaining below the high expectations that were built by new economic models and policies of development. Problems of illiteracy, inadequate drinking water, sanitation, housing, health care, power, and transportation continued to haunt the societies, and the economic ills of poverty and unemployment remained far from removed. The inequalities in standards of living, income and wealth within the less developed societies, and between them and the developed world enlarged instead of narrowing despite the best efforts, strategies and policies from both within and without.

At the end of the 1970s a slow but perceptible and distinct change also occurred on the global ideological front and economics of production of commodity industries in the developed world. Communism in the Soviet Union and Eastern Europe weakened to the extent of collapse, and staged a transition to a newer market-oriented, private enterprise economy. China realized the futility of destructive and endless war with US imperialism in Vietnam. China also felt the need for modernizing its mammoth economic machine to raise its growth rate and generate employment. In its ideological summersault, China had to depend on the US as its partner in trade and investment and be ready for market-oriented reforms acceptable to the multinational corporations.

In the developed world, a large number of commodity industries matured and faced cost constraints owing to high labor costs. Relocation of these high-cost industries with capital and technology transfers to China and other emerging market economies of Asia and Latin America seemed the best strategy for more balanced global economic development. Ricardo's principle of comparative cost advantage was to be given the largest scale application in recent economic history. It was a win-win strategy for the developed world and the emerging market economies. The term 'emerging market economies' for developing economies or the Third World nations was invented by Antoine van Agtmael, who was one of the early enthusiasts at the IFC (International Finance Corporation, an affiliate of the World Bank), promoting portfolio investment in equity shares in the emerging market economies as an alternative vehicle and catalyst for their industrial development. During the course of preparation for the launch of the 'Third World Equity Fund' in September, 1981, he sensed that the term Third World lacked the punch and sounded ideological.

> Racking my brain, I at last came up with a term that sounded more positive and invigorating: Emerging Markets. 'Third World' suggested stagnation; 'Emerging Markets' suggested progress, uplift, and dynamism. The following Monday, I sat down at my desk at IFC and dashed off a memo that made my message explicit. From now on, we would consistently refer to our Third World database as the Emerging Markets Data Base and the first index we created for emerging markets would be the IFC Emerging Markets Index. Thus, a phrase was coined. Born from conviction and based on firsthand observation in Asia.[14]

The change was not just cosmetic. It also coincided the dawn of a new era of resource transfer to the emerging market economies that changed the development philosophy and became a central feature of globalization.

The commercial debt model lay disgraced by the excessive use of debt and its onerous servicing impact. The only way through which the development of LDCs could be sustained was from more liberal trade and private investment. In this scenario, the capital market alone could release the resources required on such a gigantic scale. 'Don't put all your eggs in one basket', the age-old invest-ment maxim was followed widely, but it had to wait until Markowitz gave theo-retical expression to this simple concept in his theory of portfolio selection in 1952. The theory of portfolio diversification enunciated the first measure of risk (covariance or standard deviation of returns), and inverse relation between risk and return. The principle of diversification of investment for risk minimization became the mantra for investment for the professional investment managers of large institutional investors, but not until late 1970s when all markets, commod-ity, stock, bond, and forex, went through turbulent times. From 1972 to 1974 oil prices quadrupled, gold prices went through the roof, the US dollar fell in value in forex markets by 50 percent, S&P 500 fell by 43 percent, US long-term Treasury bonds lost 28 percent, while inflation was running at 11 percent. Risk diversification became the name of the game among institutional investors. Diversification was the mantra in investment, whether within a market or across the markets. Large investments of insurance companies, pension funds, and mutual funds in the developed countries remained invested in debt and equities within their own capital markets. Diversification stirred the idea for global port-folio reallocation among the institutional investors.[15] The capital markets of developing countries, termed as the emerging markets, were yet to be explored by the developed world. Both the imperatives of the sustainable global economic development and the principle of investment diversification gave the logical basis for the transfer of resources to the emerging markets through the capital market route. The new model of development took shape. To translate the prin-ciple of investment diversification internationally meant channeling a part of investable funds of institutional investors of the developed nations into the stocks and securities in the emerging markets.

The emerging capital markets were required to be developed in order to absorb this transfer of resources. They also needed to clear the cobwebs in their regulated financial system, and graduate their financial markets into flexible, integrated, transparent and efficient allocators of capital. Looking to the magni-tude of institutional investments and annual saving inflows, the new model could provide adequate resources for development in the emerging markets. Liberal-ization and market reforms could also attract higher private direct investment. The growth in financial markets globally and their closer integration was greatly facilitated by technology. The computer and telecom revolution could absorb ever-increasing volumes in turnover in financial markets and bring orderly set-tlements at a faster speed and lower cost. The flow of private external savings and investments through the capital markets to the emerging markets was to be the driving force of liberalization and globalization.

The shift towards new economic policy dominated by liberalization, privati-zation, and globalization began against this background in the 1980s. The removal of barriers to trade and controls on capital movements necessitated the opening up of economies with deregulation of industrial, trade and financial sectors. The new development model for the emerging market economies evolved by the ideologues in the US Treasury–Fund Bank–Wall Street centered on economic reforms with a major thrust on the free market mechanism and free foreign trade and investment. The Washington–World Bank–Wall Street Model (3W Model) was the most significant global economic and monetary initiative since Bretton Woods and Keynesianism, which changed the course of economic and financial developments throughout the world. Popularly known as the Washington Consensus, comprising ten principles – Fiscal Discipline, Redirection of Public Expenditure, Tax Reforms, Interest Rate Liberalization, Competitive Exchange Rate, Trade Liberalization, Liberalization of FDI and Portfolio Investments, Privatization, Deregulation, Intellectual Property Rights – the model was ready for launch, first in the Latin American countries, then in China in its half-baked form due to the ideological make up and commitment, and later in the East Asian countries.[16] The initial euphoria created by the East Asian Miracle gave strong credence to the success of the model until the onset of the Asian crisis in 1997. The Latin American story also showed mixed results of growth and crisis, or a boom–bust cycle.

Globalization is a process of increasing integration of different economies of the world. The emergence of floating exchange rates and the rapid growth of the euro-dollar market whose size surpassed the money supply in the US, were strong manifestations of excessive financial regulation and incoherent monetary policies in different economies. The early 1980s set the stage for globalization through gradual removal of restrictions on trade, capital movements and labor mobility.

Technology has been a great trigger in financial globalization. The transformation of the financial markets into the digital technology world of the computer, internet and telecom technology, offered unlimited scope for further expansion. A lower cost, superfast, safe, secure and transparent information highway is a boon to the globalization of markets, which have been growing at a rapid pace and without any hindrance.

The globalization proceeded in different countries or regions in different forms and shapes, with a different sequencing of policies at different speeds. The internal economic environment and equations of different sectoral regulations and freedom, varied from country to country. Deregulation involves a change in institutions that have evolved over years. The change has to be steady and careful to minimize destabilization, and coincided with proactive rehabilitation of resources. Globalization is not a single, simplistic, uniform model to be adopted for application across the borders of different nations to achieve quick, measurable and tangible returns. More often than not, the pluses in one direction are more likely to leave lots of minuses in several others. Hence, there is a need for keeping the human face intact and in good shape, while taking economic reforms to their logical end. A couple of landmines, or a few nasty potholes and risky curves are enough to turn the joyride in the process of reforms into a nightmare. The experiences in Latin America, Asia, Africa and Russia are varied and their crises manifest the lacunae in sequencing, speed and strategy of a reform process.

Globalization is not without its critics. There are overt opponents and staunch critics, such as the Left idealists and environmentalists, who are against the very philosophy of globalization, and call it a hidden plan of the capitalist system to spread neo-imperialism under the control of global corporations. There are others, and they are in larger numbers, who see globalization as a compulsive trend and need of human society with its current technological base and rate of progress which cannot be reversed, but want a change in its content and direction. Joseph Stiglitz – an insider in the process of globalization, who became an outsider after his bitter experience of fiascos and crises in Latin America, Asia and Russia – is one of the staunchest critics of the form globalization is now taking, especially in its utter disregard to the human face in the process. 'I believe that globalization can be reshaped to realize its potential for good and I believe that the international economic institutions can be reshaped in ways that help ensure that this is accomplished'.[17] George Soros, another strong protagonist of globalization but not in its current form, is also an advocate of the restructuring of institutions such as the IMF, World Bank and WTO, to be more compatible, and to eliminate the ill effects of globalization and make it more humane and productive towards the emerging markets.[18]

In a large number of countries, high-speed economic reforms, comprising the total opening up of economies, financial and trade liberalization, removal of capital account controls, and free exchange rates, have caused noticeable disruptions leading to larger unemployment that is not mitigated due to the absence of social safety nets and efforts to rehabilitate labor and other resources discarded by the new system. On the other hand, disproportionately large benefits have accrued to the new and growing sectors and those sections of population associated with them. The vigorous operation of the market mechanism has its large number of beneficiaries of population whom it embraces. But it has also kicked the market rejects in not small numbers. These market rejects are the sore point that has brought globalization its discredit. In addition, there are the poor and destitute that are outside the market system and need to be brought into it for their benefit. Market outsiders need to be made insiders, requiring more inclusive reforms. These cannot be done by the market mechanism and it needs government intervention and commitment. Disruptions are a part of the reform process, but the pace, content and sequence of reforms have been in total disregard to their ill effects on the poor and destitute. This has actually tended to accentuate inequalities after reforms and has been the worst and most neglected aspect of reforms making them unpalatable and evoking strong discontent and mass protests as well as criticisms from several economists, intellectuals, thinkers and policy makers who still support the concept of globalization. Reforms need to be accompanied by a strong, committed and adequate program of rehabilitation and support for market rejects and market outsiders. Giving the redistributive angle of globalization and its importance, Amartya Sen very eloquently says.

> I have tried to argue elsewhere that these (anti-globalization) protest movements have often been, in many ways, quite constructive, in forcefully drawing attention to problems of inequality in the world. Indeed, the real

debate on globalization is, ultimately, not about the efficiency of markets, nor about the importance of modern technology. The debate, rather, is about severe asymmetries of power, for which there is much less tolerance now than in the world that emerged at the end of World War II. There may or may not be significantly more economic inequality today, as is sometimes strongly asserted and equally staunchly denied (the evidence on this is conflicting, depending on the indicators we use), but what is absolutely clear is that people are far less willing to accept massive inequalities than they were in 1944 when the Bretton Woods agreement led to the establishment of the IMF, the World Bank and other institutions and paved the way for the present international architecture of finance and business. The global doubts partly reflect this new mood, and it is, to a great extent, the global equivalent of the within-nation protests about inequality with which we have been familiar for quite some time.[19]

The 3W Model sought to reallocate global production capacities from high-cost developed nations to the cheaper emerging market economies. Ricardo's Principle of Comparative Cost Advantage, as the logical foundation of the policy of free trade due to its economic gains, finally found a true support in the 3W Model. It seeks to bring about better allocation of global resources, more efficient production, lower prices, better global distribution of income and employment and higher global economic welfare. In line with the 3W Model, large foreign direct investments created large capacities in commodity industries in China, Asia and Latin America. China's Great Leap Forward and the Asian Miracle transformed these economies into foreign investment driven export-oriented growth machines. The share of exports in their economies and in global trade recorded a leapfrogging jump. The counterpart to export surpluses of these nations is the rising trade deficit of the US, which ballooned from $131 billion in 1991 to $836 billion in 2006. Their rising forex reserves were invested back in the US Treasuries to enable the US to finance its balance of payments. The Great Bull Market of the 1990s, the continuing stream of innovations in industries and, more particularly, in the Information Technology and Telecoms industries, vibrant capital market, and cheap money and the low interest policy of Greenspan attracted large capital flows back to the US. It is this prospect of a higher return on risk capital, higher real interest rates despite cheap money due to low inflation, and lowest risk in the US Treasuries that brought equity and debt capital back to the US from rest of the world and kept the dollar strong despite its huge and ever-increasing trade deficit. The flow of private savings from multinational corporations and institutional investors to the emerging markets set the 3W Model moving, and the return flow of public sector cash surpluses from the forex reserve accumulating central banks into the US Treasuries brought it to its logical conclusion. The 3W Model is examined later from the perspective of its new method of financing global development and its repercussions on evolving a new pattern of global financial flows.

2 Genesis of the philosophy of globalization

New experiment in economic development – from aid to trade and debt to equity

While the chronological evolution of globalization has been illustrated in the previous chapter, this chapter covers the ideological development and theoretical genesis of globalization. The evolution of globalization as the new philosophy of economic development in the emerging market economies, matching the sourcing and supporting the growth in the mature developed economies, would be better understood by a review of the experience of development over the decades until the end of the 1970s. Economic theories and policies always emerge and get shaped in response to the needs of the contemporary economic environment. A changing milieu evolves new relationships between the economic parameters unexplainable by the traditional theories and new problems remain intractable by conventional wisdom.[20] While the previous chapter covered the philosophy of globalization in the context of evolution of the international monetary system and the motivation from the developed world, the 3W Model also had an important underpinning from the needs and aspirations of the emerging market economies. This chapter looks at the experience of the earlier development models that were tried for the Third World countries. The phase of globalization can then be viewed in historical order and with a better perspective.

External aid

The development experience of developing economies, for nearly three decades until the 1970s, presents a mixed picture. Countries in Asia, Latin America and Africa followed development paths varying in shades in their thrust towards free market mechanism on the one hand, and planning and control on the other. The government involvement in economic activities and the use of a market mechanism also differed in magnitude under the influence of national political environment, and relations with and closeness to the capitalist or communist blocs. Despite whatever model they adopted, the need for an external resource for development remained imperative. Hence, beginning in the 1950s, the bilateral aid formed the major vehicle to the transfer of resources from the developed world to bridge the resource gap. The experimentation with bilateral aid raised several questions. Invariably, bilateral aid had political strings attached to it and, in the majority of cases, the aid was also tied aid, to be used in the donor country and in products specified by it. It also tended to be misallocated and misused. Although some bilateral aid schemes, like PL480, enabled several developing countries and also India to tide over their food crisis, the overall experience of bilateral aid did not vindicate it as an efficient channel to promote the growth rate in developing economies. In 1968, Gunnar Myrdal, in his most perceptive, deep and scholarly study entitled the 'Asian Drama', outlining the experience of development and economic policies observed,

> It is clear that the present system of bilateral aid has a strong tendency towards what, from an economic point of view, can be construed as misallocation. It is impossible to say how much of the economic assistance to South Asia has been misplaced, but there is no doubt that much of it has been wasted or has even inhibited essential reforms.[21]

By the late 1960s there was a growing consensus for channeling the development assistance through multilateral agencies such as the World Bank, IMF and Aid consortia.

Following the era of bilateral aid and soft loans, which were under attack for several inefficiencies, the flow of multilateral aid from global agencies and consortia took the lead in meeting the capital requirements of developing economies. The World Bank came in the forefront of this effort to multilateralize the aid flow and bring greater efficiency in decision making, allocation and utilization of aid among the recipient nations. Notwithstanding the improvement in the delivery mechanism, its transparency and utilization, the official channels of investment and lending were not adequate to meet the high and growing requirements of capital of the developing economies.

In 1969, the Pearson Commission Report on International Development recommended the transfer target of 0.7 percent of GNP of the industrialized nations in the form of official aid to developing nations. The actual experience was, however, disappointing with the percentage share declining from 0.53 percent in the early 1960s to a low of 0.32 percent in 1976. The absolute amount of official aid, however, in 1978, had doubled to $18 billion over ten years. The share of official aid in resource transfer declined from 52 percent in 1969 to 38 percent in 1975, while that of non-concessional flows increased from 48 percent to 62 percent. Several factors caused the declining flow of development assistance from developed nations. The inflationary pressures in these nations forced them to reduce deficits in their budgets. The oil crisis of 1974 brought an unexpected burden on their balance of payments. Increasing the arms race with the Communist bloc also curtailed the resources available for development aid. Finally, disillusionment with development aid necessitated a search for alternative media of resource transfer to the developing world.

Trade, not aid

Foreign trade has been the engine of growth even among the developed nations during the early stages of their development. 'In Western Europe, North America, and Australia, industrial development took place initially through a buoyant and expanding volume of international trade ... . Increases in exports once paved the way for importing capital goods that perpetuated and stimulated development'.[22] Further, foreign-trade generated economic development is more sustainable than the one triggered by foreign aid because the latter usually requires a continuous dose of assistance to meet the resource gap. The former is also built on capital formation, which sustains the output growth based on increasing foreign demand for exports.

Developing nations were the major suppliers of primary commodities, such as agricultural products, minerals and other raw materials, to the developed world. The major primary exports comprised tea, coffee, tobacco, cotton, sugar, tropical fruits, edible oils and minerals such as copper, aluminum, iron ore, and fuels such as coal and crude oil. It was thought that if these countries lacked resources for their development, the same could be raised by promoting their exports. In addition to the growth in their volumes and value addition, it was imperative to gain increases in the prices of primary products.

The problem of constraint on exports growth of the LDCs (Less Developed Countries) emerged due to a series of developments. A large number of traditional exports faced stagnant demand in the world market. Both price and income elasticities of demand for primary products remained low. This phenomenon was termed as the 'elasticity pessimism', reflecting the dim prospects for growth in primary exports of LDCs. The prices of these products were either stagnant or falling, while prices of manufactured goods were increasing. The secular decline in terms of trade of developing nations worked against their interest and retarded their development process. In fact, trade – instead of acting as an engine of growth – worked as a drag on their development, causing a reverse transfer of resources to the developed nations, while it should have been the other way round. In addition to this market phenomenon of declining terms of trade, the developing nations faced both tariff and non-tariff barriers to trade imposed by the rich nations to limit the growth in these exports and protect their local production. The thesis of secular decline in terms of trade of developing nations propounded by Raul Prebisch led to the serious effort, through multilateral negotiations, in the 1960s under the auspices of the UNCTAD (United Nations Conference on Trade Development) for tariff and non-tariff reduction. A series of rounds of UNCTAD trade negotiations worked towards removing tariff barriers, and other pricing and non-pricing arrangements to improve the growth in exports as well as the terms of trade of developing nations. Export growth was thought to be a superior vehicle of promoting growth in the developing nations rather than transferring resources directly through aid. However, despite a series of negotiations under UNCTAD and later the WTO, claims of developing nations as exporters did not meet with much success.

Except to OPEC, which has been able to dictate its own terms on pricing of crude oil, no other group of primary exporters has been able wield that kind of power in the global market. In fact, the OPEC experience is a vivid example in world trade as to how economic development of nations can change with pricing of their exports. The growth and prosperity enjoyed by Japan and West Germany in the post-war period was also based on the export-oriented growth model. Exports played a major role in the super normal growth of Asian Tigers and China since the 1980s. Their export orientation, which increased the share of their exports in GNP, was also supported by massive equity investments in export oriented sectors.

> Politically it is easier for the rich Western countries to provide grants and credits that enable their own commercial interests to increase their exports than it is for them to permit a volume of imports that may adversely affect some branch of domestic industry. Yet an increase in manufactured exports is potentially more stimulating to an underdeveloped economy than bilateral foreign grants and loans, which suffer from great uncertainty and other shortcomings. The slogan 'Trade, Not Aid' has real meaning for South Asia.[23]

What Myrdal foresaw as the strategy for growth of South Asia in 1968 became reality in the 1980s. Myrdal's dream of switching on foreign trade as the engine of growth was realized and it turned the Asian Drama into the Asian Miracle. The Asian Drama was a critical analysis of the failures of the earlier development model in Asia, and the Asian Miracle is Myrdyl's dream realized. Yet another pressing consideration for the developed nations (led by the US) actively pursuing the policy of Foreign Trade Oriented Growth in Asia was the reality of growing disparity in wages and production cost of commodities in Asia and the developed world. Ignoring Ricardo's theory of comparative costs in order to give protection to the domestic industries was becoming increasingly expensive for the developed nations. Low wage labor in Asia was making a significant difference in manufacturing costs. In order to sustain growth in its incomes and consumption, the developed world had to shift and expand the manufacturing base of a large number of commodities and consumer products outside itself, and Asia was the most attractive destination. This policy also followed the international geo-political compulsion in which both the US and China realized the futility of the bitter, wasteful, costly and endless war in Vietnam. The diplomatic coup achieved by Henry Kissinger and President Nixon through the strategy of détente paved the way for the U-turn in policy for the US and China. The US finally accepted China as a partner in trade and investment rather than a political and ideological Communist enemy.

Both the economic and political compulsions emanating from a changing economic environment, geo-political scenario and balance of power forced the developed world (led by the US) to enter first the giant Chinese Dragon, and later the smaller Asian Tigers adopting the 3W Model of foreign trade and investment-oriented growth strategy, beginning in the 1980s, that became the focus of global development. The Asian Miracle, despite the crisis of 1997, transformed the continent and became a role model for repeat in other nations.

LDC debt balloon and crisis

The euro currency debt route, which enabled the global economy to tide over the oil crisis became a major problem to the LDCs when, by the late 1970s, many countries borrowed very heavily, throwing the cautionary debt servicing norms overboard. In addition to private commercial debt, the sovereign debt, which was very small, started increasing at a rapid pace. The utilization of debt for non-project, non-productive and generalized BoP and also budgetary purposes by the governments of several nations pushed them on to a slippery path. The high level of sovereign debt and its failure to contribute to the BoP, pressed the debt servicing ratios into the danger zone. The external public debt of the LDCs soared to $580 billion in 1980. From the low interest phase, the interest rates in the US and the euro-dollar market also reached a record high in 1980 with the six month LIBOR touching 21 percent. This unprecedented and severely adverse development exerted enormous pressure on the debt servicing and forex reserves of the borrowing nations. The countries borrowed further in order to raise their level of forex reserves to avoid defaults. At the end of 1982, the nine major US banks had lent out over 287 percent of their capital to the developing countries.[24] The magnitude of the exposure of the US banks to the LDCs and primary Latin American countries and the possibility of payment defaults threatened the stability of the US banking system and raised fears of a banking collapse. In order to redress the crisis, in 1987 the Citicorp, the biggest lender, took the lead in writing off the loan losses from its free reserves. The other US banks followed suit and averted the onset of the first major banking crisis since the 1930s. This was followed by the Brady Plan of debt reduction and rescheduling in 1989 that defused the debt crisis and gave a long-term solution to the debt servicing and BoP problems of the borrowing nations by issuing the 30 year par and zero coupon Brady Bonds of the record amount of $175 billion. The LDC debt crisis of the 1980s was a big setback to the development effort as the debt model of development stood discredited and needed a better replacement. It also opened up a fresh debate on the right model for future development of the developing nations.

Equity routed growth

While external aid, trade and debt all played their due roles in the experiment in economic development for the three decades up to the 1980s, risk capital was yet to be tried and given its rightful place and predominance in the development model. Although economic theories highlighted the merits of foreign direct investment in the development of growing nations, neither direct investment nor portfolio investment ever played a dominant role in growth in these economies. By early the 1980s with the process of economic liberalization taking shape in several emerging market economies, it was time to promote growth through the risk capital.

The wave of liberalization also coincided with excess capacity, and recession in mature and developed economies. It was a natural process of tapering of their initial high growth phase. The surplus financial resources of developed nations needed an outlet for investment outside their economies. It became imperative to the developed economies to evolve a new development philosophy to sustain growth in their economies as well as to strive for higher and better growth in the developing economies. The new 3W Model primarily focused on the market mechanism in general and capital market in particular to promote investment and growth in the newly emerging markets. The need for a market mechanism and the earlier development experience of foreign aid, trade, and commercial borrowings, brought the focus of the new development model on to equity investments. The growth in the emerging market economies, through equity investments, was also in the interest in the developed economies. Emphasis was on direct investment as well as portfolio investment. Hence, the capital market became the focal point for directing investment in this new model of development. The thrust of policy on equity financing also necessitated the efficient functioning of stock markets.

The debate on advantages and disadvantages of a bank-based financial system vis-à-vis the market-based system has been continuing in Germany, Japan, the UK and the US for a long time. In Japan and Germany, the bank-based financial system is predominant, with the banks playing a major role in mobilizing savings, allocating capital, overseeing the corporate sector and providing risk management vehicles. In contrast, the market-based financial system is prevalent in the UK and the US. In this system, the securities markets are at center stage, with the banks mobilizing and allocating community savings and reducing risks. Whether the capital markets are more efficient than the financial intermediaries, such as banks and financial institutions, is an issue that is yet to be resolved. Nevertheless, the securitization proceeded in the US at a very fast pace and left the banking industry behind. 'Securitization progressed throughout the 1990s, so much so that at the end of the decade, the US financial system had become virtually "market centric", as opposed to the "banking centric" system still dominating European (especially Continental) financial intermediation'.[25]

In developing economies, the banking development has preceded the securities markets development. One of the key areas of reform concerning the financial sector relates to the securities market development. A broad-based development of the securities market is indispensable for improving the efficiency of the financial system. The wave of reform, liberalization, and globalization that swept across the emerging markets placed a major impetus on restoring or improving the market mechanism. In the field of financial reform, it involved the development and growth of securities markets. The policy of transfer of resources also underwent a change to be compatible with the new philosophy of growth. Development finance, which was routed through the aid, soft loans, and commercial debt for three decades until the 1970s, was channeled through the mechanism of equity in the 1980s. The emphasis on equity investment also came at a time when the returns on equity in the mature and developed markets were low and declining. In contrast, the emerging markets offered attractive opportunities for equity investment with a higher rate of return.

Yet another reason for the development of the equity route was that it was market oriented and hence was thought to be more efficient than other non-market transfers of resources such as soft loans and aid. Another difference between aid/loans and equity was that the former were financed by the government and government-assisted multilateral agencies, while the latter was from private sources and primarily private institutions, such as mutual funds, pension funds and investment banks. Further, the mode of injection of financial resources through the equity was itself to contribute to the development of emerging equity markets. The foreign equity flow was also to be accompanied by several infrastructural improvements and upgradation of the markets and the regulatory framework.

Global investment diversification – a panacea for balanced global development

The search for a new channel for the transfer of resources was backed by developments in investment theory and empirical results advocating diversification of an investment portfolio on a higher investment frontier, giving higher returns with lower risk. The early 1970s in the US was a disastrous period for investment and, more particularly, to the professional fund managers who managed billions of dollars of savings of individuals and firms. The shift from fixed exchange rates to floating exchange rates, the quadrupling of oil prices, recession in industries, rising interest rates, the slump in equity prices, fall in bond prices, rising inflation, all created the most complex and uncertain climate for fund managers. In this environment, Markovitz's theory of investment diversification, although published in 1952, found increasing acceptance among large institutional investors in the late 1970s.[26] Until 1979, the so-called 'prudent man rule' was interpreted as that preventing any significant investment in assets considered risky. Stocks were, until then, considered risky for pension fund investment. 'In 1979 the US Department of Labor finally clarified the concept of prudence; risky investments were deemed legitimate if they were part of a well diversified portfolio strategy'.[27] This decision paved the way for pension funds, endowment funds and trusts starting investments in listed equities but also other riskier intermediaries such as venture capital funds, buyout funds and vulture funds.[28]

The international investment also enables investors to diversify risk and attain better risk-return trade-off. This is truer of the developed and mature markets where the return on capital is on the decline and is much lower than in the many emerging markets. Hence, the concept of investment diversification got later extended for investments in equities in foreign countries and also in the emerging capital markets. Large institutional investors primarily comprising mutual funds, pension funds and insurance and investment companies with their massive investments could consider giving a small haircut to their domestic investments to invest in emerging market equities. A small percentage of their resources deployed in the emerging markets was substantially higher than the resources flowing through aid. It was the win-win strategy for both countries. The aid is funded by the taxpayers of the developed nations, for which they do not receive any tangible benefits, except that it could give rise to imports from the donor nation. In the case of portfolio investment in the emerging markets, while these nations benefit from the inflows of funds, the taxpayers in the investor country also gain due to higher return on their investments. Portfolio investments offered a win-win situation for the developed nations as well as the emerging markets. It integrated the emerging capital markets with those of the developed nations. Further, the capital flows also helped in broader based development of the market with a larger number of institutional players, larger turnover, and greater liquidity, and brought general improvement in the efficiency of the market. This, along with several systemic and infrastructural improvements in the market, lowered the transaction cost as well as the impact cost. These markets adopted a computerized trading, set up depositories to dematerialize all securities, adopted a uniform, and shorter mode of trading, settlement and payments cycles, and operated derivatives such as options and futures in both stocks and indices. All these developments brought the emerging markets on a par with the developed stock markets in trading operation. The emerging markets also became more transparent in addition to being more efficient. By 1981, the launch of the Emerging Market Equity Fund, followed by several other country funds, opened the gate of equity investments in the emerging markets and became a precursor to the Foreign Institutional Investor (FII) investment on a larger scale.[29]

The global asset allocation policy provides the benefits of wider diversification with the potential of higher returns at lower risk. A study of US domestic and global balanced portfolios for the period from 1969 to 1990 vindicates the global diversification theory. The domestic portfolio consisted of fixed allocations of US equity and bond index funds. The global portfolios additionally include a non-US equity index fund and a non-dollar bond index fund. All portfolios were rebalanced monthly. This long period saw both fixed and floating exchange rates, prolonged bouts of US dollar strength and weakness, dramatic change in average global inflation rates and substantial change in inflation differentials amongst different countries. The study showed that the global portfolio generated higher return than the mere US domestic one that had similar volatility. A 'mid-risk' domestic portfolio of 60 percent equity and 40 percent bonds generate an annual return of 10.2 percent with a standard deviation of 13.2 percent. A global portfolio that also had a 60 to 40 allocation of equity to bonds and that included non-US equities and bonds generated 10.7 percent with a standard deviation of 12.6 percent.[30]

> While the dollar returns from non-US equity and bond indexes were more volatile than returns from the respective US markets over this period, the relatively low correlation of US and non-US assets suggests that both should have a significant role in the policy asset mix.[31]

Table 2.1 Global equity valuations (3/31/2004)

	Price to earnings	Price to book value	Price to cash earnings	Estimated 3–5 year EPS growth rate
United States	20.8	3.1	13.1	12.30%
Europe	17.7	2.2	8.8	9.30%
Japan	69.1	1.7	9.1	15.50%
Emerging markets	15.8	2	9.6	16.00%

Source: Fact Set 2004; SSgA Advisor Consulting Services Research.

The period of study was up to 1990, and data which referred to the investment in developed capital markets, the US and non-US, did not cover many emerging markets. The returns in the emerging markets have been much higher than in the developed markets during the 1990s.

The emerging markets cover 3.7 billion people, 80 percent of the world's population, although its market capitalization is only 4–5 percent of the global equity markets in dollar terms. The economic growth and corporate earnings growth in the emerging market economies has been higher than in the developed world and the equity valuations have also been cheaper in the emerging markets. Table 2.1 shows that the valuations of equities in the emerging markets on all the valuation parameters, such as PE ratio, Price to Book Value and Cash Earnings Ratios, are much higher than in the US, Europe and Japan. The estimated future earnings growth of corporates in the emerging markets is also higher.

Despite the volatility in the emerging markets and the series of crises such as the Mexican devaluation in 1994, the Asian crisis in 1997, and the Russian stock market crash in 1998, the long-term returns from the emerging market equities were much better. For a 15 year period ending March 31, 2004, the MSCI Emerging Market Index (Morgan Stanley Capital International) returned, in dollars, 10.37 percent per annum, more than twice the 4.23 percent return of the MSCI EAFE (Europe, America, Far East) Index. The MSCI Emerging Market Index returned 82.16 percent, significantly outperforming the 58.15 percent return of the developed markets and the S&P 500 Index, which returned 35.13 percent. Over five years, ending March 1, 2004, emerging market equities outperformed the S&P 500 Index by more than 10 percent.[32] Another study of annual stock market returns by regions, the US (S&P 500), Europe, Australia and Far East (EAFE), and the Emerging Markets (EM) for the 15 year period from 1988 to 2002, shows similar results.

The lowest risk, 14.3 percent, is for the U.S. stock market whereas the highest risk, 23.9 percent, is for emerging markets. The emerging markets also have the highest return of 17.6 percent compared to a return of 13.6 percent for the U.S. markets. As a stand-alone market, the U.S. market is better than the EAFE region but worse than emerging markets during the 1988–2002 periods.[33]

The emerging markets equities have, therefore, been an excellent vehicle for diversification and risk management in portfolio investment of the large institutional investors. Because of their early stage of development, as well as being in the process of migrating into broader-based markets, the standard deviations in the emerging market are naturally higher. Nevertheless, equities in the emerging markets offered a relatively better investment alternative to institutional investors in the developed markets in its strategy to diversify investment globally. It served the purpose of improving their return at the same time as helping in sustained and broad-based development of the emerging stock markets and integrating them with the global capital markets. It improved the balance of payments of the emerging market economies and promoted investment rate and economic growth in these economies through debt-free financing.

The logical, statistical and empirical basis for this investment diversification strategy has been further strengthened by the relative low correlation between the emerging markets, and the US and other developed markets over a longer period. Yet another reason for the international diversification of an investment portfolio by individuals and institutions in spite of the higher standard deviation of returns representing a higher risk, in addition to higher returns, is the low correlation among different markets. The low correlation between the US market and the emerging markets, between all developed and the emerging markets and also between different regional markets, whether developed or emerging, gives further credence to the theory and policy of international diversification of investments for better returns.

> The correlation matrix shows the correlations among different markets. The correlation between the S&P 500 and the emerging markets is only 0.42. With the developed markets, the S&P 500 has a correlation coefficient of 0.58. Both of these correlations are quite low. Similarly, the emerging markets and the developed markets are not well correlated. On the other hand, the correlation between the developed markets and the world without the United States is 1.00 because the contribution of emerging markets in the index for all countries except the United States is quite small ... . The correlations suggest a continuing advantage from investing in foreign stocks.[34]

The philosophy of globalization is aimed to promote equity investment, both direct and portfolio, into the emerging market economies to meet their capital inadequacy and boost investment and economic growth rates. The net equity investment from the developed markets, which was $88.5 billion in 1992 rose sharply to $217.7 billion by 1999 to $255 billion in 2006 (Table 2.2). These investments were well rewarded both in the developed as well as the emerging world, both in terms of micro level returns on investments and also their broader macroeconomic effects on growth, BoP, inflation and employment, both in the emerging markets as well as the developed world. Compared with the earlier channels of aid, trade and debt, the equity routed philosophy of globalization has

Table 2.2 Net private capital flows to emerging markets ($ billion)

	1992	1993	1994	1995	1996	1997	1998	1999	2000	2004	2005	2006	2007*
1. Total net private capital inflows (2 + 5)	116.9	124.3	141.0	189.0	224.2	126.2	45.2	71.5	32.2	348.8	509.3	501.8	488.7
2. Bank loans and other	28.5	−14.0	−49.5	49.5	18.7	−62.1	−127.2	−136.0	−172.0	153.7	254.7	246.7	194.2
3. Net portfolio investment	53.0	81.6	110.0	42.0	85.0	43.3	23.8	53.7	58.3	39.1	55.8	69.7	63.5
4. Net foreign direct investment	35.5	56.7	80.9	96.9	120.4	144.9	148.7	153.4	146.0	156.0	198.7	185.3	211.0
5. Net equity investment (3 + 4)	88.5	137.3	190.0	138.5	205.4	188.2	172.5	217.7	204.3	195.1	254.5	255.0	274.5

Source: IMF, International Capital Markets, 2003; Institute of International Finance, Washington DC, February, 2007.

Note
*Estimate.

not only brought the largest transfer of capital in history but has also been far more benign, efficient and productive in its impact, producing and sustaining more balanced global development and much higher global economic welfare. Globalization has catapulted the global economy from the clutches of stagflation, unemployment and currency volatility of the 1970s to the higher orbit of greater growth in world trade and output, more balanced global spread of growth, unprecedented technological advances, price stability and relative currency stability barring a few forex crises. The success of China and India in globalizing with gradualism also vindicates the stand that jet-speed globalization without the parallel overhaul of the inefficient market institutions is an open invitation to higher risks.

Global flow of private savings to public deficits

Globalization, which triggered liberalization and privatization in the emerging market economies, has been sustained on the transfer of resources by the coprporates, banks and household savers and investors through the mutual fund and pension fund route from the developed world. At the micro level, savers of the developed world are transferring their surplus funds to the emerging markets. The private savings transfer is meeting the investment gap in the emerging markets. However, at the macro level, on account of the high current account deficit of the US economy, the US Government has emerged as the largest borrower in the international market. The surplus financial resources, held by the central banks of the BoP surplus nations such as China, India, South Korea and Russia, have been lent to the US by way of investment in their Treasury Bills. Since the US is facing a perpetually rising current account deficit, it is also facing a savings gap that is persistent. Hence, the US has emerged as the net borrower in the international market. Even the current account deficit is the result of private spending in the US. The private sector is globally financing growth and development in the emerging markets but the surpluses of the public sector (central banks) – more particularly, the surplus emerging market economies – are capitalizing the US in sustaining its growth and keeping the cycle of private sector flows globally moving without breaks. Growth in the US is the epicenter of this global growth cycle and any disturbance in the US growth is bound to cause disturbance in the smooth flow of this cycle. The flow of private savings from the developed world to the emerging markets has been motivated by its search for capturing higher returns and diversification to reduce risks. The flow of public savings – i.e. dollar resources accumulated by the central banks of the BoP surplus nations, including the emerging market economies, to the US Government through their investments in the US Treasury Bills and Government securities – is guided by the desire to sustain their own economic growth and not to destabilize the dollar, reducing the value of their forex reserves and also damaging the US growth machine.

So long as the forex reserves, growth in the emerging markets and monetary expansion in their economies, bring more economic growth than inflation in their economies, this shift of private savings from the developed world to the emerging markets is healthier, productive and, therefore, welcome. From the US stand-point, so long as the trade and current account deficit and foreign investment outflow (direct as well as portfolio) keep the inflation rate low without causing any recession from the initial monetary contraction of BoP deficits and from imports hurting the domestic industries, the US Government can continue to incur a higher budgetary deficit to attract dollars back to US and so not worry about its effect of raising prices and interest rates, both which are stabilized through the initial BoP deficit and subsequent foreign investment in US T bills and G Secs. The initial monetary contraction, caused by the current and autonomous capital account deficits reducing M3, is offset by monetary expan-sion when the equivalent investment in T bills and G Secs results in monetary expansion increasing M3. In the case of the US, therefore, the BoP deficit is money supply (M3) neutral on account of the role of the US dollar as a reserves asset for the global economy. An autonomous BoP deficit causes the M3 to decline and contract. However, the M3 is restored to the earlier level when this deficit leads to a subsequent substitution of foreign dollar bank deposits by the investment into the US T bills and G Secs, thereby increasing the domestic dollar bank deposits and M3. This is due to the role of the US as the reserves currency country. Other countries hold their forex reserves in the US dollar, mainly US T bills and G Secs. The growth in the US money supply is managed to match not only growth in domestic demand for money in the US, but also the demand for dollars as the reserve asset of the rest of the world. The optimal growth in the US dollar liquidity (incremental growth in M3, stock of T bills and G Secs in US, euro-dollar deposits, foreign private and central banks' holdings of US T bills and G Secs) should be such that it keeps the growth rate in the US and its trading partners robust without increasing the inflation rate and bringing relentless pres-sure on the US dollar in the forex markets. Under the philosophy of Globaliza-tion, the growth model of the international economy has been Keynesian but also encompassing Friedman's Monetarism. The aggregate spending in the global economy is driven by both the monetary policy with interest rate management and the target growth rate of money supply and liquidity, and the fiscal policy used to stimulate savings, investment and spending through government expendi-ture and tax rates.

Looking to the relationship between trade deficit and budget deficit, a higher budget deficit is more likely to cause a rising BoP deficit than vice versa. In the case of the US, the former relationship is stronger than in other countries because of money supply neutrality of BoP deficits in the US. In other countries, the BoP deficit causes forex reserves to fall, bringing monetary contraction and reducing the size of trade deficit in the second round. The former direct relation-ship is a distinct reality because higher government spending from larger deficit financing triggers both the price and income effects to raise the trade deficit. The trade deficit does not cause monetary contraction and reduce the deficit in the second round because the US trade or current account or overall BoP deficit is money supply neutral. Alternatively, an expansionary monetary policy, pursued

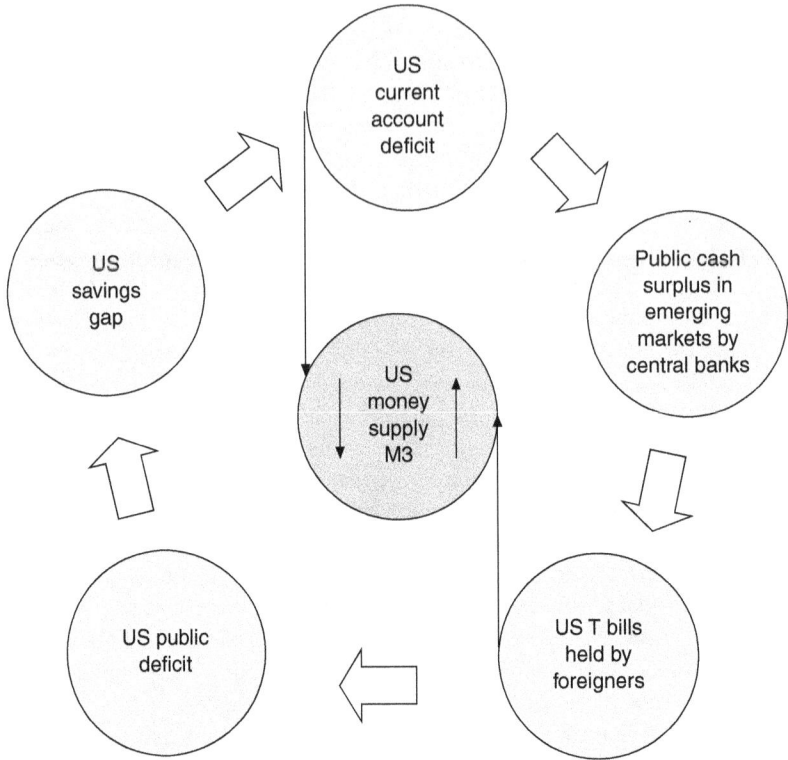

Figure 2.1 Global funds flow: private savings gap to public savings surplus to public deficit.

by the Federal Reserve with a neutral budgetary deficit to keep the unemployment rate low and growth rate high, would also bring higher trade and BoP deficit. This is unlikely to have the second round effect of raising the budget deficit.

The effect of global diversification of investments from the developed world has produced cash surpluses with the central banks of the emerging markets. These cash surpluses in turn have been invested back in the US T bills, financing the US budget deficit or increasing the foreign holdings of US T bills. Under the policy of globalization, liquidity generated by the Federal Reserve has been absorbed by the rest of the world to keep its growth rate higher and also to sustain higher growth without inflation in the US.

3 Financing globalization
Keynes goes international

Floating exchange rates and BoP disequilibria

The first sign of the need for globalization was received in 1971 from the break-down of the Bretton Woods System of gold-based dollar-centric exchange rates mechanism established in 1944. The smooth transition to the system of floating exchange rates in 1973 was welcomed with great enthusiasm, both by the policy makers as well as the economic theorists. Being market oriented, the floating rates system naturally showed short term volatility, but the long term trend in major currencies remained in line with their domestic and external monetary and economic conditions, and strengths and weaknesses. The trend of wide variations in exchange rates over the 1980s and 1990s is illustrative of the fact that fixed exchange rates would have placed enormous pressure on the global monetary system and caused severe hardships, dictated by the compulsions to use domestic policy for external adjustments. It may have also guided the global economy into severe recession in the 1980s and 1990s. These last two decades of the last millennium actually experienced exuberant economic growth primarily due to external economic adjustment being taken care of by the exchange rate movements.

Under the floating rates system, the exchange rates, although free, can be and usually are managed by the central banks. Yet another significant aspect of the present structure of exchange rates of major currencies is that the exchange rates are influenced not only by trade flows but also by the capital movements. The experience of the US dollar during 1980–85 gives a classic example of exchange rate movements contrary to the trade behavior and against the forces of comparative cost advantage. The exchange rates are more amenable to control by the central banks through their monetary policies and interest rate changes. The perfect equilibrium exchange rate arising from considerations of current account balance has lost its significance for major countries. The capital movements caused by real interest differentials have become equally dominant in the determination of exchange rates. The popular definition of an equilibrium exchange rate as one that brings equilibrium in current account in a medium-term time frame needs to be qualified. As a matter of policy, even under floating rates, countries may want their exchange rates to be overvalued to continue to have current account deficits or lower surpluses to bring in net capital from abroad for higher economic growth. Asian countries followed this model and continued with their overvalued exchange rates in mid-1990s before the eruption of the crisis in 1997.

Some countries want to keep their exchange rates undervalued, like China, which does not want to disturb its growing export surpluses that primarily generate higher growth in its economy. The logic for not having current account equilibrium by major countries (led by the US) whose currencies are international transaction currencies and global reserve assets is different. The US has to maintain a deficit in its balance of payments, either on its current account or on its capital account, in order to meet the demand for global liquidity and sustain growth in world trade, investments and finally the global economic growth. If the US reduces its trade deficit substantially, the growth in China, Japan and other Asian countries will suffer. Similarly, China has to carry its trade surplus in order to sustain its high economic growth. Revaluation of the Chinese Yuan will affect its growth and also the supplies of Chinese goods in the US, which keep a downward pressure on consumer prices.

The days of current account surplus for the US were over in 1971. Instead of incurring the capital account deficit, which it was doing earlier to supply global liquidity, it is now incurring a huge trade deficit and sending dollars abroad. Shrinking the current account deficit would hurt growth in the rest of the world. The considerations for the equilibrium exchange rate for a non-reserve currency are not the same as those for the US. The equilibrium exchange rate, therefore, needs to be viewed in the context of the whole gamut of a country's economic policies, goals and priorities, and actual macroeconomic fundamentals.

Despite the fundamental realignment of the structure of exchange rates of currencies and its success in ensuring the smoother flow of world trade and investments and their growth, the floating exchange rates have some surprises. The continuation of Germany and Japan as current account surplus nations, despite sharp appreciation of their currencies, and of the US as a trade deficit nation, over the last two decades of floating rates has been surprising. Analysis of this export surplus phenomenon transcends the conventional wisdom of exchange rate adjustment. It vindicates the theory that the overall trade balance of a country is governed by not only the level and changes in the exchange rate of its currency but also the rate and level of imbalance between its income and absorption, and macro level of savings and investments mismatch. Despite the exchange rate appreciation, both Japan and Germany have continued to generate export surpluses because of the lower absorption rates in their high-productivity, low-population growth economies. This has continued to generate savings higher than investments in these economies despite the appreciation in their currencies. These countries have low price as well as income elasticities of imports. Hence, they continue to generate export surpluses and to be capital exporting nations, although the growth in their exports is moderated by their currency appreciation. Similarly, the US has continued to face an increasing trade deficit on account of the large size of its economy, its reliance on oil imports, its high propensity to consume and import, a higher consumption growth driven by credit, low savings rate, and comparatively higher investment rate requiring resources from the rest of the world. All this makes the US economy have an investment rate higher than its savings rate, leading to a perpetually increasing trade deficit. These structural factors go beyond the exchange rate adjustments. The imbalances are healthy as long as they continue to sustain the growth in global trade, investment and economic growth. Notwithstanding the benign imbalances, the floating exchange rates have worked in encouraging a more rational pattern of trade and investments.

The opening up of the financial markets, both in the developed countries such as Japan, Germany, the UK and others, and also the emerging markets, has enormously increased the magnitude of capital account transactions worldwide. More vigorous capital flows have closely integrated global financial markets, narrowed the interest rates differential and arbitrages on returns on financial assets. Financial markets have become more efficient with low spreads in financial transactions, and lower arbitrages and differentials in returns on financial assets. They have become smoother, more flexible, efficient and also transparent. But open markets are also more susceptible to shocks from outside. The markets have, therefore, no longer remained immune to the external influences and to that extent they have been subjected to external volatility. At the same time, any internal shock or volatility also brings about quicker adjustment, since the open markets bring outside adjusting forces.

The openness of the global trade and capital movements has had a beneficial impact on the global economy. Both the US and the rest of the world have been able to have a mutually beneficial exchange of goods, services and capital, thereby spreading the economic growth emanating from the US. As the counterpart of the growing economic prosperity experienced by the rest of the world, the US economy has also been a big beneficiary of the growing global openness in the financial markets and global financial integration. It has enabled the US to draw larger resources from rest of the world at a lower cost than otherwise, to finance its increasing trade deficit. The global financial integration has enabled the US to maintain higher economic growth and price stability, through higher trade deficits and cheaper capital inflows financing them. The market determined floating exchange rate for the dollar has facilitated the pursuit of monetary policy to generate and sustain higher economic growth throughout the 1980s and 1990s. The floating exchange rates have acted as a safety valve for releasing the excessive domestic demand pressures during periods of high growth or absorbing higher external demand in times of lower economic tempo or activity.

Transformation in global trade and payments structure

Globalization has brought a profound transformation in the global trade and balance of payments structure over the 1990s. The two most significant developments in global trade in the past two decades relate to the US and China. Both are large continental economies and have shown trends in their foreign trade vis-à-vis their own economies as well as in the global trade that have been path breaking.

The US continues to be the world's largest importer, increasing its share in world imports from 14.5 percent in 1985 to 15.8 percent in 2005 with total imports of $1700 billion. US exports of $900 billion in 2005 accounted for 9 percent of global exports compared with 12 percent in 2001, the share that it had retained for the previous 15 years. US exports were $1023 billion in 2006 and grew at the compound annual rate of 5.4 percent in 11 years. The imports, however, grew at a faster compound annual rate of 6.6 percent during the same period. Looking to the size of the US economy, which is one fifth of the global economy, increasing the size of foreign trade of the US also reflects the changes brought about by freer global trade and closer financial integration of global economies.

US trade deficit conundrum

A significant trend in the global trade and payments has been the burgeoning increase in the trade deficit of the US which grew from $122 billion in 1985 to a record $450 billion in 2000, 4.5 percent of GDP and further to the record $836 billion in 2006, 6.4 percent of GDP. The US economy has been experiencing an inherent tendency towards import growth being higher than its export growth. The phenomenon it has been facing throughout the last half a century. Its diverging elasticities of foreign trade have made the US face this structural weakness. The income elasticity of US imports has remained higher than the rest of the world's income elasticity of US exports. The phenomenon of divergent income elasticities of major industrial nations was first brought out in a statistical study in 1969 by Houthakker and Magee.[35] It revealed that the US income elasticity of imports was 1.5, as against the rest of the world's income elasticity of US exports of 0.99. This gap of about 0.5 makes the US a perpetual trade deficit nation with its growing economy. The truth is better perceived, established and accepted when an empirical study of figures, which manifest economic behavior, vindicates a hypothesis and becomes a phenomenon. This phenomenon of a widening US trade gap under structural trade imbalance was further exacerbated by the recurrent bouts of a strong US dollar in the 1980s and 1990s. Further, buoyant economic growth in the US in the 1990s triggered imports growth at a rate much higher than exports, thereby widening the US trade deficit to a record level.

The recent study by IMF measuring price and income elasticities of US imports and exports during 1986–2006 shows a much wider gap between the income elasticities of US imports and exports. The estimates show the respective elasticities at 1.86 and 0.76, a gap of 1.1, which is double the earlier estimate of 0.5 of the 1950s and 1960s.[36] The IMF estimates also vindicate the theory that the conundrum of US trade deficit is deciphered by the Keynesian spending or absorption propensities in the US. The other side of the US trade and current account deficit is its savings gap caused by low saving propensity and higher investment rate. The savings gap seems to be more dominant than the trade gap in the US. The discussion on the dominance of two gaps was earlier usually restricted to the problems of developing economies. Now, because of the large and persistent US trade deficit, which is structural in nature, one has to revert to the dual gap approach and its dominance in the analysis of the Conundrum of the US trade deficit.[37] Although the IMF study also examines the price elasticities of US imports and exports and concludes that up to 10 percent real depreciation of the dollar can bring about an improvement in its current account by 1 percent of GDP, dollar deprecation is a price measure and exchange rate is relative. The partner country currency can manage its exchange rate to nullify the effect of downward pressure on the dollar. How much the dollar can go down in the global forex market depends more on the willingness of central banks of partner countries, namely China, Japan, Germany, the European Central Bank and other major exporting nations, to accept appreciation in their currencies rather than on the Fed monetary policy that paves the way for dollar depreciation. The dollar exchange rate, then, becomes a matter of the oligopolistic pricing game among the major central banks. The exchange rates changes for the dollar in adjusting its BoP imbalance, therefore, have limitations. We now see the US trade deficit more as the Keynesian savings gap puzzle than the price-elasticity-based Marshallian demand problem. The US has now reverted back to the policy of 'benign neglect' Phase II in respect of the dollar as an international currency under globalization. This brings us to the fundamental issue. Is a trade deficit bad for the US and the global economy? Even under the Bretton Woods system, the global monetary system and economy relied on the US to provide the global liquidity in the form of dollars. With its trade account in surplus in the 1950s and 1960s the US incurred a deficit in the capital account and provided grants, aid and loans to enable the deficit nations to meet their dollar needs. The system collapsed because the US trade surplus disappeared, the US BoP deficit became larger and dollar liquid liabilities held by the Central Banks increased manifold the value of US gold stocks. The gold convertible fixed exchange rate system collapsed, to be replaced by the gold free floating exchange rates. The US dollar regained the confidence it had lost in the last days of Bretton Woods, in 1971.

The 1970s were a tumultuous decade for the US as well as the global economy. During this period of a sharp swing in global payments in favor of the oil exporting nations, the global economy swung into stagflation and severe BoP crunch. The euro-dollar market and floating exchange rates rescued the global economy before it plunged into a deeper morass of the worst debt crisis. While the US banking system was putting in place the plan for rehabilitation of debt ridden economies, the seeds of the philosophy of globalization were germinating in the 3W think tank. The upshot of the matter is that from Bretton Woods to globalization the central feature of the financing of the sustained growth of the global economy continues to rest on the US. This time, however financing is through US trade deficit and direct/portfolio investments.

Export surpluses in emerging markets

The second noteworthy development has been the emergence of the Asean countries and China as large exporters in the global market. During the 1990s, these economies enjoyed supernormal growth. It was also foreign investment and trade centric growth. The process of liberalization and reforms in the Asean region and China set the stage for the Asian miracle. The growth model was foreign investment dominated and foreign trade oriented.

> The most encouraging development in globalization is that some developing countries, accounting for about 3 billion people, have succeeded for the first time in harnessing their labor abundance to give them a competitive advantage in labor-intensive manufactures and services. In 1980 only 25 percent of exports of developing countries were manufactures; by 1998 this had risen to 80 percent.[38]

The remarkable change it brought about in the structure of global trade is shown in Table 3.1 showing trade balances from 1985 through 2005.

During this period, the Asean countries and China transformed from trade deficit countries into ones enjoying large trade surpluses. Asia and China, which incurred trade deficits of $9.5 billion and $13 billion in 1985, turned into trade surplus nations with surpluses of $116 billion and $34 billion in 2000, respectively. China emerged as the world's third largest trading nation with its exports leapfrogging from $27 billion in 1985 to a record $266 billion in 2000, 4.5 percent of world exports compared to a mere 1.2 percent in 1985, and further to $726 billion in 2005 with a 7 percent share in world exports. From exports of only

Table 3.1 Global trade (im)balance (US$ billion)

	1985	1990	1995	2000	2005
Industrial countries	−43.1	−34.6	121.8	236.7	−
USA	−122.2	−110.3	−172.3	−449.6	−716
Japan	55.3	69.3	131.8	116.7	80
Germany	28.4	68.5	65.1	57.2	196
UK	−4.0	−32.6	−19.0	−48.3	−129
Developing countries	−57.1	58.3	13.8	239.9	−
Africa	15.9	17.1	2.8	16.0	−
Asia	−9.5	5.2	−0.3	116.2	180
China	−13.1	9.2	18.0	34.4	102
India	−5.6	−5.1	−6.7	−12.2	−40
Europe	1.4	−34.1	−27.5	5.0	−171
Russia	−	−	20.0	60.7	119
Turkey	−2.9	−9.6	−13.2	−22.3	−
Middle East	16.0	40.9	27.0	102.4	216
Latin America	33.7	29.2	−0.4	−0.2	57

Source: International Financial Statistics, World Economic Outlook, IMF; US Bureau of Economic Analysis.

9.4 percent GDP in 1985, the Chinese economy turned into a export oriented growth machine with exports measuring 27 percent of GDP in 2001. This is, indeed, a remarkable feat, looking to the continental nature of its economy, which traditionally does not have a share of exports in GDP exceeding 10 to 15 percent, and would not have happened without a dramatic change in the US trade and investment policy towards China. The open door policy for direct investment, liberal foreign trade, and the setting up of Special Export Zones with a global infrastructure have, over one and half decades, transformed the economy into a major force in the global economy with record forex reserves. From a trade deficit of $13 billion in 1985, China recorded a $34 billion trade surplus in 2000. Continuing this buoyant trend the Chinese trade surplus reached the record level of $178 billion in 2006 and further to $46.44 billion in the first quarter of 2007, nearly double the $23.3 billion surplus in the same period in 2006. The net capital account annual inflows, which were primarily instrumental in this Great Leap Forward, of between $4 billion to $9 billion from 1985 to 1992, rose sharply to $13 billion in 1993, further to $24 billion in 1996 and reached the record level of $72 billion in 2005. In 1997, under the huge current account surplus of $37 billion and foreign exchange reserves crossing $100 billion, China became a net exporter of capital in the world capital market. In ten years its forex reserves have grown ten times to touch $1 trillion in 2007 to be largest in the world, overtaking Japan. Export surplus has been the driving force behind the runaway growth in China's forex reserves. The forex boom has also created the problem of high monetary expansion, and the demand from its trading partners, mainly the US, for a reduction in export subsidies on goods ranging from textiles to steel, and a revaluation of the Yuan.

China's export-led growth model was also followed by the other market-oriented emerging economies of Asia, such as South Korea, Taiwan, Singapore, Malaysia, Indonesia and Thailand. Asia, which had a trade deficit of $9.5 billion in 1985 enjoyed a hefty trade surplus of $116 billion in 2000 and $180 billion in 2005 on the strength of the export-led growth. China and Asia became the major playground for transformation in global trade under globalization.

Thirdly, the traditional large exporters, like Japan and Germany, which have been generating export surpluses, continued to maintain this status despite the dramatic change in global trade picture with the emergence of Asia and China as the majors in the global export market. Naturally, their export growth rate has been blunted. Germany faced the economic burden of unification with East Germany. Japan encountered prolonged stagnation in its economy primarily due to its inability to maintain its high growth rate of exports and to substitute lower export growth by boosting domestic consumption demand. Looking to its small population size, its negative growth, changing age profile towards a retired and aged population, and natural propensity towards savings, Japan is unable to generate economic growth emanating from higher domestic consumption to substitute lower export growth. The labor cost in Japan is also many times that in China, which now – with Japanese and American technology – produces goods substantially cheaper than in Japan. The UK follows the US model. The UK trade deficit of $4 billion in 1985 has multiplied twelve-fold to $48 billion in 2000, compared with a six-fold rise in trade deficit of the US. In contrast, Japan's trade surpluses trebled and Germany's doubled. During the five years 2000–2005 Japan's trade surplus declined to $80 billion, Germany's showed a sharp rise in surplus to $196 billion, while the UK plunged into a deeper trade deficit of $129 billion.

What is a sustainable US BoP deficit?

The US trade deficit is the core around which the philosophy of globalization revolves. The whole process of global financial integration and trade liberalization rests on the US incurring a trade deficit for cheaper imports and from capital outflow (direct and portfolio) along with technology transfer to the emerging markets. Both the US trade and investments are triggers for higher growth in the emerging markets to sustain the higher trade flow and faster growth with price stability in the US. Without the trade deficit of the order of 5 percent of GDP, the US would not keep its inflation rate under 2 percent and unemployment rate below 4 percent. The US trade deficit is not a deterrent to US growth and employment. In fact it is facilitator, releasing resources from the industries in which the US has comparative disadvantage in costs to be used by the industries in which it is cost competitive. With technology gains this resource transfer from the old to the new industries has brought unprecedented productivity gains within the US that have also spurred the overall economic growth rate and reduced the unemployment rate to record low levels. The productivity gains have also crossed the US borders, spreading globally and covering the emerging markets. The floating exchange rates have ensured a timely correction of severe trade imbalances arising out of pricing differentials of exports and imports.

Hence, the US trade and current account deficit, although it is rapidly increasing, is not a worry if several other effects within the US and in rest of the world are benign. As long as the trade and current account deficits help in lowering inflation below 2 percent without raising the unemployment rate, it is most welcome. Higher US imports and investments abroad trigger growth in other nations, promoting higher growth in world trade. As long as the US trade and current account deficits do not cause the dollar glut in the forex markets and start weakening the dollar in the exchange markets, it is not a worry for the Federal Reserve. The strength of the dollar in the short term in the forex market is derived primarily from the demand for liquid investments in T bills. If inflation and unemployment numbers are strong and real interest rates on T bills are relatively favorable in the global money markets, the dollar would not weaken much even in the face of higher trade and current account deficits, which supply more dollars abroad. This brings us to the critical question as to what is the level of a sustainable BoP deficit for the US.

Keynes goes international

Globalization and benign neglect II – new Keynesian avatar

During the 1960s, the US sustained a BoP deficit despite the trade and current account surplus to meet the global demand for international liquidity. It pursued the policy of 'benign neglect' and let the BoP deficit continue as long as it did not hurt the US domestic and international interests.[39] The financial imperatives of globalization now are such that it requires the US to pursue the same policy towards its BoP. The major difference between 'benign neglect I' and 'benign neglect II' is that of the economic environment and policy constraints prevailing then and now. The earlier policy was dictated by the fixed exchange rates and gold-tied dollar for the central banks, while the policy now faces a more open environment of floating exchange rates and gold-free dollar. Under the policy of *'benign neglect I'* the US incurred a BoP deficit through its capital account to supply global liquidity. In contrast, globalization in the last 25 years has facilitated the US incurring large trade deficits, and thereby ensured supplying dollars to the rest of world.

The policy *'benign neglect II'* under globalization has a much wider canvass of operation and is more entrenched into purely economic and monetary factors which are within the will and control of authorities. In contrast, *'benign neglect I'* had a narrow range and time frame for success. It was constrained by the uneconomic commands and whims of the gold market. It was structurally obsolete but politically expedient and hence stretched to act as a bridge towards more economic and Keynesian architecture. The US was the strongest in gold globally and would not renounce its advantage in favor of Keynes' goldless global monetary system, another revolutionary idea discarding the conventional wisdom on gold, especially after the resounding success of the anti-balanced budget policy prescription from his 'General Theory'. That was too much of Keynesianism to be absorbed for the political thought and structure in democracies. Throwing overboard, by Keynesianism, both the balanced budget and gold, the two strongest pillars of the economic governance of societies that worked and served well globally for centuries, over the span of nine years from 1936–45 was, it seems, a little too audacious an agenda for democratic societies to accept. Keynes' goldless global monetary system had to wait untill 1971 when gold was repealed from its convertibility into dollars. The dollar standard with floating rates was not Keynes' dream but the system set free from the constraints imposed by gold, the enigmatic metal that ruled the monetary system of the world for centuries.

Keynesianism emerged in its new avatar under globalization through the US policy of 'benign neglect II'. The driving force of globalization is US consumption and investment spending on the macroeconomic front. On the microeconomic front, globalization relies on the advocacy by Adam Smith for the free market and by Ricardo for free trade on the principle of comparative cost advantage. Both ensure higher productivity, better resource allocation and higher global welfare. And to realize these productivity gains from more efficient use of reallocated global resources, Keynesianism in the US, the global money source, has to drive the global economy. While Adam Smith and his free market advocacy have been very well projected in the literature analysis, the genesis and spread of globalization, Ricardo and Keynes are totally ignored. The thrust of Ricardian theory underlying a freer trade regime under globalization is not as widely articulated and referred to as Adam Smith's. And the currents of Keynesianism plying under the waves of globalization have gone totally unrecognized. The spending or absorption in the US drives the US growth and facilitates globalization through its BoP deficit. This is Keynesianism going international.

While trade and current account deficits, in terms of their magnitude, trend and economic relativity are important in terms of analysis of their monetary and economic impact and also policy initiatives, what is also critical is the overall BoP deficit which is not a disequilibrium. Further, the BoP analysis of a country whose currency is used as a major trading currency and reserve asset, needs a different, much broader and holistic perspective. The BoP imbalance of country 1 cannot treated on a par with the BoP imbalance or disequilibrium of $n-1$ countries. The BoP imbalance of country 1 is the driving force of the global economy and monetary system and their equilibria. Country 1 enjoys the status and benefit of a global money supplier because of the stock of its wealth, pace of its generation and their value in the global economy which reflects its economic power. The BoP imbalance of country 1 is, therefore, a vital and critical parameter in the global economic and monetary system. If the BoP imbalance of country 1 degenerates into a structural disequilibrium, the global monetary system is in jeopardy. This is how the Pound Sterling as the global currency and money under the gold standard of the nineteenth Century gave way to the US dollar in the twentieth Century under Bretton Woods, which again came to be replaced in 1973 by the dollar standard and floating exchange rates.

The BoP imbalance of country 1, the US, therefore has a different connotation. It has to play in line with a contemporary economic and monetary milieu and, more importantly, the demands of the global economic and monetary system on the US, since the economic and monetary management globally has become more a proactive exercise than a reactionary effort. The BoP deficit of the US is as much a function of US consumption and investment spending, a part of which percolates overseas, as it is of the rest of the world's aspiration for growth and its capacity to meet the US demand for goods and investment outlets emanating from its spending. When there is a perfect match in these two demand – supply equations, we arrive at a sustainable US BoP deficit. It is neither inflationary for the global economy nor deflationary causing unemployment in the US. Any inflationary signal worldwide or unemployment numbers climbing in the US would require the US BoP deficit to be charted on a path of restraint. The policy of *benign neglect II* would then have to be renounced for correction in the deficit as was required to be done after *benign neglect I* under Bretton Woods.

Under Bretton Woods, the gold stocks of the US were the benchmark against which the US liquid liabilities abroad were reckoned. Now the gold buffer as the benchmark is renounced and is irrelevant. The US is now facing the market-determined benchmarks of inflation, real interest rate, and strength of dollar in the forex market to reckon with the rising holdings of US T bills abroad. The BoP surveillance for the Federal Reserve has become much more complex. It is called BoP surveillance because, under the policy of *benign neglect II*, there is no active BoP management by the US. The US pursues and promotes free trade and investment and manages its domestic economic growth, inflation and unemployment. It will have to have a sharp surveillance of its BoP to eliminate any sign of instability in the dollar in the global forex markets and the international monetary and payments mechanism. The BoP management will be active only when its new benchmarks begin to signal adverse change. All three benchmarks, inflation, real interest rates and dollar exchange rate, are monetary factors and hence the Fed policy is of critical importance in the active management of the BoP.

Real BoP deficit of the US

This brings us to the question as to what is the sustainable BoP deficit of the US. Before that, however, we must approach the issue of what is the BoP deficit of the US and how it is measured. Returning to the analogy of $n-1$ countries in explaining the BoP problems, the BoP deficits of $n-1$ countries and the BoP deficit of country 1 are not treated similarly. A protracted BoP deficit of $n-1$ countries needs an exchange rate or macroeconomic adjustment but not for country 1, which is supplying its currency globally and has to maintain a certain deficit to generate global growth and growth in world trade and investment. That is the rationale behind the *benign neglect* policy under Bretton Woods then, and now under globalization. Let the US continue unhindered with its natural rate of growth of its aggregate demand-consumption and investment to generate its BoP deficit, and the rest of the world will respond as to how much it requires and can absorb. The US dollar will get adjusted in the forex market on this supply – demand matrix. The dollar will depreciate if the supply from the BoP deficit is more than the demand for it. And it will appreciate if the demand is more than supply from the deficit. Although this will be the market play from all trade, investment and transfer transactions, market supply and demand is buffered by the interventions from central banks, which add or reduce their own demand for dollars. Hence, we take into account not only demand and absorption capacity of the global market economy but also the buffer and absorption capacity of the central banks. Easy absorption of dollars by the central banks has enhanced the sustainability of the persistent, large and rising US BoP deficits. The globalization has progressed in the last two decades on this phenomenon of increasing absorption of dollar assets or T bills by the central banks and a drastic redistribution of dollar assets held abroad. This global redistribution of dollar financial assets is a phenomenon that is reminiscent of the euro-dollar phenomenon of late 1960s, which was in the limelight then. It naturally means a drastic rise in US financial liabilities held abroad. It happened before the collapse of Bretton

Woods and it has happened now under globalization. Not facing the handicap from gold stocks, which it did under Bretton Woods, this process under globalization has so far brought only positive results for the global economy.

Coming to the question of the Real BoP deficit of the US, one has to revert to the definition of the BoP deficit or surplus, or BoP disequilibrium. The definition of James Meade is the most widely accepted and precise measure of BoP disequilibrium even now. Going by this definition, the balance of all autonomous transactions on the debit and credit sides, both on current and capital accounts is the true test and measure of the real BoP deficit or surplus, or BoP disequilibrium.[40] The autonomous transactions of trade and investment in BoP are all private and market driven transactions in goods, services, financial securities, and even on the real assets like land and property. The government and central bank transactions in BoP have the purpose of bridging the BoP deficit or surplus and are accommodating transactions that are not autonomous. Further, the BoP deficit or surplus per se is not undesirable. Both the BoP deficits and surpluses are a part of the evolution of the global economy and continuing growth in global trade and investments. In particularly, the current phase of globalization relies heavily on the growth in world trade and investments to realize its gains and to distribute these among all the trading partners. One should not, therefore, be overly critical of the US BoP deficit without recognizing its relevance in the global context and the phase of globalization.

In the 1930s, Keynes gave the gift of budget deficit to the US for curing depression much before any other country adopted his bitter medicine, which involved breaking the commandment of a balanced budget in favor of a much maligned deficit financing by the government. Keynes comes back to the US again. And now the prescription is trade deficit. In the 1980s, under globalization, the US needed a BoP deficit for more equitable growth in the global economy under globalization. In two stages of budget deficit and trade deficit, over fifty years, Keynes lifted the US and global economy from a economic depression in the 1930s to sustainable growth and then to globalization in the 1980s for progress towards optimum global welfare. The US trade deficit seeks to achieve better global distribution of growth and global resource allocation. Globalization without Keynesianism would be an impotent philosophy with poor results for global productivity and growth. Under globalization, Keynesianism has received a new and international dimension. Although Keynes restricted his General Theory to an analysis of a domestic economy and its atrophy or negative growth, his principles when extended to the international economy give the magic formula for growth under globalization. The US BoP deficit under the drive of the Keynesian principle of unhindered consumption and investment spending growth in the US is the main force that moves the phase of globalization forward with higher Smithian and Ricardian global gains in productivity and growth.

Different countries with different phases of their economic development, varying natural resource and production endowments, diverse consumption trends and patterns, and different sizes in the global economy, will have BoP deficits and surpluses of various magnitude and trends. If the BoP deficit or surplus is continually out of line with the domestic and global economic and financial environment and has more deleterious effects than beneficial, it would be a matter of concern requiring correction of the BoP disequilibrium. But the BoP deficit of a country, whose currency is used as international money and a reserve asset, is to be seen in a much wider and global context. The BoP deficit of the US is also to be seen in the light of the aspirations of the rest of the world to have growth without inflation. Since a large part of that growth is emanating from the US propensities to import and also invest abroad, it is a much simpler exercise of matching the supply of dollars from the US BoP deficit with rest of the world's demand for dollars. If this demand is higher than the supply, the dollar will start appreciating, which would again reduce the growth process. Under the early Bretton Woods system, the US met this gap by sending soft loans and aid abroad. This ended up with central banks holding more US T bills. However, the US loans and aid were actually accommodating items not emerging from the market system and were also from US budgetary allocations. The US budgetary allocations for meeting the rest of the world's demand for dollars fell out of favor in the US. No large budget allocations have come for incurring the BoP deficit in the US in recent times. The Brady Bonds issue of the record $175 billion in 1989 to help the US banks and the Latin American countries out of the debt crisis, in which the US banking system would have been in deep crisis forcing the US and the global economy into another recession, was not directly a budgetary support but relied heavily on the collateralization of 30-year US Treasury Par and Zero coupon bonds. The Brady Bonds was yet another Keynesian prescription.

Post Bretton Woods, the global economy entered the phase of a market dominated economy. Globalization is being taken to its logical conclusion. Under this system, if the rest of the world's demand for US dollars is higher than the US supply, the US will have take monetary measures to drive the US growth higher so to raise the US BoP deficit higher to match the demand. Fortunately, the US growth in the last one and half decades, since the early 1990s, has been a record high for a prolonged period in recent US history. One of the important effects of globalization has been to raise the US propensity to import and propensity to invest abroad. The trade liberalization in the US and investment liberalization in the emerging market and transition (erstwhile USSR) economies and China have raised US import and foreign investment propensities. This has generated greater BoP deficit in the US and this trend is the driving force of globalization. The propensities to import and absorb foreign capital have also gone up in all countries following globalization and, more particularly, the emerging market economies. Globalization has raised substantially the volume of global trade and investment in absolute as well as relative terms in all economies. The US buys goods and sends capital abroad, and this supply of dollars is matching the rest of the world's demand for US dollars. The global growth is without price inflation and unemployment. The worry is whether the US supply would be larger than the rest of the world's demand. Such a situation would throw signals of inflation and unemployment. A higher trade deficit may cause unemployment in the US. A higher US demand for exports of emerging markets than they can supply and higher inflows of capital than they can absorb would throw up signs of inflation. It is this BoP deficit of the US that will be a worry, and would be a disequilibrium requiring correction or adjustment. It could be called the unsustainable level of US BoP deficit or disequilibrium. Hence, as the process of globalization progresses under market-dominated economies, inflation and unemployment levels in the US and globally are critical signals of the measure as to what is the sustainable level of US BoP deficit.

Measuring the US BoP deficit, which has now to be viewed differently, requires balancing the autonomous transactions in the US BoP. Usually, trade deficit or current account deficit figures are widely quoted, indicating the size of US BoP deficit. This is an important indicator since the current account transactions have immediate bearing on the GDP figures; the current account deficit reduces the GDP. However, the capital account also comprises transactions that are market related and autonomous. If we take all capital account transactions of the private individuals and bodies and do not include the capital transactions of the US and other foreign governments and their central banks (since there transactions are largely of an accommodating nature), we get the balance on the capital account from autonomous transactions. It means that if we keep the account of governments and central banks separate in the capital account, and balance the current account and changes in private assets and liabilities in the capital account, we have a true measure of US BoP deficit. The counterpart of this deficit is the rise in the foreign government holdings of US Government securities. The balance of payments has always to balance as an accounting statement. Every debit or payment has a corresponding credit or receipt.

In the Bretton Woods era, the US BoP deficit was measured in two ways – official settlements balance or liquidity balance. These concepts have now been abandoned and the Bureau of Economic analysis gives data on the current account, and on the capital account in the form of the changes in US and foreign private and Government assets and liabilities.

Table 3.2 shows a secular trend in the US balance of payments from 1960 to 2006. The US trade deficit, which is the balance on goods, which was in deficit by $25 billion in 1980 rose persistently to $111 billion in 1990, then quadrupled to $452 billion in 2000 and reached a record $836 billion in 2006. The current account deficit has also shown a similar rise. The current account deficit increased from $79 billion in 1990 to $856.7 billion in 2006 accounting for 6.5 percent of GDP. The US is a net receiver on the services account and the surplus on services account was $70.7 billion in 2006. On the unilateral transfers the US is in deficit due to outward remittances of migrants working in the US. The deficit on remittances was $84.1 billion in 2006.

However, if we take autonomous capital account transactions, the deficit on the current account is considerably moderated due to the net inflow of private capital into the US, both in equity and debt – direct as well as portfolio investments through the stock market transactions. It is this net foreign capital inflow

Table 3.2 Secular trend in US balance of payments US international transactions (billions of dollars, credits +; debits −)

	1960	1970	1980	1990	1995	2000	2006ᵖ
Exports of goods and services and income receipts	30.6	68.4	344.4	707	1004.6	1421.5	2058.8
Exports of goods and services	25.9	56.6	271.8	535.2	794.4	1070.6	1436.8
Goods, balance of payments basis	19.7	42.5	224.3	387.4	575.2	772	1023.7
Services	6.3	14.2	47.6	147.8	219.2	298.6	413.1
Imports of goods and services and income payments	−23.7	−59.9	−333.8	−759.3	−1080	−1778	−2831.4
Imports of goods and services	−22.4	−54.4	−291.2	−616.1	−890.8	−1448	−2202.1
Goods, balance of payments basis	−14.8	−39.9	−249.8	−498.4	−749.4	−1224	−1859.7
Services	−7.7	−14.5	−41.5	−117.5	−141.4	223.7	−342.4
Balance on goods	4.9	2.6	−25.5	−111	−174.2	−452.4	−836.0
Balance on services	−1.4	−0.3	6.1	30.2	77.8	74.9	70.7
Balance on goods and services	4	2.3	−19.4	−80.9	−96.4	−377.6	−765.3
Unilateral current transfers, net	−4	−6.2	−8.4	−26.7	−38.8	−58.6	−84.1
Balance on current account	3	2.3	2.3	−79	−113.6	−415.2	−856.7
US-owned assets abroad, net (increase/financial outflow	−4.1	−8.5	−85.8	−81.2	−352.3	−560.5	−1045.8
US official reserve assets, net	2.1	3.3	−7	−2.2	−9.7	−0.3	2.4
Gold	1.8	787	.....	.....	.....	.....	.....
Special drawing rights	.....	0.2	1.1	−0.2	−0.8	−0.7	−0.2
US private assets, net	−5.1	−10.2	−73.7	−81.4	−341.5	−559.3	−1053.4
Direct investment	−3	−7.6	−19.2	−37.2	−98.8	−159.2	−248.9
Foreign securities	−0.7	−1.1	−3.6	−28.8	−122.4	−127.9	−277.7

continued

Table 3.2 continued

	1960	1970	1980	1990	1995	2000	2006^P
US claims on unaffiliated foreigners reported by US nonbanking concerns	-0.4	-0.6	-4.0	-27.8	-45.3	-138.8	-44.4
US claims reported by US banks, not included elsewhere	-1.1	-1.0	-46.8	12.4	-75.1	-133.4	-482.4
Foreign-owned assets in the United States, net (increase/financial inflow (+))	2.3	6.4	62.6	141.6	438.6	1046.9	1764.9
Foreign official assets in the United States, net	1.5	6.9	15.5	33.9	109.9	42.8	300.5
US Government securities	0.7	9.4	11.9	30.2	72.7	35.7	243.8
US Treasury securities	0.7	9.4	9.7	29.6	69.0	-5.2	118.3
Other foreign assets in the United States, net	0.8	-0.6	47.1	107.7	328.7	1004.1	1464.4
Direct investment	0.3	1.5	16.9	48.5	57.8	321.3	183.6
US Treasury securities	-0.4	0.8	2.6	-2.5	91.5	-70.0	29.4
US securities other than US Treasury securities	0.3	2.2	5.5	1.6	77.2	459.9	621.2
US currency	.....	.....	4.5	18.8	12.3	5.3	12.6
US liabilities to unaffiliated foreigners reported by US non-banking concerns	.....	2.0	6.9	45.1	59.6	170.7	176.5
US liabilities reported by US banks, not included elsewhere	0.7	-6.3	10.7	-3.8	30.2	117.0	441.2
Real BoP Deficit	-1.3	-8.5	-24.2	-52.7	-126.5	29.6	-445.7
Real BoP Deficit as % of GDP	-0.3	-0.8	-0.9	-0.9	-1.7	0.3	-3.4

Source: Bureau of Economic Analysis, Government of US.

Note
^P = Provisional.

into the US that provides its BoP considerable resiliency. The US is also a large private investor abroad. Table 3.2 shows US private assets, net (net US private investments abroad) and other foreign investment in the United States (net foreign private investments in the US). If we balance these net inflows and out-flows, we get the net private capital movement in the US BoP. We are not con-sidering the changes in US official assets abroad and foreign official assets in the US. These we regard as the accommodating items in the US BoP. If we balance the net private capital movements, we find that the US has a net surplus on the private capital account. Except for 1980 and 1995 when it showed deficits of $26.6 billion and $12.8 billion, the surplus on private capital account was $26.3 billion in 1990, a massive $444.8 billion in 2000 and $411 billion in 2006. This moderates the US real BoP deficit as shown in Table 3.2. A large real BoP deficit of $126.5 billion in 1995 turned into a surplus of $29.6 billion in 2000. The real BoP deficit of the US has remained between 1 percent to 2 percent of GDP. The year 2006 has shown a rise in the real BoP deficit to $445.7 billion, 3.4 percent GDP.

The above analysis shows that the US BoP deficit is not yet as worrisome as is often presented. As against the trade deficit of $111 billion in 1990, the real BoP deficit was only $52.7 billion with private capital inflows into the US including direct investment of $107.7 billion. In 2000, the record trade deficit of $452 billion turned into a real BoP surplus of $29.6 billion due to a huge

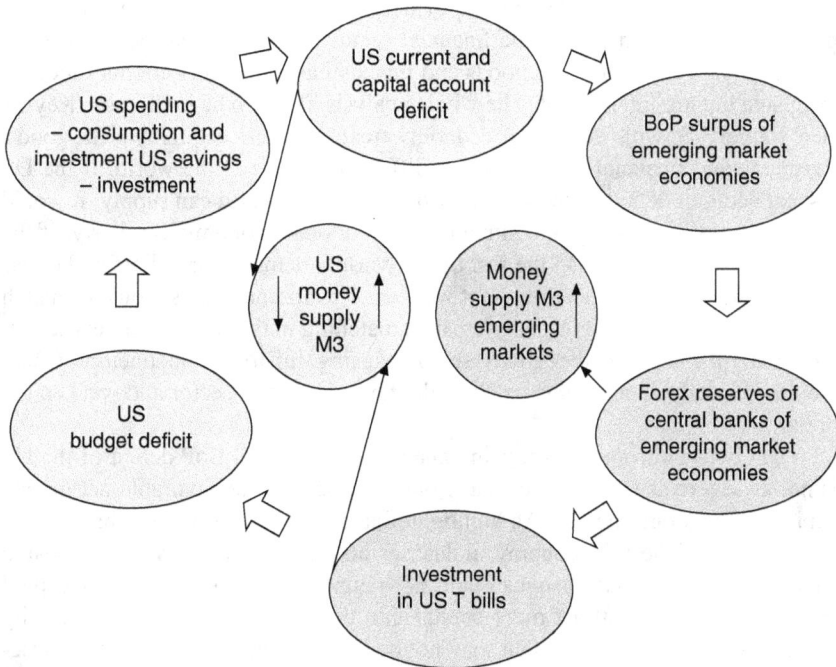

Figure 3.1 Financing globalization.

capital inflow of $1004 billion comprising direct equity and bond investments. This was despite the large private capital outflow of $559 billion from the US. The upshot of the matter is that strong net private capital movements into the US have been considerably moderating the impact of a high current account deficit on the overall balance of payments, which does not show a very high deficit. The buoyancy of the US capital market and technological lead which the US is maintaining helps in having a moderate real BoP deficit and keep the US dollar from any strong pressure in the forex market. The role of the US capital market and innovations in the global economy is discussed in the next chapter. In 2006, despite the very high private capital outflows from the US of $1053 billion, a strong private capital inflow of $1464 billion helped reduce the record current account deficit of $857 billion to the real BoP deficit of $445 billion, accounting for 3.4 percent of the GDP from the current account deficit of 6.5 percent of GDP.

Both the current account as well as the real BoP deficit have relevance. While the trade and current account deficit emanates through US consumption and investment spending, it reflects the aggregate demand pressure on the rest of the world. The real BoP deficit reflects the US liquidity supply in the rest of the world. The former deficit is in the goods and services sector and the latter deficit is in the global liquidity sector. If the rest of the world's supply in the goods and services sector and its demand for US financial securities match the US current account deficit and real BoP deficit respectively, we have equilibrium. The mismatch on the goods sector would be evident in the form of inflation and unemployment. The mismatch on the financial securities front would be reflected in the dollar exchange rate. The goods and financial assets sectors are not mutually exclusive but are interrelated. The whole analysis can then be built in the Keynesian framework with the global economy treated as one economy with goods, payments and financial flows between different regions of the world. If the US current account deficit is short of what the rest of the world can supply, it would not cause any excess demand situation in the global economy. Similarly, if the real BoP deficit is less than the rest of the world's demand for dollars and dollar financial assets, the dollar would not weaken. The absence of a serious mismatch in the goods sector would usually create a matching in the financial assets sector. And the mismatch in the goods sector causing inflation and unemployment would definitely create a mismatch in the financial assets sector and weaken the dollar.

It can be seen from the foregoing analysis that the real BoP deficit of the US is not as severe as it appears or made out to be, due to the favorable net private capital inflows into the US. As highlighted later in Chapter 4, the vibrant innovative spirit of the US economy, industries and universities, fostering research supported by financial systems such as venture capital, keep the US capital market buoyant and attract more capital into the country. Although the gravity of the US current account deficit may not be severe, it has brought about a structural change in the status of the US and its international investment position. This is discussed in the next section.

US – the largest borrower and debtor nation

Globalization has contributed to enlarging the US trade deficit. The US economy has been able to maintain the growth momentum of 3.7 percent over last two and half decades while keeping the price inflation rate low at 2.8 percent due to the burgeoning trade deficit, which increased supplies of goods, matching the rising demand. This trend has put pressure on the balance of payments of the US. The current account surplus of the US, which was $4.6 billion in 1981, turned into a deficit of $9 billion in 1982. The current account deficit rose to $41.6 billion in 1983 and further to $113 billion in 1995, accounting for 2.8 percent of GNP. Since 1983, the US emerged as the net importer of capital for the first time in the century. Its status of the exporter of capital, which it maintained for about a century, came to a close. The US became a net borrower in the international market with foreign capital inflows helping finance its trade and current account deficit. Compared with the net foreign private investment outflow from the US of $5.2 billion in 1980, there was a net foreign private capital inflow into the US of $42 billion in 1983. The US has been a net receiver of funds in the capital account since then. Its net private capital inflow went up consistently to a high of $152 billion in 1987, declined later to $26 billion in 1990. In 1991, the US private capital account showed a net outflow of $9.5 billion. A surplus of $45 billion in 1992 went on increasing thereafter to $224 billion in 1998 and further to a record $444 billion in 2000.

Table 3.3 shows changes in the international investment position of the US from 1976 to 2005. The changes in the US global investment status has come through changes in its balance of payments.

Compared with the net international investment holdings of $164 billion in 1976 and $361 billion in 1980 (Table 3.3) the US position in 1985 reduced to $54 billion and in 1990 the US became a net debtor country, to the tune of $245 billion, from the net creditor one earlier, indicating the amount by which the foreign investments were more than the US investments abroad. Owing to the persistently rising trade and current account deficit, US borrowings abroad increased. In addition to US borrowings, the foreign equity investments in the US have also increased more than US equity investments abroad. We see the US net debtor position rising from $245 billion in 1990 to $496 billion in 1995, further to $1387 billion in 2000 and to $2694 billion in 2005. Out of $2694 billion net debtor position, foreign official and private holdings of US Treasury securities alone are $1992 billion, i.e. 74 percent. The foreign holdings (official and private) of US treasury securities which were $438 billion in 1990 more than doubled to $1025 billion in 2000 and further nearly doubled to $1992 billion in 2005 (Table 3.3).

The major financing of the US current account deficit and inflow on capital account has come from debt securities and, more particularly, from investment in US treasury bills. Official holdings of US treasury bills have risen from $111 billion in 1980 to $625 billion in 2000 and a record $1288 billion in 2005. Private holdings of treasury bills have also shot up from $16 billion to $400

Table 3.3 International investment position of the United States (billions of dollars)

	1976	1980	1985	1990	1995	2000	2003	2004	2005
Net International Investment Position:									
At current cost	164	361	54	−245	−496	−1387	−2157	−2484	−2694
At market value			97	−165	−343	−1588	−2372	−2542	−2546
US owned assets abroad:									
At current cost	457	930	1287	2179	3452	6229	7641	9053	10,009
At market value			1302	2294	3930	7394	8297	9973	11,079
US official reserve assets:	44	171	118	174	176	128	184	190	188
Gold	37	156	86	102	101	72	109	114	134
Foreign currencies	0.3	10	13	52	49	31	40	43	38
US private assets:									
At current cost	368	693	1080	1920	3191	6016	7372	8780	9743
At market value			1095	2035	3669	7180	8028	9700	10,817
Direct Investment abroad	222	388	371	616	885	1529	2063	2367	2454
Portfolio Investment:	44	63	119	314	1170	2385	2953	3437	3525
Bonds	34	44	75	117	393	532	874	917	988
Stocks	10	19	44	197	777	1853	2079	2520	3087
Foreign owned assets in US:									
At current cost	292	569	1233	2424	3948	7617	9798	11537	12,702
At market value			1206	2459	4274	8982	10,669	12,515	13,625
Foreign official assets in US:	104	176	203	373	683	1015	1567	1982	2216
US government securities	73	118	145	291	507	749	1192	1500	1649
US Treasury Securities	71	111	138	286	490	625	990	1261	1288
Private Foreign Assets in US									
Direct Investment in US	48	127	247	505	680	1418	1586	1709	1874
US Treasury Securities	7	16	88	152	330	400	543	640	704
Corporate and other bonds	12	9	82	239	459	1076	1707	2059	2275
Corporate stocks	43	65	125	222	511	1547	1701	1929	2115
US currency	12	24	46	86	170	252	318	333	352
Foreign official and private holdings of US Treasury Securities	78	127	226	438	820	1025	1533	1901	1992

Source: Bureau of Economic Analysis, Government of US.

billion and to $704 billion during the same period. The foreign official and private holdings of T bills rose from $438 billion in 1990 to $1992 billion in 2005. In January 2006, these were $2.19 trillion, 51 percent of total outstanding treasury bills. This figure was $1.58 trillion, 44 percent of the total outstanding bills in January 2004.

More than half of US treasury securities are now held outside US. Overseas holdings of US dollar currency notes have also risen from $24 billion in 1980 to $170 billion in 1995 and further almost doubled to $352 billion in 2004. A study estimates foreign holdings of dollar currency to be between 50 percent to 70 percent currency issued in US, and at $500 billion in 2005.[41] While the accumulation of official holdings of US treasury bills by the central banks is more a matter of policy, dollar currency circulation outside the US is in response to market demand for dollars for transactions and as store of value. The former phenomenon is a result of the supply of dollars generated by the trade deficit, the latter development of dollarization is caused by the demand forces arising from the substitution of weak and constantly weakening domestic currencies by the US dollar.

More than half of US treasury securities are now held outside the US. Overseas holdings of US dollar currency notes have also risen from $24 billion in 1980 to $170 billion in 1995 and further almost doubled to $333 billion in 2004. Compared with the total US dollar currency in circulation in 2004 of $720 billion, 46 percent is held outside the US. Federal Reserve estimates of foreign holdings of dollar currency vary between 50 percent to 70 percent. While the accumulation of official holdings of US treasury bills by the central banks is more a matter of policy, dollar currency circulation outside the US is in response to market demand for dollars for transactions and as a store of value. The former phenomenon is a result of the supply of dollars generated by the trade deficit, the latter development of dollarization is caused by the demand forces arising from the substitution of weak and constantly weakening domestic currencies by the US dollar.

Not only has the Fed adapted to the forces of globalization, but since the US is a major actor and player in the philosophy, the Fed is also playing the major role in ensuring smooth functioning of the mechanism that handles the financial flows and the transformation therein caused by speedier globalization. It is interesting to note the recent comment by the Fed Chairman, Ben Bernanke,

> Certainly, the financial environment in which U.S. monetary policy is made has been irrevocably changed by the remarkable increases in the magnitudes of financial flows into and out of the United States. A quarter-century ago, foreign holdings of U.S. financial assets were limited, and therefore, the influence of foreign investors and foreign financial conditions on U.S. financial markets was in most cases relatively modest. As I have already noted, that situation has changed markedly, as global financial markets have become increasingly integrated and both foreign and domestic investors have become more diversified internationally. Today, foreigners hold about

one-quarter of the long-term fixed-income securities issued by U.S. entities of all types and more than half of publicly-held U.S. Treasury securities. Cross-border financial flows are enormous and growing: For example, in 2006, foreigners acquired on net more than $1.6 trillion in U.S. assets, while U.S. investors purchased more than $1 trillion in foreign assets. Given their scale, capital inflows and outflows certainly influence long-term U.S. interest rates and other key asset prices, both by affecting the underlying supply – demand balance between saving and capital investment and by helping to determine the premiums that investors receive for holding assets that are risky or illiquid.[42]

International liquidity – a strong shift to Asia

Under the policy of globalization during the 1990s, the Asian countries have been at the forefront of economic growth, world trade, global investments, and international liquidity. Trade and investment liberalization has triggered this rally in Asia. Despite the Asian crisis, which affected the so-called Tigers, the recovery was very prompt and promising, bringing them back in to their race to high growth. Exports-led growth in Asia enabled it to increase its share in the world trade from 10 percent in 1990 to 16 percent in 2001. Japan's export growth story, which lifted its share in world trade from 7.3 percent in 1972 to 8 percent in 1990 pales in comparison. Japan's share later fell to 6.5 percent in 2001. Japanese exports gave way to other Asian nations for their growth. The US has continued to maintain its status of the world's largest exporter despite the decline in its share in world exports from 12 percent to 9 percent in the last six years.

The forces of globalization have brought a dramatic change in international reserves position over the last one and half decades. There has been a sharp rise in the international reserves of developing nations, which held $1529 billion, 59 percent of the total world reserves of $2592 billion in 2001, compared with $270 billion, 41 percent of total reserves in 1985 and $50 billion, 23 percent in 1972. Much of the increase in reserves has been cornered by the fast growing Asian Tigers and oil-exporting OPEC nations. China alone with $258 billion in 2001 held 10 percent of total reserves and with Hong Kong's $132 billion held 15 percent of global reserves, a formidable position in the global financial market. The 1990s have been a high growth period for China and the Asian Tigers. They have collectively dominated a larger share of international reserves. China, Hong Kong and the Asian Tigers (Korea, Malaysia, Singapore, Indonesia, Thailand and Philippines) increased their reserves from $136 billion, 37 percent of reserves of developing countries and 13 percent of global reserves, to $728 billion, 47 percent of reserves of developing countries and 28 percent of global reserves in 2001. During the period, India's forex reserves increased from $2.1 billion to $55 billion, with the corresponding shares in reserves of developing countries rising from 0.6 percent to 3.4 percent and in global reserves from 0.2 percent to 2 percent. India's performance has been more impressive with its

Table 3.4 Forex reserves held by central banks ($ in billions)

	2007*	*2003*	*2000*
China	1070	403	166
Japan	909	674	347
Taiwan	268	207	107
South Korea	244	155	96
Euro Zone	450	233	240
Russia	311	73	28
India	200	96	40
Hong Kong	135	118	108

Source: International Monetary Fund.

Note
* March end.

share in global reserves increasing tenfold during the 1990s. The trend to rising forex reserves of the emerging markets has continued unabated. By March 2007, China, the world's largest holder of forex reserves, follwed by Japan, crossed the $1 trillion mark and India had $200 billion. Russia has also been a large forex accumulator with reserves of over $300 billion (Table 3.4).

The transformation of global trade and liquidity pattern under globalization is a clearly evident result of the policies of liberalization in foreign investments in the emerging markets and in foreign trade in the developed world. While investment liberalization created capacities for higher output, freer trade readily absorbed the capacities. With the considerable liberalization of imports by the developed world, global trade flows showed a sharp rise. Trends in global trade and liquidity under globalization are also a pointer to the emergence of Asia and the Indian subcontinent as the major economic growth centre in the world in the coming decades. The growth momentum of the US economy would undoubtedly continue to be the driving force behind the sustained growth trajectory in the region. China and the Asean countries would be more susceptible to the US economic outlook and growth than India, which is not as trade oriented as the former, and less US centric in its linkages in trade and investment. The region would enjoy the state of a secular current account surplus zone on account of both, the higher goods as well as factor traffic. Greater mobility of human resources and capital would outpace the growth in commodity traffic. As long as the surplus capital in the developed world finds more lucrative investment options in the region, the capital account would generate greater BoP surpluses in the emerging market economies. Greater mobility of Human Resources would show a sharper rise in inward remittances in the HR exporting economies.

Central bankers in the region have a natural aversion to revalue currencies in the wake of BoP surpluses, lest it would jeopardize growth, which is the top economic and political priority. The surge in international liquidity in the region is a long-term phenomenon it would have to learn to live with and manage without causing a liquidity overhang having a serious inflationary potential. The prediction of numbers is fraught with risks. The crude oil price is a critical factor that can seriously influence global trade, investment and liquidity dynamics. It can greatly erode the gains from a higher global trade of the emerging markets. Economic variables usually show a trend, but can often beat the trend taking unpredictable turns violating the results of number crunching exercises involving mathematical models and probabilities.

Reallocation of global capital and liquidity

Floating exchange rates and global forex reserves

The floating exchange rates that replaced the Bretton Woods fixed and pegged exchange rates system in 1973 gave greater flexibility to the exchange rates mechanism and brought timely correction of balance of payments disequilibria. Advances in technology in communications and computers, gave unprecedented thrust to the mobility of capital internationally. Technology enabled large volumes of transactions to be conducted globally at split-second speeds. The switchover to floating rates and scalable technology promoting low-cost and high-speed global mobility of capital required several developed countries, such as Japan, Germany, the UK, and France, which had regulations and controls of different degrees in their financial systems that were inconsistent with the evolving global financial environment, to liberalize and deregulate their financial system.

In a financial system, controls that work against the strong market forces always help in the creation and proliferation of parallel financial markets. It was, therefore, a prudent policy to deregulate the financial system in line with the global trends. Liberalization of financial controls globally since the early 1980s brought about not only proper realignment of exchange rates among different countries but also redeployment of global capital, savings and liquidity, opening up capital markets in the developed countries as well as the emerging market economies, and opening new vistas for development of capital. Greater capital flow among nations has also narrowed arbitrage opportunities, large differentials in interest rates and returns on equities, and helped in a broader based and more balanced development of global capital markets. Swifter and longer tenure flows of both debt and risk capital have resulted in greater integration of capital markets in different countries. Both the capital lending and user countries have benefited from higher returns on, and lower cost of, capital, respectively. The global capital has been more efficiently distributed among different countries and different uses and users. The test of success of globalization lies in its effect on promoting higher global economic growth, more equitably distributed between different countries, and increasing the productivity of capital. If globalization has given higher economic growth and improved allocation of capital to different nations based on their growth potential and produced higher return on capital, then it would pass the test of its success.

Under the impact of the operation of floating exchange rates and the process of globalization, both short term and long term capital have been reallocated among different countries. It was theorized that the need for international liquidity and global forex reserves would be minimized under the system of floating exchange rates. The experience of the last three decades does not support this hypothesis. The demand for international liquidity has continued to remain high despite the floating exchange rates, and the central banks have been managing a higher level of forex reserves. Rather, the supply of international liquidity in the form of the US T Bills generated by the sustained rise in the US trade and current account deficit has been easily absorbed by the other central banks as their forex reserves on account of a number of factors.

First, removals of forex controls and financial liberalization across the countries have increased the volume of capital flows, including volatile, and sometimes dominant short-term flows. The magnitude of the capital account in the balance of payments of all countries under floating rates has shown dramatic growth compared with the trade account transactions in the balance of payments vis-à-vis such positions under fixed exchange rates. Some volatile capital flows have brought a perceptible impact on exchange rates. The demand from the central banks for forex reserves has naturally risen to meet a higher level of volatility in capital account.

Second, under the current floating exchange rates system, the exchange rates are not totally left to the market forces, but are usually allowed to change in line with the fundamental changes in the balance of payments by the central banks. The central banks have been, therefore, having a much bigger cushion of forex reserves in order to insulate exchange rates from capital flows, which are productive and are needed, or are temporary in nature, or destabilizing in potential and which are not needed. Over the last decade, large volumes of capital flows have gone into the kitties of central banks by way of forex reserves instead of appreciating their currencies. The resultant monetary expansion has not caused inflation in these countries due to the prevalence of overall excess capacity in production globally. It has worked in the direction of promoting economic growth in these countries, especially in China, South Korea, India and other Asian nations, which have been heaviest guzzlers of forex reserves.

Third, even under floating exchange rates, Asian countries kept their exchange rates stable until the Asian crisis of 1997, which forced on them the fresh level of exchange rates. China and Hong Kong have continued to keep their currencies fixed for more than two decades despite their favorable foreign trade and balance of payments performance. Stable rates have also enabled China and Asian countries to sustain their high economic growth rates. These countries have managed exchange rates of their currencies in line with their capacity of resource utilization, growth aspirations, inflation situation and tolerance, and desire to keep exchange rates stable or variable.

On account of all these factors, the floating exchange rates have necessitated and absorbed higher global liquidity despite the theoretical model arguing for years that the floating rates system would be a great economizer of international liquidity requirements. The new model of floating exchange rates has gone against Friedman's standard purely market dominated and oriented floating exchange rates model. Friedman calls the new model *dirty floating*. Despite its ideological distance from the pure market model, the floating rates model under globalization has shown good results. We do not know what results Friedman's model devoid of central bank intervention would have brought.

Despite the above systemic peculiarities of the contemporary system of floating exchange rates, there has been greater flexibility in exchange rates behavior than ever before, and it has enabled the economic policy makers to be more focused towards domestic macro-economic goals of faster growth and price stability. With any fundamental changes in balance of payments, the float has allowed a gradual shift in exchange parities. This has happened in respect of currencies of not only emerging markets but also the major currencies, like the US dollar, yen, pound sterling, deutsche mark and euro, which have shown major movements in both directions over the last decade. More recently, the euro has moved from a low of $0.89 to a high $1.29 in two years, giving a 45 percent swing in the exchange rate.

Liquid dollar twins

The main channel of financing globalization, as we have seen, is through the US T bills. This has given a new and added dimension to the growth of liquid dollar assets outside the US. The phenomenon of the operation of US dollars outside the US is not new. The euro-dollar deposits and banking system developed in the late 1960s in London and later spread to other important international banking, off-shore banking centers and tax heavens. So much was the growth of euro-dollar market nearly matching and rivaling the US domestic banking system and M3 that the Federal Reserve allowed the creation of off-shore centers, first in New York, to be called International Banking Facilities (IBFs) in 1981. It allowed the euro-dollars to fly back to the US. It is estimated that 60 percent of off-shore bank deposits comprise US dollars. The Bank for International Settlements (BIS) reported cross-border liabilities of BIS-reporting banks for 2005 at $19,888 billion (Table 3.5). If we consider 60 percent of this, we get the size of euro-dollar deposits of $11,933 billion. The US money supply M3 was $10,241 billion in 2005 (Table 3.5). Hence, we have the size of the euro-dollar deposits little larger than the money supply in the US. While the euro-dollar banking system is one segment of the dollars outside the US, the US currency notes leaving the US shores have also proliferated outside. The estimate of the 'greenbacks' outside the US is between 50 percent to 70 percent of US currency in circulation.[43] This phenomenon has grown rapidly due to growing acceptance of the US currency anywhere in the world and also because of the growing weakness of local currencies in several emerging market and transition economies. The latter is known as 'dollarization' and is increasing globally. It is estimated that out of the US currency notes of $800 billion in circulation, more than $400 billion are outside the US.

The third segment of the parallel dollar market is the foreign holdings of US T bills. This is a new phenomenon that developed under globalization. Under this component, nearly 50 percent of US T bills outstanding are held outside the US. In 2006, foreign holdings of US T bills were $2.1 trillion, 51 percent of treasury bills outstanding. All three components represent liquid dollar assets outside the US. It means that US dollar liquidity in terms of currency, bank deposits and T bills outside the US is almost equal to the liquidity within the US. We get liquid dollar twins; one within the US and one outside the US. The globalization over the last few years has increased the size of the parallel liquid dollar market. It also indicates that we are slowly moving towards a global village, a world with a single currency and no exchange rates. It has implications for the course of monetary policy by the Federal Reserve as well as the thrust and direction of globalization.

Prerequisites of a strong US dollar

On the face of the figures and data, the US is facing a precarious balance of payments situation. Its trade deficit is continuously enlarging and reached $617 billion in 2004, 5.3 percent of GDP, which is alarmingly high for any nation. It rose to $836 billion in 2006, 6.3 percent of GDP. Its forex reserves have been steady between $22 billion and $25 billion, which give only 2.5 weeks import cover and would be considered as a warning signal for any country for adopting strict balance of payments corrective measures to pre-empt any foreign currency crisis. It has been the net borrower in the global capital market since 1983, net debtor since 1990 and the world's largest borrower.

Against these several handicaps the US balance of payments faces in the global market, there are a number of key strengths the US has which weigh against its weaknesses. One has to see whether these strengths are heavy enough to ward off any trigger to the dollar crisis.

The BoP analysis of the US made earlier clearly brings out that despite the high current account deficit, the real BoP deficit of the US is not very large. It has been very marginal until 1990, when it was 1.7 percent of GDP, showed a surplus of 0.3 percent in 2000 and was in deficit by 3.4 percent in 2006 (Table 3.2). The high current account is not a worry but would be a concern arising from two alternative or simultaneous developments. First, if the high current account deficit starts hurting the US by creating larger unemployment than the resistance level, it would start weakening the dollar. It would be necessary for the US to abandon the *benign neglect II* philosophy to allow the US dollar to depreciate for improvement in its trade and current account deficit. This development is on the goods sector. Alternatively, there may be an imbalance on the financial sector or liquidity front or sector. If the autonomous private capital account shows a net deficit instead of surplus, causing higher private capital outflows supplying more dollars, it would enlarge the real BoP deficit. This would increase the US T bills accumulation abroad, worsen the net debtor position further, and due to higher supplies of dollars than the demand in the forex market would start weakening the dollar. The real BoP deficit may rise because of a worsening situation on both the goods and financial securities fronts or levels. Alternatively, one may worsen and the other improve, which is happening now, to bring down the real BoP deficit. Hence, the strength of dollar really depends on the real BoP deficit.

Yet another formidable monetary strength of the US is its official gold stocks. Despite its low forex reserves, US federal reserves have the world's largest holding of gold, of 262 million ounces, now worth nearly $180 billion, accounting for 28 percent of the gold holding of all central banks of 941 million ounces. In comparison, the Euro Area with 402 million ounces has nearly one and a half times the US holdings.

Money in international markets is exchangeable not only against goods and services but also financial instruments, like deposits, treasury bills, bonds and equities, and also physical assets like land and real estate. In addition to the current account, the physical and financial wealth and their relative prices and prospects become important in exchange rate determination. In spite of a rising trade deficit and also a current account deficit during the 1980s and 1990s, the US dollar has continued to remain strong due to higher real interest rates attracting debt flows, higher rates of profits on investments, the availability of relatively cheaper equity giving lucrative returns, and relatively cheaper and elastic supply of land, housing, real estates, and public infrastructure.

It is this stock and supplies of financial and physical assets in the US, their relatively higher real rate of return and relative elasticity in their stock as well as supplies, which has enabled the US to keep the dollar stronger despite its worsening fundamentals in the classical sense of deteriorating trade and current account balance.

Under the pre-war gold standard and the post-war Bretton Woods system of the gold-dollar standard until 1971, the strength of the US dollar emanated from the gold stocks of the US. Its *seigniorage* was limited to the value of its gold. In the post Bretton Woods floating rates system, the US is trading on value and returns on its financial and physical assets. Further, more important than its stock of financial and physical wealth, is also the capacity of its industrial and technical research infrastructure, which constantly innovates and creates opportunities for massive investments in several industries. The US has been in the past, and continues to be, the world's leading powerhouse of innovations, generating and sustaining investments and growth in its economy and also in the global economy. The decade of the 1990s witnessed an unprecedented investment activity in the US emerging from computer hardware, software, and internet and telecommunication industries. It kept the US economy buoyant throughout the 1990s with one of the longest bullish stock markets in US history.

The innovations do follow a cyclical pattern of ups and downs. Since foreign investments have been playing an important role in innovation-based investments in the US, the demand for dollars is also influenced by this cycle of innovations-based investments. In a rising cycle of innovations in the latter half of the 1990s, the innovation-oriented investment demand for US dollars was at its peak in recent US history. Post 2000, the low ebb of innovations has been a factor lowering the demand for the US dollar in the forex market.

The capacity of the US to leverage on the *seigniorage* it enjoys on dollar is finally dependent on its monetary policy, which determines its real interest rates and exchange rate, real return on capital and physical assets and also innovations, which drives its investments. The dollar is, therefore, driven by the innovative spirit of the US. The spirit of enterprise and innovation is the driving force of US economic growth and strong dollar. During the pre-war and Bretton Woods periods, the US enjoyed a trade surplus, and the dollar was, as a result, in short supply in the forex and international markets. The US incurred a deficit in its capital account by lending, investing and giving foreign aid. It supplied dollars abroad and generated its exports growth until 1971.

Post Bretton Woods, the situation was exactly the reverse. The US started incurring higher and higher trade deficits, and supplying more dollars abroad in the forex and international markets than its demand. To keep the US dollar strong as well as sustain its trade and current account deficit, the US needed to reattract the dollar through its capital account. Whatever went through the trade account had to come back through the capital account to keep the dollar strong and stable. Its inability to attract dollars back to US would make the dollar weaker in the international market.

Tight money policy and high interest rates charted by Paul Volcker kept the US dollar strong during the 1980s by attracting primarily bond investments in the US. The 1990s was the decade of a stock market boom that coincided in the latter half of the decade with the TMT investment boom. The investment and equity boom attracted dollars back to the US and kept the exchange rate stable and dollar strong. Even with interest levels at record lows compared with the highs of 1980s, the real interest rate differentials still worked in favor of the US, owing to a lower inflation rate encouraging foreign central banks to invest their dollar balances accumulated through large US trade deficits in US treasury bills.

The slump in the stock market, a sharp correction in TNT stock valuations and a low ebb of innovations in the TNT industries in 2001 weakened the attraction for dollars to move to the US. The dollar started bleeding on the capital account and witnessed a trend of weakness in the forex and international markets during 2002–2003. This helped the euro to strengthen. The euro rose from a low of $0.89 in 2002 to $1.34 in 2004. Several central banks also readjusted their forex holdings in favor of the euro and away from the US dollar, a factor that helped the euro strengthen further.

The success of globalization underscores the importance of a strong US dollar. Although the US dollar does swing from one end to the other in order to correct mismatches between the overseas demand for, and supplies of, the dollar, the fundamental strength of the US dollar is the anchor of the global monetary system and is intact. As long as the US can leverage its enormous national wealth in supplying dollars to the rest of the world through its trade deficits without causing global inflation, the strength of the dollar will not be jeopardized.

March of the euro

Former French President Charles de Gaulle was one of the staunch critics of the dollar standard and the benefit of *seigniorage* it gave to the US. He was also an ardent supporter of the gold standard. Despite the constant European efforts, neither pound sterling nor French franc or even D-mark could develop as a strong currency to rival the standing of the US dollar. The only way the European nations could stand and meet the American challenge was through the Common Market, later evolving into the European Economic and Monetary Union with a common central bank and a common currency. The countries' geographical smallness and proximity to each other made them the perfect candidates for an economic union. But in the 1960s and even in the 1970s, this was considered something of an ideal organization or a dream difficult to realize considering the large number countries in Europe with different languages and political systems and ideologies. Yet with slow and steady, but definite, progress the governments of 13 European countries gradually realized this dream in 1999 with the establishment of European Central Bank and the euro as their common currency. Robert Mundell had developed the concept of an *Optimum Currency Area* in 1961 and Europe was the right region for trying its political acceptability, and economic feasibility and success. The European Central Bank also sees the adoption of Keynes' plan of 1944 to create an International Clearing Bank (ICB) with an international currency, first called 'grammor' and then 'bancor'.[44] Although not realized on an international scale, the European Central Bank with the euro accomplished Keynes' dream on the European scale. As we move on with the evolution of the global monetary system, it will not be long before we will have the global central bank in place of the IMF.

Over the last few years, the European dream of a strong currency seems to be coming true. In just five years since its creation, the euro currency has become one of the leading mediums of exchange and a store of value in Europe in private transactions, and an important reserve asset among the central banks. With the strengthening of euro against dollar since 2002 and more recent appreciation since 2006, the euro reached a peak against the dollar at 1.3558 in May 2007; the euro has also become increasingly attractive as the reserve asset for both private investors as well as the central banks. The euro notes in circulation crossed the figure of €610 billion, equivalent to $800 billion of 'greenbacks' in circulation, in January 2007. Hence, like the dollar, the euro will also now enjoy the *seigniorage*.

The euro is now poised to rival the dollar as an international currency. An important implication of this is that if euro starts displacing the dollar as a reserve asset, the dollar will weaken in the forex market but as the foreign-held T bills are unloaded, their prices will fall and the yield rates will go up. This will also reduce the M3 in the US. But the excess supply of dollars in the forex market will bring a downward pressure on the dollar exchange rate. The exchange markets and money markets are interlinked. When foreign central banks unload their T bills, the rising supply and falling prices of T bills will raise the yield rates and thereby improve the relative return on US T bills. On the other hand higher demand for euro securities will increase their prices and reduce their yield. When they buy euro securities they will have to weigh the return on the euro vis-à-vis US T bills. Rising interest rates would again make the dollar stronger. This see-saw will go on in the forex and money markets for dollars and euros. It will stabilize at dollar-euro exchange rates when the demand and supply of dollars and euros match, to eliminate the interest rate or yield rates differentials between the dollar and euro money markets. The euro money market is now relatively small and it has to develop larger supplies to meet greater international demand.

An important implication of the switch from dollar to euro as a reserve asset is that it will limit the ability of the US to sustain its trade and current account deficit. However, there are several handicaps. As mentioned earlier, the euro securities market must develop with adequate supplies to meet international demand as a reserve asset. Further, there are several other hindrances in the march of the euro as an important international currency and a reserve asset. The inertia in favor of the dollar, its low transaction cost, anti-growth bias of the European Central Bank, and its complex governance structure representing many countries are likely to weigh against the euro in its competition against the dollar.[45]

Yet the euro is marching forward and is stronger. In 2006, for the second year in succession, the euro overtook the dollar as the world's pre-eminent currency in international bond markets. Outstanding debt issued in the euro was worth the equivalent of $4836 billion at the end of 2006 compared with $3892 billion for the dollar. Outstanding euro-denominated debt accounted for 45 percent of the

Table 3.5 Global money and forex reserves

Year	Global forex reserves SDRs* ($ billion)		USA M1 ($ billion)		USA M3 ($ billion)		Cross-border external liabilities of BIS-reporting banks ($ billion)	
1980	321		419		2000		1192	
1990	655	7.4%	843	7.2%	4089	7.4%	6481	18.5%
1995	988	8.6%	1152	6.4%	4647	2.6%	7831	3.9%
2001	1728	9.8%	1203	0.7%	8065	9.6%	11,187	6.1%
2005	3284	13.7%	1456	4.9%	10,241	6.2%	19,888	15.5%

Source: IMF, International Financial Statistics; BIS, Annual Reports.

Note

* Including gold stocks. The figures in percentages are compound annual growth rates.

international – or cross-border – market, compared with 37 percent for the dollar. New issuance in 2006 accounted for 49 percent of the global total. This is a massive rise for the euro which, in the bond market, had just 27 percent of the global pie, compared with 51 percent for the dollar a few years back. The most important reason for the popularity of the euro is the stability in the interest rate of the euro. Over three years, from 2003–2006, interest rates for the euro varied by 1.5 percent, between 2 percent and 3.5 percent. In contrast, the Fed funds rate fluctuated by 4.25 percentage points, ranging from 1 percent in the middle of 2003 to 5.25 percent at the beginning of 2007.

4　US capital market

Trigger for global growth

Monetary policy triumphs – interest rate reverts

With globalization, financial markets the world over became more open, transparent, flexible, responsive, and sensitive to changes and the smallest policy moves from the central banks (and more particularly, the Federal Reserve, the world's largest central bank and the supplier of global liquidity). Increasing integration of the markets following the process of financial liberalization and deregulation globally also compounded the influence of the demonstration effect of interest changes. The floating exchange rates offered greater freedom and maneuverability to monetary authorities in the supply of liquidity and its cost. The fast-changing financial environment also meant more frequent changes in the monetary stance of the central banks. The world's largest and strongest controller of liquidity and interest rates, the Federal Reserve, was quick in adapting to the new rules of the game. In the late 1970s, the Chairman of the Federal Reserve, Paul Volcker, abandoned interest rates as a tool of monetary control to switch over to monetary targeting. Nevertheless, during the era of record asset price inflation, which the US experienced in the 1980s and more particularly in the 1990s, Alan Greenspan, who succeeded Paul Volcker in August 1987 – only a few months before the October 1987 stock market crash – had to revert to the weapon of the discount rate and more particularly the Fed Funds rate as the primary tool of monetary management with much greater frequency than at any time in the US monetary history.

The Federal Reserve, instead of being reactive in its policy approach began to be more proactive in its influence. Upswings in the equity markets worldwide and more openness in these markets further increased the importance of interest changes made by the Fed on account of their pervasive influence on the global stock and capital markets. The Fed's benchmark interest rate, which determines the yield curve for the Government securities, from Treasury bills to 30-year bonds, became the topmost item on the watch list of global financial managers. Moreover, as the entire structure of interest rates of bonds reacts to the benchmark of a risk-free rate structure for the T bills and G Secs, the focus of the Federal Reserve monetary policy on the Fed Funds Rate as a guiding factor in the financial market became more prominent. The Fed used the Fed funds rate, both as a lever to arrest the overheating of assets markets, especially the stock markets, to impact inflation, as well as to revive the sluggish economy, rejuvenate investment climate and reduce unemployment numbers.

> Greenspan had come to understand that controlling the fed funds rate was the key to the Fed's power over the American economy .... Buying or selling of US Treasury bonds, so-called open market operations, gives the Fed a brutal tool. Changes in the fed funds rate usually translate into changes in the long-term interest rates on loans paid by consumers, homeowners and businesses. The FOMC's (Federal Open Market Committee) monopoly on the fed funds rate gives the Fed control over credit conditions, the real engine of capitalism. Though the changes in the rate were not announced in 1987, private market watchers in New York closely monitored the Fed's open market operations and soon figured out the changes. The discount rate was the rate that the Fed communicated its intentions publicly; the fed funds rate was the way the Fed actually imposed those intentions .... . The FOMC, and now Greenspan, had the full weight of the law nearly 75 years of history – and myth – behind them. They could work their will if they choose.[46]

Thus came the historic reversal in US monetary policy and management wherein, it was not the Fed's discount rate but the Fed funds rate that became the main tool of controlling monetary and liquidity conditions in the US. This switch over to the interest rate and, more particularly, the Fed funds rate as the weapon of monetary control also occurred owing to the growing importance of the demonstration effect of the Federal Reserve's announcements of interest rate changes and the predominance of the expectations factor exacerbated by the digitally connected borderless money markets.

Dividend of cheap money policy

One of the most overriding factors that enabled the US economy to achieve record and sustained economic growth in the 1990s has been the low interest and cheap money policies pursued by the Fed. The low interest policy stimulated corporate investment and coincided with the phase of several technological breakthroughs and innovations, it brought unprecedented productivity gains and higher and sustained economic growth in the US economy. Cheap money also kept the growth in consumer spending and housing demand high, thereby, promoting higher investment and contributing to higher economic growth. The low interest rate and cheap money policie triggered a long and historical bull phase in the US stock market in the 1990s. The Fed Funds rate, which was 7 percent in February 1989, was lowered to 6.5 percent in December 1990. It was successively cut by 0.5 percent to 4.5 percent by December 1991 when it was further reduced by 1 percent to 3.5 percent. Yet another cut of 0.5 percent was effected in 1992 to bring it to the lowest level of 3 percent, where it remained unchanged through 1993. Between 1994 and 1999, The Fed funds rate varied between 4 percent to 5.25 percent.

During this period, Dow Jones enjoyed one of the fastest, sustained, and longest rallies in the US stock market history. From a level of 2590 in January, 1990 Dow Jones ran higher every successive year with different degrees of steam until it reached a peak of 11,497 in December 1999 (2736 – January 1991; 3223 – January 1992; 3310 – January 1993; 3978 – January 1994; 4001 – January 1995; 5395 – January 1996; 6813 – January 1997; 7906 – January 1998; 9358 – January 1999; and the peak of 11,497 – December 1999).

Despite cheap money, the inflation rate remained one of the lowest due to the high growth in output, rising trade deficit and real effective appreciation in the US dollar, which kept imports cheap. Higher growth in imports increased the supplies of goods and kept inflation low, but only at the cost of a higher trade deficit. The low cost of financing gave a boost to housing and consumer spending, both of which helped corporate America capture higher earnings growth in each successive year, and thereby sustain the stock market rally. The growth phase was also induced by revolutionary changes in computer hardware, software, the internet, and telecoms, which attracted huge investments. ITT investments (Information Technology and Telecoms) also gave quick financial and economic results, both to corporate America as well as the US economy. These sectors showed a high growth in profits, which helped the stock market boom, and yielded high productivity gains, boosting the overall economic growth, to a record level for a sustained period throughout the 1990s, the period in which President Bill Clinton, who turned the US fiscal deficit into a robust surplus, led the Bullish American economy and Alan Greenspan managed the Stock Market, US Dollar and inflation.

In February 2000, the American economy would officially have enjoyed the longest expansion in its history. The White house wanted Clinton-Greenspan team to be part of the celebration … . Clinton and Greenspan were almost glowing at each other, … linked surprisingly to each other's greatest success, wrapping themselves in each other's legacies …

'You know' the President said, addressing Greenspan to his immediate left, 'I have to congratulate you. You've done a great job in a period when there was no rulebook to look to'.

'Mr. President' Greenspan replied, 'I couldn't have done it without what you did on deficit reduction. If you had not turned the fiscal situation around, we couldn't have had the kind of monetary policy we've had'.

Who would have thought, seven years before at their first meeting in Little Rock, that such economic conditions were even possible – steady economic growth, low inflation, and unemployment hovering at unheard of 4 percent and Dow above 11,000. More than 20 million new jobs had been created since Clinton took office. Some economists would have put the odds at 1 in 1 million. Greenspan, ever a stickler about probability, couldn't even calculate it.[47]

During 2000, the continuing stock market rally invited a note of caution from the Fed Chairman on the risk of the market undergoing a correction due to what he then called, and is now a popular term or jargon, '*irrational exuberance*'. The Fed Funds rate was raised by the Fed three times, from 5 percent to 6 percent in 2000, to ward off further speculative build up in the stock market. When the market did correct in 2001, the Fed again swung in to action to use the Fed Funds rate cuts and arrest the steep fall in the market and growth rate in the economy. During 2001 the Fed went on vigorously to cut the Fed Funds rate by as a many as record 11 times, by 0.25 percent to 0.5 percent each time, to a record low of 1.75 percent, in its desperate attempt to arrest the declining stock market and economy, and to ignite recovery. The Fed Funds rate was lowered further to 1.25 percent in November, 2002 and to the lowest level of 1 percent in June, 2003. The next section deals with the Keynesian analysis of boom and slump, and the rationale of the ineffectiveness of interest rate tool for igniting recovery and why it fails to give an effective response.

Since 2004, the rate was progressively raised from 1.25 percent in June, 2004 to a high of 5.25 percent in June, 2006. The stock market remained weak in 2002 when the Dow fell and closed at 8348 for the year. During 2003 to 2005 the market remained range bound with the Dow hovering from 10,400 to 10,700. The year 2006 showed Dow rising by 16 percent when it closed for the year at 12,459.

Interest rate illusion

One of the most striking aspects of the Fed monetary policy under the Greenspan era, especially during the 1990s, was the high frequency of change in interest rates. Interest rates also reached their lowest level in the US in recent history. The concept of the *interest rate illusion* is brought in here to demonstrate how the Fed was, on many occasions, not able to achieve the results it aimed through frequent interest rate changes due to this illusion. The interest rate illusion masked the effects of frequent interest changes on consumption and investment. It did, however, carry out its effects better on the securities prices both in the equities and bond markets.

Keynes coined a term *money illusion* when he found that an average household is more concerned about its money income and not its purchasing power or real income. Money wages were more important than real wages in guiding consumer behavior in consumption and saving, he observed in the depression years of the early 1930s when he initially considered increasing employment by reducing money wage rates. A similar illusion is also evident in respect of interest rates. The interest rate is a price for the use of money. It is the price for parting with liquidity, which gives command over resources. However, unlike other prices it is expressed in percentage terms. The price is expressed for a period, usually a year. It is a time-related price expressed in percentage terms. A change in interest rate is also expressed in percentage terms. The actual change in interest rate in percentage terms is different from what is commonly expressed. For example, a 1 percent fall in the interest rate from 10 percent to 9 percent is a 10 percent fall in interest. Further, a 1 percent reduction from 9 percent to 8 percent works out to be a higher fall, i.e. 11.11 percent, from 8 percent to 7 percent, a 1 percent reduction comes to 12.5 percent. A further decline of 1 percent from 7 percent to 6 percent, measures as 14.29 percent. Next a 1 percent reduction from 6 percent to 5 percent increases to a value of 16.67 percent. Hence, a 1 percent fall in interest in a declining interest rate phase goes on progressively rising. A 1 percent reduction in interest from 4 percent to 3 percent, works out to be 25 percent. The *interest rate illusion* is an illusion that masks the realization of progression or regression involved in each successive round of the same percentage interest rate decrease or increase respectively. As shown earlier, each successive 1 percent decrease in the interest rate from, say, 10 percent becomes effectively larger and larger, and each successive increase of 1 percent from 10 percent becomes effectively smaller and smaller. Although, the economists, mathematicians or finance professionals are not required to be educated about it, when we are reckoning with the market and public reactions, we are dealing with all its participants and the mass market and the mob, which is subject to the *interest rate illusion* like Keynes' *money illusion*.

When the Fed cut the Fed funds rate every time by 0.25 percent or 0.5 percent, it meant a higher and higher cut in percentage terms at lower and lower levels. A progressive cut of 0.25 percent or 0.5 percent each time worked out higher in terms of interest cost. When the Fed cut the Fed funds rate by a record 4.75 percent during 2001, from 6 percent to 1.25 percent, each time by 0.25 percent or 0.5 percent, the same cut was getting bigger and bigger every time. Actually, the 4.75 percent cut from 6 percent to 1.25 percent meant a whopping 79 percent cut in interest cost. That was the kind of big push the interest rate cuts of 2001 intended to give. Nevertheless, despite this vigorous move, the investment climate remained lukewarm, vindicating Keynes' hypothesis that at low levels of interest rate, investment is interest inelastic, although each successive cut at low levels of interest means more and more. In this 'investment trap', the expectations on income and spending growth are more important than the rate cut. So also is its effect on consumer spending. Small changes in interest rates are unlikely to affect immediately consumer spending momentum due to the interest illusion. These changes, however, have an instantaneous impact on the prices in the securities market, which basically deal in a stock of financial assets. Consumer spending and investment are flows and not stocks, and therefore, their reaction to small interest rate changes is likely to be marginal due to the mask effect of the interest rate illusion. Galbraith called it the *monetary illusion.* Writing about the ineffectiveness of an interest rate rise in curbing consumer spending in his famous book *The Affluent Society* in 1958, he observed.

Thus a man who signs a note for $1800 on the purchase of a new car to be repaid over twenty-four months, and who agrees to an 'add-on' of 6 percent of this amount as interest, will have a total interest bill of $216 and monthly payments of $84. If the interest charge is increased by one-third to an add-on of 8 percent, his total interest obligation becomes $288, but the increase in monthly payments in only $3. The one-third increase in interest brings but a one-thirtieth increase in the payment. This increase can easily be offset by a lengthening of the term of repayment. In practice it is submerged by a variety of additional inspection, insurance, and other charges. Since the customer in contemplating the purchases is aware, not of the interest rate, but of the monthly charge, it will be seen how readily a very large increase in interest charges can, in practice, be offset. During the period of active monetary policy in the early fifties, increased finance charges were regularly followed by large increases in consumer loans. Want creation, and the process of financing it, was still acting to exaggerate rather than to restrain the inflationary effect of consumer spending while its conflict with the machinery of consumer want creation remains unresolved and, in degree, even unrecognized, and while we concede the paramount importance of the latter. And though the reasons have not been fully seen there is, in fact, considerable agreement that monetary policy does not make any effective contact with consumer borrowing and spending.[48]

Like the money illusion, the interest rate illusion influences saver and investor behavior. This illusion does not follow economic logic, like the stock market in *irrational exuberance*. Hence, a conventional economic reaction in responding to the normal remedy cannot be expected. The interest rate works very similar to a brake. It can slow the economic momentum of growth and avoid overheating the economy. It can check consumer price and asset price inflation. Moreover, it cannot restore the lost momentum of economic growth. Lowering the interest rate is like releasing the brake: it would only continue maintaining a lower momentum of growth but not accelerate it. To accelerate growth we need a fresh trigger or thrust. This vindicated the Keynes' hypothesis of Liquidity and Investment Trap and the inability of monetary policy to revive a sluggish economy. This is Keynes' main argument and he forcefully brought out this weakness of monetary policy and impotency of the low interest rate in reviving business confidence and investment in *The General Theory*.

> If reduction in the rate of interest was capable of providing an effective remedy by itself, it might be possible to achieve a recovery without the elapse of any considerable interval of time and by means more or less directly under the control of the monetary authority. But, in fact, this is not usually the case; and it is not so easy to revive marginal efficiency of capital, determined, as it is, by the uncontrollable and disobedient psychology of the business world. It is the return of confidence, so to speak, in ordinary language, which is so insusceptible to control in an economy of individualistic capitalism.[49]

Even after 72 years it seems that Keynes is referring to Greenspan's dilemma in 2001. Surprisingly, these comments do not come in Keynes' main writings on *The General Theory* but in one of the concluding chapters, entitled 'Notes on the trade cycle'. His comment further as to why there is a collapse at the top of the boom is also most relevant in the current context.

> ... it is an essential characteristic of the boom that investments which will in fact yield, say, 2 percent. in conditions of full employment are made in the expectation of a yield of, say, 6 percent., and are valued accordingly. When the disillusion comes, this expectation is replaced by a contrary 'error of pessimism', with the result that the investments, which would in fact yield 2 percent. in conditions of full employment, are expected to yield less than nothing; and the resulting collapse of new investment then leads to a state of unemployment in which the investments, which would have yielded 2 percent. in conditions of full employment, in fact yield less than nothing.[50]

Keynes brings out clearly how non-fulfillment of overly optimistic expectations of returns from investment causes a slump in fresh investment, leading to a declining spiral of income and output, or in current common business terminology, lower consumer confidence or spending power, causing a fall in the normal rate of return on investment. He goes on to explain that during the later stages of a boom, the optimistic expectation of future rate of return is so strong, offsetting the rising supplies and higher costs of the products and also rising interest rate, that when there is disillusionment in the overbought market, it falls suddenly and with catastrophic force.[51] Keynes' analysis is so eloquent and far reaching that it is still relevant in explaining the ups and owns in our stock market. Greenspan aptly termed the foregoing phenomenon *irrational exuberance*, Keynes called it *misguided state of expectations* or *speculative excitement*.[52] Commenting further on the remedy for the boom he writes, 'The right remedy for the trade cycle is not to be found in abolishing booms and thus keeping us permanently in semi-slump; but in abolishing slumps and thus keeping us permanently in quasi-boom'.[53] This is what the sustainable growth path is which the global economies have been achieving in the Keynesian era.

Although interest rates serve as a very potent tool of asset price control and spending momentum in an economy, it is blunted in extreme circumstances when the interest illusion creeps in. Up to a certain threshold limit, small interest changes fail to curb asset price inflation or avert the slump in asset prices, and remain ineffective in taming the booming economy or reflating the sluggish economy due to the mask effect of *interest rate illusion*. This is vindicated by the experience of the Fed policy in the 1990s, although the overall effect of the Fed policy throughout this long period has been positive and successful.

The inability of interest rates to spur investment and economic recovery was vividly demonstrated in Japan during the 1990s when it went through its worst recession and period of economic stagnation, caused primarily by a sharp deceleration in its exports growth. Japanese economic growth was fuelled by its buoyant export sector. Globalization created large production capacities in China, South Korea and other Asian nations, which produced goods at lower cost, hurting Japan's higher cost exports. Globalization did affect Japan adversely. The low interest rate policy in Japan with the interest rate bordering 0 percent for a long time could not stimulate either consumption or investment to generate economic growth. Only a Keynesian remedy could resolve Japan's long recession.

The declining interest rate phase benefits fresh borrowing and adversely affects fresh lenders. Moreover, economics is not a one way street. It also compensates those whom it affects adversely. For every 1 percent decline in interest rate, which hurts a saver by reducing his fresh interest earnings, he is more than compensated by capital appreciation on his old savings contracted at a higher rate. The capital gains on old debt work out larger than the decline in earnings on fresh savings. This is a percentage game. It has different implications for households, corporations and government. The reverse happens in a rising interest phase. The rising interest causes capital loss on the old savings although new savings get the higher rate.

Bull market of 1990s

The decade of 1990s witnessed one of the longest and most vigorous bullish phases in the US stock market history, which coincided with one of the longest periods of sustained economic growth in the US. While the cheap money policy created an environment for faster economic growth and prosperity, there were other factors and developments that sustained growth and the bull market of the 1990s. To find out which came first, whether growth or bull market, is a 'chicken or egg' puzzle. Undoubtedly, however, both phenomena reinforced each other in spinning the wheel of economic prosperity that was unprecedented in US history.

The key factor that encouraged a sharp rise in equity investments and a buoyant capital market was the support from the institutional investors. Throughout the 1990s, the strength of the growth of the global economy and capital markets emanated from the US stock market, the largest stock market of the world with sustained high return on the equity it offered. The growing importance of institutional investors in the global capital market is illustrated by its increasing size and operations. The total assets of the top 300 institutional investors in the US went up from $535 billion in 1975 accounting for 35 percent of GDP to $8 trillion in 1993 with its share in GDP of 110 percent. Pension funds, mutual funds, and insurance companies in five major industrial nations had assets under management close to $13 trillion in 1993. The global equity market capitalization in the same year was $14.1 trillion and the outstanding stock of government debt in the seven largest industrial nations was $9 trillion. By 1998, assets managed by institutional investors more than doubled since 1990 and reached a figure of $30 trillion, about equal to the global GDP.

Institutional investors, primarily comprising pension funds, mutual funds and insurance companies have became a strong force in the capital markets as well as in the financial markets of the world during the 1990s. The assets of institutional investors from OECD countries rose from $16 trillion 1992 to $27.3 trillion in

Table 4.1 Financial assets of US institutional investors (in $ trillion)

	Pension funds	*Insurance cos*	*Mutual funds*	*Total*
1992	3.0	2.2	1.6	8.0
1995	4.2	2.8	3.5	10.5
2005	7.3	5.6	8.9	21.8

Source: Investment Company Institute, USA.

2000, an average annual growth of 11 percent. The US alone, which accounted for $8 trillion in 1992, 50 percent of the total, had $19.5 trillion in 2000, 71 percent of total OECD institutional investors. The share of these assets in GDP in US went up from 124 percent in 1991 to 207 percent in 2000. Table 4.1 shows the growth in the financial assets of institutional investors in the US.

During the 1990s, the investment in equity by institutional investors showed higher growth. The equity holdings of institutional investors went up from $4 trillion in 1992 to $16 trillion in 1999. The share of their equity investments went up from 30 percent in 1992 to 48 percent in 2000.The bull phase of the 1990s showed more spectacular results to equity investors, perhaps unprecedented in the US stock market history. The Dow Jones, which was 2500 in 1991 rose persistently to 11,700 in 2000, giving 17 percent compound annual rate of return and 37 percent average annual return, the highest ever return given by any financial asset over a period of a decade in recent history, except perhaps gold when the gold price went up from $35 an ounce in 1971 to high of $850 in 1980.

The buoyant stock market and phase of innovation in the internet and telecoms invited large foreign investment in the US. A trend, which is distinct, noteworthy and revealing, is that during 1995 and 2000, there was a remarkable increase in foreign private investment in the US. While the foreign official holdings went up in the US, Government securities went up from $507 billion to $749 billion, the foreign private direct investment rose from $680 billion to $1418 billion, investments in equity stocks went up from $511 billion to $1547 billion and in corporate and other bonds went up from $459 billion to $1076 billion (Table 3.3). In addition to the investments by retail and institutional investors in the US, large overseas investments in the US equity and sector stocks, and relative switch from debt to equity was one of the driving forces of US equity and TMT boom.

Record growth of mutual funds and index funds

One of the main segments of institutional investors that rode the wave of growth was the mutual fund industry. In 1982, before the US bull market began its ride, the mutual fund holdings of $40 billion in the total equities of $1.3 trillion was 2.8 percent. By 1998 with the mutual fund equity holding of $2.5 trillion, they controlled 21 percent of corporate America. Compared with 1992 when mutual funds accounted for 6.1 percent of financial assets of US households, by 2000 this share almost doubled to 12.2 percent. Mutual fund investments in equities in the US went up from $309 billion in 1991 to $3.3 trillion in 2000. Pension funds, which invested $1.3 trillion in equity in 1991, had $4.2 trillion in equities in 2000.

The decade of the 1990s witnessed the real thrust to the mutual fund mobilization in the US. The US mutual fund assets, which were $1.1 trillion in 1990, doubled to $2.2 trillion in 1994, and further doubled to $4.4 trillion in 1997 and rose to $7 trillion in 2000. The number of US households owning mutual funds more than doubled during this period from 23.4 million to 50.6 million. The number of mutual funds in the market rose from 3081 in 1990 to 7791 in 1999. Equity mutual funds in the US, which numbered 340 in 1982, rose to 3952 by 1999, more than the stocks listed on the NYSE, with 120 million shareholder accounts, compared with 62 million in 1982. Prolonged stock market rally and continuing increase in bond prices during a declining interest phase caused a shift of household assets from real estate and other tangible assets to the financial assets, and primarily to mutual funds. The households showed an increasing preference towards mutual funds rather than direct stock investment. Net cash flows to mutual funds, which were $44 billion in 1990, rose sharply to a record of $477 billion in 1998 and were $489 billion in 2000. Equity funds that attracted 30 percent of mutual fund mobilizations in 1990 received 51 percent of cash flows in 1999. In 2000, which was a year of rising interest rates, the size of bond funds reduced due to falling NAVs of bond funds caused by declining bond prices, and equity funds got $310 billon out of total of $389 billion, i.e. 80 percent.

During this period the US stock markets – both NYSE and NASDAQ – experienced record growth in their turnover. The turnover rate (total shares sold in a year divided by the total number of shares) nearly doubled in the NYSE from 42 percent in 1982 to 78 percent in 1999, while in the NASDAQ, which was a citadel of technology stocks, turnover went up from 88 percent in 1990 to 221 percent in 1999.

Since 1999, due to the leapfrogging advances in internet technology, online trading in equities showed a spectacular growth. From 3.7 million online accounts in 1997 to 9.7 million in 1999. By 2001, with rapid growth in internet technology and infrastructure, the online trading accounts rose to a whopping 21 million. This encouraged day trading, even by the smaller investors, in large numbers.

The equity mutual fund mobilization in the US, which rose sharply, raised the institutional demand for stocks. Investment and return in the stock market often become circular and self-fulfilling. Expectations of higher return raise prices and fulfill higher returns, which raise prices further until this positive cycle is broken at some point.

The same logic applies to index funds. Rising index fund mobilization itself raises the index due to investment of these funds in the index stocks. In view of the rising index, small and mid capital stocks, with earnings growth higher than index stocks and a PE ratio lower than index stocks, attract buying which give returns better than the index. This cycle continues so long as the positive flows into the index funds are maintained, and it is the future confidence level and risk perception that maintains the positive flows and keeps the cycle moving up.

In 1975, John C. Bogle launched the first index fund at his mutual fund company, Vanguard. The philosophy behind index funds is that the index funds offer a better and safer vehicle to investors at lowest cost than pure or plain vanilla equity funds. The majority of actively managed equity funds were found to be underperforming the index, while only a small percentage of total equity mutual funds outperformed the index. Further average returns on all equity mutual funds were found to be lower than the returns from the index. Bogle used the S&P500 to make this comparison. Vanguard, the pioneer in index funds, has since then emerged as one of the largest mutual funds due to growing popularity and better returns offered by these mutual funds. In 1995, Bogle published results, which showed that S&P500 had outperformed 96 percent of all actively managed equity funds.[54] Further, index funds also have a low cost ratio of 0.25 percent compared with the average of 1.25 percent to 1.5 percent for actively managed funds. Owing to growing investor acceptance and fancy, the size of index funds in the US increased by more than sixfold, from $30 billion to $200 billion during 1995 – 98. The share of index funds in all equity funds rose from 3 percent in 1995 to 5.4 percent in 1998. Out of the cash inflow in equity mutual funds in the US of $50 billion in 1998, index funds received nearly 25 percent, one quarter of the total. Annual return on S&P500 for 5 years ending 1997 was 23.1 percent compared with an average equity mutual fund return of 18.5 percent, an annual out performance of 5 percent.

The S&P500 includes 500 of the largest corporations of the US and is, therefore, dominated by large stocks, which account for 75 percent of US market capitalization compared with 90 percent 25 years back. There are about 60 different indices tracked by index funds but the vast majority of assets are indexed to S&P500.

The rising size of index funds in progressively increasing mutual fund mobilizations during the 1990s, with the share of index fund mobilization going up to 25 percent, created demand pressure on the stock market in general and index stocks in particular. Increasing return from index becomes a self-fulfilling equation. So long as the earnings growth in index stocks supports the confidence reposed by the investors, the rising trend in index remains sustainable.

401(K) and capital gains tax

A revolutionary change in pension plans in the US was the unprecedented growth in defined contribution plan under 401(K), under which employees were offered the opportunity to make their own contributions from their pay checks towards a tax-deferred retirement account. These must be allocated to equities, bonds, or money market accounts. During the 1990s, a large portion of defined contributions under 401K went to equities or equity funds shoring up the demand for equities.

One of the reasons for the proliferation of mutual funds, especially equity funds, was the growing investments from 401(K) pension funds. Mutual fund retirement assets, which were $350 billion in 1991, spiraled to $2.5 trillion in 1999. This accounted for 36 percent of mutual fund assets and 20 percent of US retirement market. In 1999, 50 percent of these 401(K) investments were made in equity, which shows the growing size of household savings deployed in the US equity markets through professional institutional investors.

The popularity of 401(K) was also encouraged by a positive development on the tax front. In 1997, the capital gains tax rate was cut from 28 percent to 20 percent. Unlike 1978 and 1980, when tax cuts on capital gains brought the market down, the effect of the 1997 tax cut on the stock market was favorable, perhaps because of the expectation of a further cut. The already buoyant US stock market viewed this move positively, giving a further boost to the market.

Employee stock options

One factor, which has also contributed to the bullishness in the stock market in the 1990s, was the extensive use of employee stock options by the corporates. The philosophy behind the employee stock option is to make the employees a part owner in the companies. It is a motivation factor to elicit greater commitment, and vigorous and concerted effort in work by all employees towards consistent improvement in the performance of companies. When employees become the co-owners or shareholders in the companies, they could share the prosperity in the company not only through a share in the profits but also higher valuations of its shares in the stock market. While the options do generate greater motivational force from employees towards better financial results, it also lures the management in to projecting superior earnings forecasts, which may be out of line with reality since option holders have an inherent interest, or vested interest in the share price going up after the employees have exercised their options. During the 1990s, increasingly large numbers of companies offered stock options to employees – and also in large numbers compared with the share capital of companies – than ever before. This was more so in the technology and other new economy companies. In several such new ventures, managements and also investment analysts tended to have biased and optimistic earnings projections. In a bull phase, stock options did contribute further to the bullishness because of the larger stake of employees in the valuations of their stocks.

Innovations and growth

Process of creative destruction

The market oriented economy driven by the capital market is sustained by innovations. Capital investment emanating from new and innovative technology has been the engine of growth in the US. Innovations in a capitalistic society are an ongoing process on which the competitive economy thrives. Joseph Schumpeter described innovations in capitalism as the evolutionary process of '*creative destruction*' that fuels its growth and changes its structure.

> The fundamental impulse that sets and keeps the capitalist engine in motion comes from the new consumers, goods, the new methods of production or transportation, the new markets, the new forms of industrial organization that capitalist enterprise creates ... process of industrial mutation – if I may use that biological term – that incessantly revolutionizes the economic structure from within, incessantly destroying the old one, incessantly creating a new one. This process of creative destruction is the essential fact about capitalism.[55]

Although the process of creative destruction is continuous, at times there have been such sequences in interrelated innovations that have a chain effect, resulting in bunching of innovations. The decade of the 1990s and, more particularly, the second half of the 1990s close to Y2K, brought such a chain effect of innovations in Internet, Information Technology and Telecoms (ITT) that galvanized the investment climate in the US and propelled the stock market boom. One of the fundamental factors behind the sustained economic growth of the US economy throughout the 1990s has been a series of innovations in technology in computer hardware, software, internet and telecommunications in quick succession promoting high and increasing capital spending, and also generating quick returns. The service sector of ITT brought in unprecedented gains in productivity, which contributed to higher overall economic growth. The ITT revolution of the 1990s shrank both space and time. Distances were shrunk with instantaneous fixed and floating communication. Time condensed due to the real time processing of vast information. It generated gains in productivity, which were comparable to the revolution caused by the railroads, telephones, and electricity generation in the US in the 1880s.

The new industry attracts fresh investment as long as the market demand and its growth are not met by the existing production capacity. As soon as the market is saturated and its growth is met by the existing excess capacity, only a nominal additional investment is made in the industry. Schumpeter's innovation cycle still has a great influence on the behavior of the modern, high technology, and increasingly service oriented economy, like the US. In order to sustain the cycle of growth, there has to be an uninterrupted sequence of new discoveries, to keep investment levels high. Near saturation of the market in ITT by 2001 and the absence of a fresh flow of breakthroughs in technology resulted in a failure to attract additional investments, which were a feature of the industry during the period of a peak in the growth cycle in the late 1990s.

Wealth effect – Keynes effect?

The positive wealth effect of rising stock prices during the 1990s gave crucial support to both economic growth and sustenance of the stock market rally. Higher and well-spread consumer confidence and a sense of well being boosted consumer spending and its growth throughout the 1990s. In addition to investment spending and productivity growth, strong growth in consumer spending emanating from the wealth effect did play a crucial role in keeping the economic momentum high.

The wealth effect is the tendency to spend more due to an increase in the value of assets, physical or financial, or wealth arising from the rise in their prices. When it is realized, it becomes capital gain. In economics, capital gain or loss is treated as monetary gain or loss. The wealth effect indicates that it is not necessary to realize capital appreciation to spend more. The increase in the value of wealth is enough to prompt more spending. It has a powerful effect on the growth momentum of the economy through the two most important and critical Keynesian elements driving the real GDP growth. Capital gains have a strong influence on the propensity to consume and the incentive to invest, which are two key determinants on income, output and employment and their growth. Its effects on the economy are similar to business profits which drive capital investment and growth of trade, commerce, and industry. However, capital gains are more pervasive in their effect on the economic system. It covers both households and business and, therefore, has a much wider impact in terms of its spread as well as its effects on growth. While capital gains, realized or unrealized, in business primarily contribute to further investment, capital gains of households promote higher consumption in addition to investment. Capital gains arise out of assets price inflation, and therefore, act as a powerful accelerator of economic growth. This wealth effect is well documented by Keynes and, in the environment of stock market collapse and economic depression in the early 1930s, his thoughts were more on the negative wealth effect and not the positive one arising from the stock market boom.

> Unfortunately a serious fall in marginal efficiency of capital (expected rate of return on real investment) also tends to affect adversely the propensity to consume. For it involves a severe decline in the market value of Stock Exchange equities. Now, on the class who take active interest in their Stock Exchange investments, especially if they are employing borrowed funds, this naturally exerts a very depressing influence. These people are even more influenced by their readiness to spend by rises and falls in the value of their investments than by the state of their income. With a 'stock minded' public, as in the United States today, a rising stock-market may be an essential condition of a satisfactory propensity to consume; and this circumstance, generally overlooked until lately, obviously serves to aggravate still further the depressing effect of a decline in the marginal efficiency of capital.[56]

After discovering and highlighting first the relationship between consumption and income, contradicting the classical economic view of relating consumption as the counterpart of saving with the rate of interest, Keynes went further in *The General Theory* and even documented the powerful influence of the wealth effect on propensity to consume and hence on the economic growth. He also portrays how boom and slump in the stock market have a strong impact on the overly optimistic and pessimistic expectation of return on real investment, finally influencing the growth cycle of the economy.

The stock market boom during the 1990s was one of the factors that contributed to the long and sustained period of high economic growth in the US that has no historical parallel. It is also possible to argue that sustained economic growth also created conditions for the stock market to rally for a long period throughout the decade of 1990s. This becomes a 'chicken or egg' story; which came first? Then, what about innovations? The role of innovations in capital investment and growth momentum of the capitalist economy was analyzed earlier. The bunching of innovations in the ITT sectors in 1990s was unprecedented. The level of investment which these sectors attracted in the US from within and abroad broke all earlier records. The IT, Telecoms boom, which permanently changed the structure and functioning of the economy, was the biggest in the history of industrial economy. And what about Fed Chairman, Greenspan, who orchestrated the most congenial monetary policy for 12 long years from the post-1987 stock market crash to the market peak in 1999 for sustained economic growth, touching a high of 4.5 percent, inflation below 2 percent and unemployment below 4 percent? That leaves out the biggest kingpin of the 'Goldilocks' economy of the 1990s. President Clinton, who with his vision, used all his intellect and skills to navigate the most difficult U-turn for his gigantic ship and turned the record budget deficit into an enviable surplus. The upshot is that one can debate whether the stock market boom, the wealth effect, innovations, monetary policy, or budget surplus played a dominant role in the 1990s 'Goldilocks' economy, but all these factors had their role to play, and the wealth effect undoubtedly contributed to the growing economy.

The wealth effect could also be negative. Apart from lower investments in the lead sector of growth, ITT, the general investment climate after the year 2000 remained dull due to the negative wealth effect eroding household wealth, dampening consumer confidence and lowering consumer spending. The stock market bearish trend, which began in 2001 and carried through first half of 2003, brought the negative wealth effect into play and restrained consumer spending growth. The NASDAQ and Dow fell from their peaks of 5048 and 11,400 in 2000 to their lows of 1300 and 8500 in 2002. This further lowered capital spending in the old economy and curtailed the overall economic growth rate.

The absence of a strong wealth effect emanating from the stock market, which remained buoyant throughout the 1990s, was a major cause for concern for sustaining higher economic growth in the US and the global economy. The US economy needs a stimulus in consumer spending and a spurt in capital expenditure to achieve higher economic growth.

Globalization – new Keynesian growth model for the US

In the Bretton Woods model of development, the economic aid from the US was offering liquidity to the international monetary system and it enabled the aid recipient nations to import US goods. It promoted economic growth among aid receiving nations and also enabled the US to finance its export surplus. Circumstances changed totally by late 1970s. The US emerged as the major net importing nation, and not a net exporting one with persistently enlarging trade deficit. At the same time, US capital and technology was required to be exported to countries with lower production costs in the emerging market economies. The 3W Model sought to achieve the same.

Globalization enabled the US to incur higher trade deficits year after year and keep the rate of inflation low. The US trade deficit increased from $111 billion in 1990 to the record $836 billion in 2006. Japan and West Germany were the leading trade partners of the US during the 1970s and 1980s. In the 1990s, China and other Asian countries provided a much broader canvass for US trade. Tremendous growth in the output capacities in China and Asia did not pose any supply constraint for meeting commodity consumption growth in the US. Globalization had made several industries in the US less competitive due to high wage costs. Technology growth, and its spread and trend were also gradually transforming the character of the US economy from the commodity economy to a more mature, and sophisticated service economy. This trend was not unanticipated but followed the prognosis made by several economists, management experts, thinkers, intellectuals and even far-sighted politicians. The enlargement of the service economy is the last stage in the development of a mature, technology driven, capital rich economy. In this process, the enlarging flow of commodity exports from China and Asia enabled the US to incur a higher trade deficit, augment its domestic supplies of commodities, and keep the rate of inflation at historically low levels for an extended period of more than a decade.

What is remarkable is that the sustained low rate of inflation was achieved during a period of higher growth in money supply. The potential of the process of globalization was best exploited by the US for the global economy through the cheap money policy charted by the Fed with the active support of the US Treasury. The glorious 1990s would not have been a reality without the carefully crafted, and highly flexible and proactive low interest policy pursued by the Fed. This policy faced the biggest opposition from the IMF, which was suffering from the inflation paranoia.

> The IMF simply had no understanding of the changes that were then occurring over the preceding decade in the US economy that allowed it to enjoy faster growth, lower unemployment, and low inflation all at the same time. Had the IMF's advice been followed, the United States would not have experienced the boom in the American economy over the 1990s – a boom that brought unprecedented prosperity and enabled the country to turn around a massive fiscal deficit into a sizeable surplus.[57]

Greenspan's astute and adroit handling of cheap money policy played the trick. Rates of interest declined to historically low levels. The stock market remained buoyant. Higher consumption and investment were supported by cheaper imports from China and Asia, and an increasing trade deficit. In the wake of a phase of low interest rates globally, relatively higher real interest rate differentials and a lower risk element in the US treasuries, and rising value of equities in the US stock market attracted record debt and equity portfolio investments into the US. The large and increasing trade and current account deficits did not pose any threatening problem due to the strength of the US dollar in the currency markets supported by commensurate inflows of foreign portfolio investments into the US. The liquidity that went out of the US economy and financial system by way of the trade deficit raised the foreign exchange reserves of China and Asia, but came back to the US through the investments in US Treasuries, bonds and equities.

Under globalization, the US financial system and the global capital and forex markets have shown tremendous responsiveness and resiliency in reacting to the challenges, and sometimes to threats, emerging from time to time. The US financial system has been successfully and efficiently recycling the current account surpluses and forex reserves of China, India and other Asian countries and thereby maintaining the growth momentum of the US and global economy without eroding the strength of the dollar and its purchasing power.

5 Changing face of currency markets

Superliquid forex markets

Blessed with liberal economic policies under globalization and supercomputer technology, financial assets have become globally 'superliquid'. While economic policies have improved access to different financial products across the countries and currencies, such technology has accelerated the transactions velocity of money and financial assets. Supported by the technology, the dynamics of the market have undergone a sea change. The markets have become timeless, spaceless and super-efficient. All this has naturally made the international markets more volatile since they have become more responsive, sensitive and susceptible. It is more true of financial markets than commodity markets. This is because, in the post 1974 oil crisis era, the growth of money and financial assets has been much faster than the real output growth. The market capitalization of financial assets as a percentage of both GNP as well as money supply has increased substantially in developed and also emerging markets. The global financial market has been working like a large reservoir of interconnected pools. Any change in the level and pressure in any one pool affects the others. The degree of influence of a change in pressure in any one pool would depend upon the size of the pool in relation to the total reservoir and the degree of change in pressure in the pool.

The decline in transactions cost in the financial markets has also led to increasing the frequency of switches from one instrument to another. The market turnovers have scaled upward for the same stock of financial assets. By the conventional definition of rising turnover-stock ratio, the markets have become superliquid. This phenomenon of superliquidity of markets raises an issue of the market crash caused by panic, herd mentality and disequilibrating movements. Information and high technology have made the global markets and also the national markets having a significant international presence much more volatile and destabilising. When the bad news breaks out, the sudden surge of sell transactions, which the technology causes globally, brings about a sharper fall in the market, which goes on compounding and finally culminates in a crash. This was evident in the 1987 stock market crash in the US triggered by the programmed trading. High-tech, superliquid, hypersensitive global markets, therefore, need more effective circuit breaking mechanisms, as suggested after the 1987 crash to restore more sanity in the market mechanism following the events causing panics. The Mexican, Asian and Russian crises sent a panic wave among the institutional investors. The emerging markets investments were viewed with suspicion and apprehension. The lesson from the crises to the Central Bankers was that the exchange rate of a fundamentally weak currency cannot be sustained for long, and gradual, more frequent but smaller adjustments of exchange rates in currency management are superior to building the disequilibrium for a sharper rate adjustment over a longer period.

Latin American syndrome and Asian drama

The experience of massive devaluation of the Mexican Peso by 50 percent in 1994 amply demonstrated the lessons in currency behaviour in the world of floating exchange rates and the precautions needed to guard against a sudden jerk in exchange rates. While the trade transactions were still a significant factor, the more dominant stressor has been the portfolio investment flows, in addition to the short-term investment flows. Following the Peso devaluation, the perception of international investors for emerging markets took a complete U turn for some time. The avalanche even damaged major global equity markets due to the sudden loss in the market valuation of the portfolios of large pension funds, mutual funds and other institutional investors. The magnitude of valuation loss and realised financial deficit suffered by these institutional investors also affected the confidence of the international investment community.

Both the experience of the Mexican Peso and Asian currencies indicates how difficult it is for a Central Bank to withstand the market pressure on its currency value. The float of offshore liquid funds available for arbitrage and short-term gains is too large for control, even collectively, by the major world central banks. The exchange reserves of these central banks remain abysmally in short of the global market liquidity, making them powerless against strong market forces. The global currency market reigns supreme, and directs and dictates to the central banks the action they ought to take. In fact, the occasional bursts of currency crisis serve as a constant reminder to the central banking authorities to initiate corrective action to align the discordant monetary policies, balance of payments trends, and currency values.

The currency upheaval in the Asian continent was also an unexpected jolt to the speeding Tigers. In recent times, the Asian continent has, only infrequently, been the battleground for testing the currency equilibria in the forex markets. For nearly a decade, the Asian Tigers rode the wave of uninterrupted economic prosperity on the back of currency tranquility. While the mightier currencies, such as the yen, D-mark, sterling and now the euro, could swing against the US dollar in a range of up to 30 to 40 percent in a year, the smaller currencies need to take the lesson of remaining rightly realigned against the new exchange equation. The problem is that when the matter of exchange rate change comes up for a decision, it is very difficult to overcome the politically irresistible obsession for stability in the currency. It is this obsession for stability that always blinds the economic logic and brings the currency finally in the zone of instability.

Currency stability in these economies, which are getting more and more open and are tending towards full convertibility, can only be achieved through exchange rate equilibrium. A pegged exchange rate accompanied by protracted exchange disequilibria is an open invitation for the speculative attack and currency turbulence finally leading to heavy currency depreciation. Both the Mexican and Asian crises amply demonstrated this. Although the gravity of both the crises, their magnitude and contagion effect were different, the laws of economic and currency gravity remain the same irrespective of the region and country.

Global fund management – influence of portfolio management

International investment is becoming increasingly complex due to the diversity of instruments across the countries, sectors, and time zones. The global fund manager's task is fraught with a variety of risks, which change their composition, complexion and magnitude from minute to minute. In this scenario, one would not expect the task of the global fund manager to be any easier than that of an acrobat. Increasing integration of the global economy and the opening up of several closed economies has no doubt offered opportunities for growth and greater risk diversification, but at the same time it has also added more variables into the fund manager's investment equations. The global investment game has become more astute than it has ever been.

Further, in liberalized and open global financial markets, currencies have not remained only a vehicle of trade and investment transactions. Currencies have become an investment asset. Individuals, banks and corporations have been keeping a portion of their assets in a stronger currency. This has added a new dimension to the traditional demand – supply equation for foreign exchange. Investors are moving in and out of currencies not for short-term speculative gains but as a part of the strategy of asset or wealth management centering on the principle of diversification.

The currency ball game has also changed significantly over the last decade. Even under the floating exchange rates in the 1980s, the central banks could orchestrate exchange rates on gentlemen's agreements. The market forces were not as dominating in influence if misalignment in exchange rates was within reasonable limits. Often, the exchange rate remained a duopolistic game between the major central banks. This scenario has undergone a complete change. Not only has the global economy become closely integrated today, but it has also become more vulnerable and, therefore, more responsive to external shocks and changes. The international capital flows of portfolio investment as well as arbitrage, hedge and speculative debt, equity and foreign exchange exposures have increased very substantially over the decade. Because of a large and increasing asset base of international portfolio in the emerging markets built over the last decade, ever since the emerging market economies opened up and became hosts to the portfolio investment from the developed markets, the need to cover these exposures in the forex market has also become more paramount than ever before. Further, as the base of portfolio investment gets larger and larger, the consequent volume of transaction in the forex markets also increases in magnitude. Although many investors do not always cover their exposures in good times when the currency is stable, in times of shakiness there would be an avalanche of cover transactions in the forex market, enough to take toll of a currency. This happened in Mexico in 1994 and was repeated in Asia in 1997.

Mismatch of spot and forward markets

The emerging markets were new in this game. The new game also meant understanding its new rules, new equations, and preparing for new adversities. The forex game has to be win – win game, since in addition to the usual economic logic of international trade and investment, it is now also increasingly governed by the science of modern portfolio investment theory. As the base of portfolio investment gets larger and larger in the emerging markets, the influence of the global fund managers in the forex markets becomes increasingly higher. Since the emerging markets are the net recipients of foreign portfolio investment and commercial borrowings, and their overhang is very large, there is greater demand for foreign exchange than supply in the forward market, which eventually also affects the spot exchange rate. Hence, attacks on currency surface not only from traditional short-term capital flows but also because of the imperatives of covering the impending loss on the overhang of existing asset exposure of international investors. Moreover, these forward covers influence the forex markets more, depending on the magnitude of foreign portfolio investment and commercial borrowings. These demand – supply mismatches in the forward market have been a feature of not only emerging economies but also the currencies of large economies in times of weakness. The signs of imbalance and weakness further aggravate the magnitude of mismatches. It finally culminates into an uncontrollable spiral of disequilibrium and lower level equilibrium until it settles down to a more stable level.

In addition to these covers, there are the hedge fund operators who are in search of profitable opportunities to invest for short gains. And a weak currency waiting but reluctant to be depreciated is the most likely target for the hedge fund manager's activity. Billions of dollars of the commercial banks, currency speculators and hedge fund operators constantly circle the globe, at the speed of light, entering currencies edging up and exiting currencies sliding down. In this multi-trillion dollar global forex market, no central bank is invincible. If Soros can bring the old Lady of Threadneedle Street to her knees, the central banks of the emerging markets face very little prospect of winning the battle against the Soroses and, more importantly, the market forces they represent. The modern central bankers now have to learn to deal with not the mightier counterparts among their species, nor the conventional Gnomes of Zurich, but the Hedge

Fund operators, who are the players representing the new and more powerful forces in the global investment and forex game.

Dynamics of a forex crisis

There are peculiar dynamics in the foreign exchange market, known as its disequilibrating nature. In a typically foreign exchange deficit country, the excess demand for foreign exchange is always met by the central bank by supplying US dollars or other currencies at an exchange rate which it is supporting. In these countries, the foreign liabilities also exceed the foreign assets. So long as the exchange rate is stabilized by the central banks by a reasonable loss of forex reserves, the normal transactions in the forex market continue. However, the moment there are signs of weakness in the currency and the seed of speculation of depreciation in the currency takes root in the market, not only do the normal transactions get disturbed, but the abnormal transactions also begin to be more overpowering. This phenomenon, caused by the change in the sentiment, brings disequilibrating movements in the market and finally settling the exchange rate at the new equilibrium. When the expectation of currency deprecation gets closer to reality, the exporters defer the sale of foreign currency and importers start covering even future purchases. This severely multiplies the usual deficit in the spot forex market, and it brings downward pressure on the exchange rate. Added to these normal transactions in the spot and forward markets, is the avalanche of forward cover transactions on the demand side arising out of foreign liabilities (the overhang of portfolio investments and commercial borrowing) with very little cover on the supply side, that draws the foreign exchange rate further down until it settles at the lower equilibrium level. While the activity on the spot forex market sucks the liquidity in the economy and raises the call money and other short-term rates, the forward market behavior increases the forward market premium. Nevertheless, the interaction between the money market and forex market also causes short-term capital inflow if the interest differential between the local and foreign money markets is greater than the premium on the forward rate in the forex market. This is a welcome respite for a weakening currency. In fact, in this crisis situation, the central banks do not usually intervene to lower short-term interest rates by open market operations in order to promote short-term capital inflows that tend to offer some relief in stalling the sliding exchange rates. Unusually high inter-bank rates are, therefore, a common phenomenon in the currency attacks and the central banks tend to encourage it as a countervailing force or measure. This is, however, not a long-lasting solution because the capital flight motivated by falling currency is more overpowering than the short-term capital inflow for interest gain, which is risky if the forward cover is unavailable at a premium lower than the interest differential. When the build up of mismatch between demand and supply emanating both from spot and forward transactions in the forex market goes on progressively cumulating despite intervention, the central banks do not succeed in this game and the currency achieves new equilibrium under the market pressure.

In the forex markets, the mightier currencies must wisely follow or else are forced to follow the market laws and pressure for ensuring smoother adjustment to eliminate painful corrections later. After learning from their experience in the 1980s, the central banks of the developed nations have been wiser in following the market signals and allowing their currencies to slide up or down to the new equilibria. This has also given them greater freedom to run their monetary policies to promote economic growth or curtail inflation, and allow exchange rate adjustments to take care of external payments pressures. Over the last few years, we have seen some of very large adjustments in currencies like the yen, D-mark, sterling and also the euro against the US dollar. The central banks of these nations have very wisely avoided the temporary palliative of artificial currency support. In the long run, this has avoided the panic currency attacks that are more painful than the smoother and gradual market adjustment route. The German unification brought pressure on the German economy and necessitated the D-mark–US dollar rate to slide down from its earlier strength. The Bundesbank followed the market rules and allowed the D-mark rate to depreciate from 1.38 to 1.84 in 1995. When the Japanese surplus became a problem for the US as well as Japan in 1995, the yen appreciated and the yen – US dollar rate fell from 140 to a record low of 82.5. As that seemed too strong a rate for Japan, depreciating its huge holdings of the US Treasury Bills in terms of yen, the rate again moved to 127. Sterling had to bend from $2.0 to $1.43 in 1993 under the famous Soros effect. However, it improved later with a remarkably economic buoyancy and swelling current account surplus, to a high of $1.71 before declining to $1.64 again later. The euro recently moved from $0.89 to $1.29 in two years.

The exchange rate seesaw is now common due to myriad factors influencing international payments flows. The emerging markets need to recognize this. In fact, the frequent changes in currency parities of the major currencies is one important reason why the emerging markets pegging their currency to one currency, like the US dollar, need to adjust their pegs more frequently, or allow them to crawl gradually. When the circumstances demand, the mechanism of crawling peg or small and frequent changes seems to be the most practical solution to the currency problems of the emerging markets.

Empirical analysis of forex market behavior

Analyses of returns on equity over a long period do not show any serial correlation. Returns in one period do not influence the returns in next period. This indicates that one cannot forecast returns from past data. Footprints in markets in the long periods are not useful in predictive models. The stock market in longer periods follows the random walk hypothesis. The experience of forex markets is, however, is different and may be unique. Whatever is true for a longer period may not be so for a shorter duration. For shorter periods, market behaviour tends to be trend reinforcing. Exchange rates do not follow the random walk hypothesis, especially at high frequency. The most significant auto correlations appear at the 30 minute interval. Low frequency data have much lower significance levels.[58] Further, the auto correlations were found to be both negative and significant for the D-mark and yen against the US dollar.

This is due to two reasons. First, interventions by the central banks; and second, contrarian positions taken by the some operators. Currencies have no longer remained as a vehicle of international transaction for trade and investment but have emerged as a separate class of asset that can value add in investments. Hence, there is more interest in currency positions as an asset class today, apart from conventional demand/supply sources arising from trading and the usual lending and investment transactions.

The currency markets are the best platform to test the behavior of markets. They are now global, very liquid and appear homogeneous. Stock and bond markets are more heterogeneous since each stock and each bond has its own peculiar characteristic, history, background, dynamics, volatility and hence, different risk-return profile.

Yet all markets, including the forex markets, are also heterogeneous in a sense that its participants are non-homogeneous. They can be grouped by their investment objectives, time horizon and constraints. This heterogeneous market hypothesis explains why forex markets do not follow the market efficiency test. Different market participants react differently to new information, while their reaction time differs. Money managers have been exploiting these arbitrage opportunities and inefficiency in short time scales through high frequency trading. This strategy has been supported by more than a decade of intensive empirical and mathematical research on the world's largest database of high frequency and forex data. Although a number of trading rules have been developed for high frequency trading, they have not displayed significant profits after transaction costs. Further, changes in currency markets in recent years have been more closely integrating different foreign markets. Different time horizons of different investors and a change from a trend-following market to a contrarian market have also reduced the arbitrage. As time passes, there is a technological decay of these trading rules, which become more prevalent and later obsolete.

The dynamics of the market have undergone a remarkable change over the last decade. Advances in computer and telecoms technology have halted the separation of markets. Technology has been harnessed to make markets more accessible, faster in response, wider in participation and turnover and, above all, relatively less costly than earlier, despite the huge spending on technical infrastructure. All these have gone towards improving the efficiency of the market structure and function. Forex markets in particular, operate a round the clock, around the globe, at the speed of light. The market efficiency is also visible in lower spreads, better price discovery, lower impact cost, lower volatility, higher liquidity, larger growth in turnover, a wider and larger base and cheaper transaction cost. A number of statistical and empirical tests have proved these benefits across different markets and different countries.

Research in market behavior has achieved more sophistication due to technology enabling more elaborate data about markets. Open, high, low, and close data has been replaced by high-frequency tick-by-tick data about rates and volumes,` enabling more micro-probing of market behavior. Yet, despite considerable statistical research, empirical analysis and studies, the outcome is inconclusive and the fact remains that markets by their very nature are unpredictable and cannot be captured in predictable laws of behavior. And forex markets are no exception.

6 Lessons from the Asian crisis

Following the policy of modernization in China, one of the biggest experiments in liberalization and reforms in its pure form of the 3W Model began in the East Asian countries in the late 1980s and accelerated during the 1990s. Freer trade and capital accounts attracted large foreign direct investment to raise the overall rate of capital formation. The share of net private capital flows in GDP rose from 0.6 percent in 1985–88 to 6.6 percent in 1993–96. East Asia became important in the global context as a major destination for private capital flows, and its share in total capital flows to developing nations increased from 12 percent in the early 1980s to 43 percent during the 1990s.[59] A Large investment in export oriented industries taking advantage of low wage costs boosted exports. Economic growth rates nearly doubled from the pre-globalization era. The Asian miracle became the role model of globalization for the other emerging markets to follow. This image was shattered by the sudden eruption of a currency crisis in Thailand in the summer of 1997, which quickly spread to other East Asian economies. The Asian miracle suddenly became the nightmare, evoking global attention and international effort to curtail its further contagion and bring the region back to normalcy.

Following the Latin American debt crisis of 1980s, the Asian crisis was the second largest financial crisis affecting the global economy. It became pervasive among the Asian countries due to the contagion effect. A degree of homogeneity of these countries in the structure of their economies as well as their growth model, philosophy and policies, caused this contagion effect. The Macroeconomic data of the Asian countries reveal striking similarities in their growth financing policies. The Asian economies achieved substantially high economic growth, ranging between 6 percent and 9 percent during 1991–96. Maintaining high investment rates ranging between 35 percent and 42 percent, while domestic savings rates ranged between 29 percent and 36 percent, generated these high economic growth rates. The savings gap, ranging between 5 percent and 7 percent of GDP, which was also the current account deficit, was needed to be financed through external resources. The financial liberalization, underway since the early 1980s, had made the foreign investment climate conducive to financing the huge current account gap. By any historical standard, the current account deficit of 5 percent to 7 percent was very large and required sustained foreign investment flows.

Like India, the Asian economies also had restrictions on foreign investments in the corporate sector. In the 1970s, the Malaysian government actively pursued a policy to reduce foreign investment in Malaysian stocks. However, following the new model of development under globalization, it brought about a sharp reduction in the foreign holding in Malaysian companies from 55 percent in 1970s to 25 percent by 1990. In 1974, India also pursued the policy of lowering foreign ownership in corporate equity below 49 percent. Offering foreign equity to the Indian investors through public issues was called FERA (Foreign Exchange Regulation Act) dilution in India. The CCI's (Controller of Capital Issues) conservative formula for pricing these issues and broad-based share allotment norms transformed the Indian equity market, spread the equity culture by substantially enlarging the equity investing population and provided a wider market base following the market listing of many foreign companies.

The 1980s marked the reversal of the old policy for encouraging foreign investment to push investment rates and economic growth into a higher orbit. Thailand relaxed restrictions on foreign equity holding, repatriation of profits, dividends, and conversion of foreign exchange gradually during 1980s. Foreign ownership limits were removed, except in areas of domestic consumption, finance and telecommunications. Malaysia removed the 30 percent cap on foreign ownership in 1991. Indonesia raised the foreign ownership limit to 49 percent in all companies except finance and banking companies. In South Korea, the foreign equity limit, which was as low as 10 percent of equity, was gradually raised, step-by-step, through the 1990s, to 55 percent, with a 3 percent increase each time.

In addition to the liberalization of equity flows through direct investment and portfolio investment, it was imperative to attract more foreign resources through the debt route. The corporate sector and commercial banks were given a liberal mandate for external borrowings. Higher interest rates in the Asian economies offered attractive opportunities for lending by international banks and investment institutions. The interest differential between foreign and domestic interest rates among the Asian nations was as large as 4 percent to 5 percent.

Heavy current account deficit and its financing

The current account deficit, although high by historical global standards, was managed by external resources through a cocktail of direct equity, portfolio investment, long-term bonds, and short-term debt. Asian countries faced the average current account deficit during 1993–96 of 4.6 percent compared with 1.1 percent in 1985–88, and it was nearly twice the figure of the current account deficit of the Latin American countries.

What was more critical was the financing of the current account deficit and the composition of the capital inflows. Here again, the magnitude of both long-term and short-term capital flows in terms of their share in GDP was bigger in the Asian countries than in the Latin American region. The share of portfolio equity and bond investment and short-term debt was unusually high. This was risky, looking at the volatile nature of these flows.

While the net long-term capital flows were 6.9 percent of GDP during 1993–96, portfolio equity was 2 percent, portfolio bonds 1.4 percent and short term debt 2.3 percent. Along with the shift towards more volatile foreign capital, the direction of investment also underwent a change from foreign trade oriented and productive sectors, which contributed to balance of payments and GDP, to the less productive sectors with less or no contribution to BoP, and more risky and speculative sectors.

Both the banking and the corporate sectors relied heavily on short-term external borrowings. Financial liberalization through decreasing reserve requirements for banks had brought an enormous increase in their lendable resources, which needed to be deployed. A surge in monetary aggregates and liquidity also brought about high and rapid growth in the non-banking financial sector and its lending.

Heavier exposure of banks to real estate sector

A factor that contributed to the fragility of the banking system and made it more vulnerable to crisis was the heavy exposure of banks to risky sectors. Attracted by a large interest rate differential, foreign banks lent extensively to risky sectors, such as equity securities and real estate.

> Banks in Mexico, Asia, and Russia contributed variously but massively to the emergence of lending, equity, and real estate bubbles by disregarding elementary rules of prudent management. In all cases they took on excessive exchange rate risks; in many cases they undertook reckless maturity transformation; and generally, they disregarded credit risks.[60]

Lending to the property sector accounted for 20 percent of the total loans of the banking sector in Indonesia during 1991–95. This share was 18 percent for Thailand, 17.5 percent for Malaysia, 11 percent for Philippines and 5 percent for South Korea. Korean banks, which did not have a large exposure to real estate, had a larger exposure to bonds and securities (16 percent) compared with their Asian counterparts. The construction boom generated by heavy bank lending had brought such an increase in supplies of both residential and commercial space in the region that, by 1996–97, the supply of space outstripped the demand by a large margin, leading to a collapse in property prices.

The other side of bank lending is the borrowing of the corporate sector. While the banks overlent to certain sectors, which created the boom–bust situation, the corporate sector also generally borrowed very heavily during the high growth period and also raised their short-term borrowings in local as well as foreign currencies beyond the healthy levels. High debt-equity and interest coverage ratios caused a liquidity crisis in many corporates when the interest rates went up after the forex crisis.

Strong fiscal balance – a plus that couldn't help

One of the very strong features of Asian countries was the fiscal deficit, which was moderate in the early 1980s and turned into a surplus by late 1980s. In 1994, Thailand had a budgetary surplus of 1.8 percent of GDP, South Korea 0.6 percent, Malaysia 2.4 percent, Philippines 1.1 percent, and Indonesia 0.8 percent.

> The overall public sector budgets in the region which had exhibited deficits not out of line with those of other middle-income developing countries at that time, moved steadily into surplus after mid-1980s. By the late 1980s, several countries in the region had achieved sizeable fiscal surpluses. As the economies of these countries grew and the tight fiscal stance restrained (and at times reversed) the growth of public sector debt, public sector debt/GDP ratios fell throughout the region. As a result, by the mid 1990s several countries in East Asia had achieved ratios of debt/GDP substantially below those of many industrialized countries. This tight fiscal stance permitted the depreciation of the real exchange rate, and helped to prevent the emergence of exchange rate misalignment.[61]

Nevertheless, as current account deficits continued to worsen by the mid-1990s, debt servicing ratios became threateningly dangerous. With volatile capital also dominating the capital account, balance of payments showed signs of cracks that could trigger an avalanche of panic-ridden capital outflows capable of throwing the currency rates into a deep depreciation zone.

Pegged exchange rates – insurance against devaluation?

On the macroeconomic policy front, a factor, which initially contributed to the heavy inflow of external capital, but later triggered the forex crisis in the Asian region, was the policy of pegging currencies to the US dollar for a longer period than sustainable. The policy of central bank intervening in the forex market by supplying foreign exchange to avoid currency depreciation requires adequate forex reserves and a substantial inflow of foreign capital. The latter is possible only when the return on capital is adequately higher than the expected rate of currency depreciation. Hence, it is a Catch 22 situation. Inflows are required to boost forex reserves to support currency, and inflows will be substantial only if currency is stable. The government/central bank having a gentlemen's agreement that the currency will not be devalued in the medium term until the foreign capital earns positive and marginally higher returns can only solve the stalemate. It acts as an insurance or guarantee against the risk of devaluation. The currency is then pegged and monitored and regulated to move within a narrow band.

Guides of peg success

The success of the policy of pegged exchange rates is dependent on a number of factors:

i Inflation differential

The degree by which domestic inflation is higher than that of its trading partners determines the inherent external strength or weakness of the currency. Higher inflation would make currency inherently weaker, although it is held steady by forex intervention. Higher domestic inflation with fixed exchange rates weakens the balance of payments and, if continued for a longer period, would be a perfect recipe for forex crisis. With prices remaining relatively stable compared with trading partners, a fixed rate peg becomes sustainable.

ii Behavior of the US dollar – the peg currency

When a currency is pegged to the US dollar, its currency behavior is in sync with the US dollar's behavior with other currencies. When the US dollar is depreciating, the pegged currency also automatically depreciates with other currencies. This automatic depreciation provides the exchange rate flexibility or depreciation required to offset domestic inflation. This phase is benign to the pegged currency. The malign phase begins when the US dollar starts appreciating. In the wake of domestic inflation, which inherently weakens the currency, dollar appreciation makes the currency actually appreciate in the forex markets, working against all the fundamental laws of exchange rate and balance of payments behavior. In a pegged exchange rate system, this phase sets a time bomb for a forex crisis. This phase is, therefore, dangerous, and the fixed peg system has to switch over to managed flexibility through either a crawling peg or small and frequent changes. The Asian crisis was actually simmering in 1996, when the US dollar started strengthening and causing appreciation in the real effective exchange rates of Asian currencies, when they needed a small depreciation.

> In spite of Mexico's negative experience with rigid exchange rate regime, all five of the East Asian nations had a rigid – de facto, pegged, or quasi pegged – exchange rate system with respect to US dollar. Whereas this system worked relatively well while the US dollar was relatively weak in the international currency markets, things turned to the worse when, starting mid 1996, the dollar began to strengthen relative to Japanese yen. Naturally, as the dollar appreciated relative to yen, so did those currencies pegged to it. This strengthening of the East Asian currencies squeezed competitiveness of exports and fed back into larger current account imbalances.[62]

After the Mexican crisis, there was great concern among economists about the sustainability of the real exchange rates under the fixed peg rated system, incompatible with the balance of payments position. Economists like Dornbusch argued, 'Crawl now, or crash later'.

iii Broad basing the BoP

During the period of high economic growth financed through foreign capital and fixed pegged exchange rates, it is imperative to broad base the balance of payments by lowering or eliminating the current account deficit. If the BoP is transformed in this fashion, the pressure on currency can be avoided by pre-cluding volatile flows triggering a crisis. However, the continuation of a current account deficit and persistent reliance on foreign capital to balance it, is unsus-tainable for a longer period. Broad basing the BoP involves reducing the trade deficit through higher exports growth and curtailing imports growth through expansion of output of import substitutes. Raising the invisible receipts through service exports and inward remittances from non-residents also helps in redu-cing the current account deficit to a manageable level. This makes the BoP less vulnerable to the sharp changes in capital flows, be they short-term capital flows or portfolio equity investments, either of which can be switched quickly. The increase in the share of current account transactions in overall BoP transac-tions also makes the exchange rate more resistant to volatile capital flows in the capital account. Such a change also makes currencies less vulnerable to spec-ulative attacks. Since these attacks can be taken care of by the normal or autonomous current account transactions, the drawdown of forex reserves by the central bank through exchange rate intervention is also not necessary to ward off undesirable speculation and the wide variation in exchange rate not supported by the fundamentals.

Financial liberalization and capital account convertibility initially increase the size of the capital account in the overall BoP transactions compared with the pre-liberalization era. However, in the next phase, the current account also has to grow. One of the objectives of liberalization is to render long-term sustain-ability to the BoP. The foreign capital flows have to be directed not only into productive sectors but also towards improving exports, substituting imports and raising invisible receipts. These results can take two to three years following the initial capital inflows. A reasonable broad basing of BoP arising from these changes can render the pegged rates system more sustainable.

iv Adjustment of pegs

Depending on the foregoing three factors, namely, inflation differentials, the movement of the peg currency–US dollar and magnitude of broad basing of BoP, there has to be adequate maneuverability for adjustments in pegs. The best insurance against a sudden currency attack or recurrent attacks is the flexible adjustment of the peg periodically.

v Controls on capital movements

The system of pegged exchange cannot work on totally free capital movements. Exchange rates are barometers against which capital flows take place and as the capital flows influence exchange rates, excessive movements are themselves checked by the changes in exchange rates. Free flows of capital, therefore, requires floating exchange rates, which takes the heat off the short term, volatile and excessive capital movements by bringing an appropriate change in exchange rate. Under the system of pegged exchange rates, the central bank has to be armed with the tools of discretionary capital controls in order to check speculative and destabilizing movements in capital. In order to discourage speculative, short term in-and-out capital flows, James Tobin had proposed a uniform transaction tax on all spot conversions of one currency into another. The idea received renewed attention only after the Mexican crisis of 1994. Tobin's argument was as follows:

> The essential property of the transactions tax – the beauty part – that this simple one-parameter tax would automatically penalize short-horizon round trips, which negligibly affecting the incentives for commodity trade and long-term capital investments. A 0.2 percent tax on a round trip costs 48 percent a year if transacted every business day, 10 percent if every week, 2.4 percent if every month. But this is a trivial charge on commodity trade or long-term foreign investments.
>
> In support of Tobin's position, Jeffrey Frankel (1996) noted that if – as survey data suggest – expectations of exchange rate movements over short horizons are extrapolative, but mean-reverting over longer horizons, then such a tax would help to reduce the volatility of exchange rates by driving short term extrapolative speculators from the market – reducing the influence of Chartists in favor of Fundamentalists.[63]

However, even transaction tax would be incapable of curbing capital flows arising either from the euphoria of high interest differential or fear of large currency devaluation. It would also interfere with the normal spread between bid and offer quotes in the forex market and increase the spread due to tax. Higher spread is also likely to affect the liquidity in the forex market. This leaves the choice of no other alternative but capital controls to deter destabilizing movements in capital flows that bring adverse pressure on exchange rates.

Reality of the Asian peg

In the case of Asian economies, all the above five prerequisites were not met. First, the inflation differentials between the Asian economies and their trading partners worked against the former, causing appreciation in their real exchange rates. Second, since the Asian currencies were pegged to the US dollar, the behavior of their currencies against other major currencies was tied to the movement of the US dollar. So long as the US dollar remained stable or relatively weak, it enabled Asian currencies to remain competitive. As the US dollar started strengthening in 1996, the real effective exchange rates of all Asian currencies started appreciating and required immediate redressal by depreciation in their currencies vis-à-vis the US dollar to avoid exchange rate disequilibrium from worsening. Third, despite high economic growth and high capital inflows, these economies could not broad base the BoP, and current account deficits and debt servicing ratios continued to be high.

> The roots of increased vulnerability lie in East Asia's success in attracting private capital flows, based on strong macro-economic fundamentals and structural reforms in 1980s. In the initial phase, East Asia was quite successful in managing inflows to avoid increased vulnerability. In more recent periods, there was a shift in the pace and pattern of investment, and in the structure of financing, that led to a surprisingly rapid build-up of vulnerability. Investment rates rose from already high levels, and were directed towards non-traded end potentially risky sectors, with evidence of falling productivity. Although domestic savings continued to provide the bulk of financing, current account deficits widened, reaching high levels in some countries. More pertinently, there was a very heavy reliance on debt finance from domestic and foreign intermediaries, and in the most vulnerable cases, much of it was short term and unhedged.[64]

Fourth, as the exchange rate disequilibrium was building up as a result of pegged rates, with a continuing current account deficit and real effective exchange rate appreciation following the strengthening of US dollar, there was an imperative need to correct disequilibrium quickly by small adjustments (depreciation) in exchange rates vis-à-vis the US dollar. This would have avoided the disequilibrium from building up and finally culminating into a forex crisis. Lastly, because of full convertibility of the currencies, there were very few controls on capital movements.

> Virtually all emerging market countries which joined the globalized world got their priorities wrong. They freed their capital account transactions and lifted a large part of administrative controls on domestic financial intermediation without establishing a solid institutional framework that would enable them to absorb large scale capital imports in an orderly way. The disproportion in numbers did the rest. During the single year of 1995 Thailand took up $36.3 billion in new banking funds. Its GDP stood at about $160 billion.[65]

The capital controls would have helped in containing the crisis and also stopped its contagion effect. After the crisis, all the Asian countries promptly reimposed controls on capital movements, adopting the Indian wisdom. 'The need for prudent capital controls in the emerging markets is now widely recognized even in the IMF and also the Wall Street–Treasury Complex, which earlier advocated gung-ho international financial capitalism'.[66]

The Asian crisis put a damper on the policy of gung ho liberalization and capital account convertibility without adequate domestic institutional and policy preparation. It also strengthened the case of the India model of liberalization and reform, which was going ahead step by step but attracted criticism for being too slow in pace before the Asian crisis. With wider experience, the Indian model of gradualism in reforms finally received the stamp of approval even from the 3W circles.

7   Reform of the IMF

The IMF, which governed the global monetary system under the Bretton Woods agreement, contributed to the global economic prosperity for two and half decades until it developed cracks in 1971 when the US dollar was required to be made non-convertible into gold. Demonetization of gold from the international monetary system also meant the abolition of the fixed exchange rates system. The switchover from the fixed and adjustable exchange rates system to floating exchange rates was, however, smooth and without much disruption in the global trade and financial world. The last three decades of floating exchange rates have witnessed a greater amount of flexibility and more frequent changes in exchange rates, more in line with the market signals than with the discretionary adjustments by the IMF and the member central banks. Naturally, the central banks have enjoyed greater freedom in pursuing their monetary policies, targeted more towards economic growth and inflation control, while the balance of payments disequilibria have been taken care of by the floating exchange rates mechanism. Yet, when the central banks desired to closely monitor the exchange rates of their currencies, the monetary policy was also required to be moderately bent towards this end.

Although the shift towards the floating exchange rates, which was a systemic change in the early 1970s, marked some dilution of the IMF's authority, nobody questioned the role of the IMF. The Asian Crisis and the IMF's effort in tackling the same brought this issue in to sharper focus. Both the academic economists as well as politicians in the US were critical of the IMF's policies, and some have questioned its very existence and role in an increasingly market-oriented functioning of the global economy and monetary system. Traditionally, the most vociferous critics of the IMF loans and conditionality have been the parties of the left, who argued that the conditionality meant less welfare for the Poor. After the collapse of the Iron Curtain, the break up of the USSR and marketization in China, the Left critics of the IMF have been dwarfed by the new free market economists and the Republicans among the US politicians. This curious turn in the IMF's critics is a clear reflection of the ideological change in the global economy over the last two decades.

The Asian Crisis in 1997 was the repeat of the first Latin American debt crisis of the 1980s and the Mexican crisis in 1994. There are striking similarities as well as dissimilarities between the two. Compared with the hyperinflationary situation, larger government budgetary deficits and larger external public debt, the Asian countries presented a sharp contrast. Asian countries enjoyed moderate inflation, government budgetary surpluses or very small deficits, and smaller external public debt. The domestic savings rate enjoyed by the Asian Tigers was also higher than that of their Latin American counterparts. While the Asian Tigers were characterized by the better fiscal prudence, both groups shared the similar external debt profile, which could not be serviced easily. Compared with the misutilization of private debt in the Asian countries, it was public debt that became unproductive in Latin America. The most important common factor, which triggered the crises in both groups, is the prolonged fixed pegging of the exchange rate to the US dollar and the inability to make adequate and timely adjustments in the peg. The accompanying factor is the failure of surveillance of the external debt position and its servicing capacity, the size and composition of forex reserves and pressure on the exchange rates, both nationally by the governments and central banks as well as internationally by multinational banks, rating agencies and multinational agencies like the IMF and the World Bank.

After the Latin American debt crisis of the 1980s, which followed the explosive growth in the euro-currency market, the international agencies realized the need to monitor the data on external debt, debt profiles and servicing capacities of borrowing nations by setting up the Washington-based Institute of International Finance. Both this agency as well as the international rating agencies rating credit worthiness of sovereign borrowers seems to have failed in giving warning signals and ringing the alarm bells in 1994 about the Mexican crisis and for the Asian trouble in 1997. Not only did the market mechanism fail to ring the alarm bells before the crisis, but also to monitor the global monetary system. The IMF also could not gauge the gravity of the crisis in terms of both its magnitude and coverage until it erupted. Although the market mechanism has its checks and balances, it invariably moves in waves and cycles. At its peak in the economic cycle, the crisis is one of the ways in which the market corrects, although it is more pervasive in its damage.

The stiff conditionality of the IMF, such as deflationary fiscal adjustments comprising a cut in essential subsidies, increasing taxes at the lower ends, reducing welfare spending, do shift the cost of adjustment more towards the Poor and also defer the investment recovery process. However, it is questionable whether to allow the crisis ridden economies to be swayed by the market forces in the hope of getting them corrected naturally.

Keynes spent his lifetime on the theory to prove that the market mechanism is prone to failure, causing a destabilizing equilibrium, which can only be corrected through financial, non-market and state intervention. While Keynesianism has been reversed in several areas of economic policy by resurrecting Adam Smithism, it cannot be thrown overboard in tackling a macroeconomic crisis. Further, a totally free market mechanism without prudent and enlightened regulation is an open invitation for the boom and bust cycles, which redistribute income and wealth more unequally. Vigilant surveillance and continuing monitoring would ensure healthy regulation by avoiding erratic macroeconomic behavior and promoting sustained macroeconomic activity. When the market runs riot and turns anarchic, it needs the Keynesian discipline and formula to bring it under control and in a state of sanity and healthy equilibrium. Adam Smith without Keynes is returning to eighteenth century economics in the twenty first century.

In a ballooning global economy and financial system, the IMF has been reduced in both its size and its influence. The market comprises several participants of different sizes, with many of them being far larger than the IMF. The market participants work on the principles of risk and return and minimize risks by diversifying. The only feature that distinguishes the IMF and its member central banks is that the market principles do not primarily guide their thinking, policy, and activity, and they may have to act contrary to the market principles for the very reason of saving of the markets from calamities and unstable equilibria. One cannot rule out the role of global agency and, hence, the IMF has to take the new avatar under the new rules of the game.

For more than two and half decades, the IMF has always remained in the background as a curious but uninfluential umpire. There has not been any serious discussion on the reform of the IMF in view of a sea change in the global monetary scenario. The last epoch-making event, which goes in the annals of IMF and global monetary history as an internationally collaborative effort in giving a new turn to the evolution of a global monetary system, was the creation of SDRs in the late 1960s. It gave the system additional liquidity when the US dollar was weakening. Since then, the euro-currency system, which grew by leaps and bounds, dwarfed every other national monetary system and the IMF. The global monetary system took the new twist, which probably even Keynes, the founder father of the IMF, may not have imagined in 1944. The cross-border banking system has emerged supreme and as a critical driving force of the global economy and financial system. Floating exchange rates and global financial integration have transformed the functioning of the international monetary system. The market-driven system has taken over discretionary changes in the system. Nevertheless, when the market mechanism malfunctions and fails under crisis, discretionary support and policies become necessary for correction. The eruption of the Asian volcano and the Russian crisis, in the form of occasional bouts of market failure, once again brought the IMF into focus and kicked off the controversy on its role and emerging function in an increasingly integrated global financial system. The system needs better surveillance and an alarm mechanism to avoid crises, and corrective modalities to restore equilibrium. Can the IMF as the global organization and economic think tank of global financial system deliver this?

The biggest challenge the global monetary system faces today is to evolve the IMF into a global central bank, redistribute its resources more equitably, create a truly global centre for creation of international money and global liquidity, and thereby reduce the overdependence of the global system on the US dollar.

One of the most significant events after the formation of the IMF, which established stable exchange rates and a mechanism for giving BoP support to the needy member nations, was the creation of Special Drawing Rights in 1967. Keynes had envisioned a new international currency, named Bancor, to be the focal point of the global monetary system. It was to act as the measure of value in which all other currencies were to be expressed and also to be the means of settling international accounts between the member countries. The IMF was to create the Bancor and act as the central bank of the central banks of all member countries. At Bretton Woods, Keynes' idea of creating an independent international currency, global central bank and transnational source of global liquidity had to face a retreat, in view of the powerful US lobby to enthrone the US dollar as the international reserve currency, monetary unit of measure. As a result, the US enjoyed the *seigniorage* in the use of its currency as the global reserve asset. During the early 1960s, when global liquidity requirements raced faster than the supply of liquidity by the US through its balance of payments deficit, the global financial community again realized the need to create a separate independent source of liquidity from the IMF. By the end of the 1960s, when US balance of payments suffered heavier deficits, the US dollar repeatedly faced attacks in the currency markets. Averting the exchange crisis required maintaining the gold price at $35 an ounce by the joint action of the US and European central banks to sell gold in the market from their reserves. This alone could maintain the confidence of the market in the US dollar. Both the paucity and redundancy of the US dollar created problems in the smooth functioning of the global monetary system. During this period, Robert Triffin mooted the idea of reviving Keynes' proposal and argued a strong case for creating a new international monetary unit, the means of payments settlements among the member nations, and a source of liquidity, called Special Drawing Rights (SDRs).

In 1967, the IMF Board of Executive Directors approved the creation of SDRs as a new source of increasing international liquidity, by creating a new reserve asset. Initially, a SDR was equivalent to 1/35th of an ounce of gold. However, later when gold was demonetized by the US from the global monetary system, a SDR was redefined in terms of a basket of 16 currencies. SDRs were created by the IMF and allocated to the members on the basis of their quotas in exchange of their national currencies. For the first time it meant creation of money by an international agency, international money, to be used by the member countries in times of need. It created international liquidity, which was in short supply in the late 1960s. One of the main criticisms of the SDRs was that they may be inflationary since they created international money and increased global liquidity. SDRs created in 1969 did provide some respite to the global economy from the inadequate growth in international liquidity. However, the US dollar was the main source of global liquidity and the US could provide more dollars to the rest of the world only by incurring deficits in its balance of payments.

After the demise of Bretton Woods and the emergence of floating rates, the issue of SDRs was relegated into the background. Further, the SDRs created over the last 35 years remained a small percentage of international reserves. SDR creation has only touched the periphery of the global liquidity, and has not addressed the fundamental issue of creating a source of liquidity and its better distribution, wherein no single country enjoys *seigniorage* in its creation, and international liquidity is allocated not only on the basis of the existing size of the member economies, but also their underdevelopment, potential to grow faster and the magnitude of their BoP problems. Developed economies, which are large and do not face acute balance of payments problems, do not need SDR allocations. There should be separate criteria than the ones used currently for determining the size of SDR creation and its allocation among counties.

SDRs should work like international money, more traded, and more held as assets in private hands and central banks. Currently, SDRs figure in the portfolio of only central banks as a reserve asset. SDRs are used to settle international payments in other important currencies, especially the US dollar. Today, SDRs are used to draw dollar balances for making international payments. They are used as an adjunct to the dollar and do not function as an independent means of payment or settlement. Euro-dollars developed as a market phenomenon due to their attractiveness and efficiency. They emerged as an important and useful vehicle of recycling the petrodollars in the mid-1970s and saved the global economy from plunging into deep recession after the 1974 oil crisis. The euro-currency markets have grown by leaps and bounds since then and have been the critical and vital segment of global money and capital markets. There is no reason why SDRs cannot function as a new global currency with a little push from the Governments of member countries and initiatives of the private commercial and investment banking community. This joint public–private initiative can write a new chapter in the evolution of global money, foster the international monetary order, reduce the overdependence of the global community on the US dollar, and promote a more equitable distribution of *seigniorage* arising from the creation of international money.

The new international money, if it is called the Bancor, will be the most befitting tribute to Keynes for his contribution in giving us the tools of economic management that helped create the prosperous post-war global economy. Alternative names could be Ecu (economic currency unit) or Erth, or Gcu (global currency unit). The IMF could evolve into a Global Central Bank (GCB). The value of the Gcu or GQ or Gq would be determined by a basket of ten to 15 major currencies. The Gcu could be traded in the exchange market and commercial banks could accept Gcu deposits. The use of the Gcu as a reserve asset would relieve the pressure on the US dollar, and the central banks could hold a portion of their reserves in Gcu. The existing resources and quotas of IMF can be more equitably distributed according to the purchasing power GDP of countries. The GCB could also create global liquidity by the creation of Gcu depending upon the need for such liquidity.

Part II

The Indian economic experience

8 Economic liberalization

A new mantra of development

Backlash of control Raj – middle path in economic policy

The policy of keeping equidistant from both the Soviet socialist centrally planned economy, and the US free enterprise capitalist market economy, has been the cornerstone of the Indian economy ever since it embarked on planning for economic development in 1951. While the Soviet model of planning largely subverted the market mechanism, the Indian model was more market friendly and used the market mechanism with regulations and controls. The Soviet and Chinese development models made little use of the market pricing mechanism in the pre-globalization era. However, it would be erroneous to think that, although the free enterprise economies did not interfere with the market pricing, they did not exercise the planning process. In the US and other free enterprise economies, the government involvement in the economic activities was critical, although limited. The private enterprise did rely on government spending and did carry out elaborate planning for their enterprise growth. The duopolistic or oligopolistic nature of large corporations necessitated an intricate and elaborate planning and business strategy exercise in line with the government policy and budgetary spending.[67] While the communistic planning process was more centralized, business planning of large corporates in a free enterprise economy was decentralized at the unit and industry levels. The latter process was much more efficient because of its micro approach, and it enabled different units within the industry to visualize their own perception rather than having a common scenario perceived by the central planning, which carried a heavier risk in cases of failures in projections. Risks in planning and projections were more widely distributed in the free economy than in the centrally planned economy.

India traversed the path, which was midway from these two processes for nearly three and half decades before the onset of liberalization in 1984. During this period of planned development, it kept its age-old market institutions alive and nurtured them. It followed the planning process undertaken by the government at the macro level. It introduced pricing, production and distribution controls at the micro level only in certain commodities and services wherever it thought necessary. It permitted private enterprise to expand and grow within the contours of the Five Year Plan priorities and targets.

The post-war economics was dominated by Keynesian theory, thought and policy. Mature economies needed to spend more to grow and not be thrifty. Developing economies on the contrary needed more capital and investment to grow faster and, hence, had to be thrifty. The focus of planning and policy was on capital accumulation and investment rate. Domestic resources were not adequate to meet investment targets envisaged by the Plan growth rates. Domestic savings needed to be supplemented by the transfer of resources from the developed economies and international agencies such as the World Bank, IMF and other aid consortia. The 1950s and 1960s were dominated by aid and soft loans from the developed economies for economic progress in developing countries. Different countries followed their own model of development.

Planning by direction

Indian development was characterized as planning by direction. It involved using the market mechanism, which was regulated to direct the resources of both public and private enterprises. Further, the public sector was to have the dominant position capturing the commanding heights of the economy, and the private sector was required to supplement it. In this scenario, the private sector was actually supported by the public sector. With tariff protection, and the second best, intermediate, and low-cost technology, India produced goods affordable to the purchasing power of its consumers, and dictated by its income distribution and income growth. High income tax rates and limits on corporate remuneration did limit the size of the market and its growth. In addition to price and distribution controls, incomes were also regulated. Rent controls fixed rentals. Wages were determined and revised with trade union negotiations. Managerial remuneration faced ceilings prescribed under the Company's Act by the government, and profits were controlled by price controls as well as high corporate and income tax rates. The regime of controls and high income and indirect tax rates gave rise to black markets, smuggling, and tax evasion, contributing to the growth of the parallel economy whose magnitude increased substantially.

The economic logic for the policy of price, production and incomes regulation was to release scarce resources towards the investment and output levels and the pattern envisaged by the Planning Commission through the mechanism of markets. The markets were not to be subverted, nor were they to be unleashed, but they were put on a leash. The greed of the market was to be tempered to the need of the market.

With investment outlay being the key parameter of the Plan, the major initiatives in investment were left to the state-owned enterprises in key and heavy industries, leaving the private sector to cater to consumer industries and those supporting the public sector. The private sector would not have been able to undertake the scale of investment required by the industries solely allocated to the public sector, without the support of the multinationals.

This was the strategy that emerged and was followed in India due to a number of factors. It was driven by the continental size of its economy, with a large and diverse resource base, its geopolitical position, its ethos derived from its cultural, philosophical and saintly tradition (which put the societal welfare before the self), ideological disposition of its political and economic leadership, memory of foreign aggressions, and history of colonial rule, mass exploitation, and casteist and racial segregation. Newly independent India could hardly think about the capitalist model of development when it had an ideal example of socialistic, egalitarian society in the successful Soviet model closer to its soil. The matter of choice was, to what extent and in what manner would the model be adapted to suit Indian needs.

Lacunae in plans

The success of economic plans has to be seen in the light of its several economic parameters and not just growth rate. The other important parameters being employment generation, income distribution, price stability, and balance of payments. The development plans in developing economies including India were based on the Harrod–Domar capital–output ratio and Lieontief's input–output ratio models. Keynesian theory also helped in the planning mechanism. Essentially a demand theory, it analyses how aggregate demand behaves and why deficient demand causes underemployment equilibrium. It illustrates laws and behaviour primarily of an economy, which is mature, and facing excess output capacity. The syndrome of unemployment, which it sought to analyze, was essentially unemployment arising in capital rich nations and not capital poor nations. Keynesian theory is, however, useful in developing economies to examine the pressure of aggregate demand of a given investment program pursued to achieve the target rate of economic growth. The Keynesian tools helped in matching the demand side with the supply side produced by capital–output ratios and the input–output matrix. The matching was based on the estimates of several economic parameters.

The success of planning, therefore, hinges on the predictability or accuracy of several economic parameters that go in the planning process. A minor deviation would not pose any problem, but any significant variance or deviation of estimates of economic parameters is likely to throw the plan out of gear. It is these mismatches, which have been the cause of pitfalls in planning, whether it is in Latin America, Africa or Asia, or under centralized communistic planning or democratic decentralized planning. Plan outlays did not solve the unemployment and underemployment problems because the investment outlays either overestimated the employment generation from forward or backward linkages or underestimated labor market growth. Alternatively, the planners thought that the plan was the best that can be done, and the problem of unemployment was unsolvable within the prevalent environment of population growth, demographic profile and available resources and technology.

Price stability became a sacrifice when the plan investment pattern did not produce output to match the demand generation from its multiplier effect on nominal income. It could be because of either the financing pattern crossing the cautionary limit on deficit financing, creating excessive monetary expansion, or a faulty investment pattern creating output not matching the demand pattern, or an inability to import more due to external constraints.

The question of income distribution is also linked to the earlier goals. Since the employment generation remained slow and price inflation surfaced uncontrollably, the income distribution became more skewed. The balance of payments got adversely affected because of the inaccurate estimation of price and income elasticities of imports and exports based on past data, an unexpectedly high rate of inflation, and the tendency to keep the exchange rate unchanged, all of which hurt the trade balance.

Despite great advances in econometrics, the use of these tools for future trends, estimates, and projections suffers from several limitations. The past trend may not be repeated in future, and more so in growing economies where a move from one stage of development to another causes far-reaching changes in economic systems, institutions, practices, behavioral patterns, and technological levels, all of which influence and build a new relationships between economic variables, which diverge from the past trends and set a new pattern. These parametric surprises have caused the planning to be ineffective even in the communist economies, resulting in large variances of the actuals from the targets.

Why market mechanism?

The risk of error in the estimates and judgments in planning, and the elaborate process of adjustments and correction that planning necessitates, have been amply demonstrated over long and wide experience, indicating why economic planning in many countries failed to achieve its objectives. Apart from this, the economic efficiency of capital investments through the Plans was also found to have been much lower than the overall efficiency of, or return on, capital in the economy.

The plea for a return to a market mechanism in the allocation of investment is based on a premise that the disaggregated decision making is more efficient, flexible, adaptive, and dynamic than the central plan. It also minimizes the risk by diversifying business decisions at innumerable micro points that collectively make the market. The mismatches in estimates and actuals in demand–supply are evident on an ongoing and continuous basis. This disaggregated decision-making by the large number of units that comprise the market avoids the risks of errors emanating from the central plan which, once prepared, becomes difficult to adjust easily.

The superiority of the market mechanism also lies in the speed of adjustment it can bring in investments and the diversification of decision-making, reducing the wastage caused by errors. However, if the planner can make mistakes, so can the private corporations and entrepreneurs who are market participants. Yet, the market mechanism, because it is disaggregated in nature, reduces the overall waste in resource allocation and utilization caused by the risk of errors of estimates and judgments in business. Further, the loss in private investment is borne by investors who have both the ability as well as the awareness of the degree of risk they are taking in anticipation of profit. In contrast, the loss in public investment is borne and shared by the tax payers and community at large. The loss in public investment, therefore, involves higher social cost, which is inherent in the central planning process.

Economic planning, controls and state ownership of business enterprises, although at one time (especially since the 1950s and for nearly three decades) they intermingled with each other, have become to a large extent mutually exclusive under the new economic philosophy of liberalization. Liberalization has to do more with controls and state ownership of business than planning. The content of planning undergoes a change, but economic planning as a concept and tool is indispensable, both in the public as well as on private corporate enterprises. Economic planning, which earlier used to encompass investment targets of private and public sector enterprises in several industries will now have to be primarily focused on sectors such as infrastructure, health, education, human resource development and defense. These sectors, including defense production, have also been open for greater participation by the private sector. Liberalization, therefore, encompasses the removal of controls and restoration of the market mechanism, which is more efficient. It also stresses privatization or disinvestment of public enterprises so that the planning is divorced from public investment in industrial enterprises. This naturally reduces the size of the plan outlay.

In the field of economic policy globally, the decade of 1980s witnessed growing acceptance and implementation of policies of economic liberalization. The Soviet Union, the largest and oldest economy exercising centralized planning, showed its willingness to adopt Perestroika and Glasnost and move towards a market-oriented economy. Whether the disintegration of the Soviet Union was the result of its arms race with the USA and/or deficiency of its Planning Model and/or its implementation is now a matter of history and research. The *avante garde* of planning turned the course and paved the way for several others to follow. China devised its own model of modernization and reforms by opening doors for massive trade-based foreign investment primarily from the US by creating Free Trade Zones in the early 1990s and at a much faster speed than India.

All along, there has been growing acceptance of the invisible hand of Adam Smith who wrote in 1776 that the market mechanism guided by enlightened self-interest unhindered by government intervention would bring public good together the with private profit motive. However, the free market mechanism discussed in theory, though it is the best in terms of economic efficiency, productivity, allocation and growth, is not what exists in the real economic world. Several imperfections of the market mechanism emanating from imperfect competition, asymmetric information, absence of level playing field, and destabilizing behaviour, do not give credence to the belief that the market can always deliver a social good. Further, the market is blind and impersonal to its participants. It does not always address the issue of economic and social equity.

Nor are they competent to ensure social justice. These 'public goods' can only be provided by a political process ... . Even creation and maintenance of market requires political action. This point is well understood by market fundamentalists. What is less well recognized is that the globalization of markets without a corresponding strengthening of our international political and social arrangements has led to a very lopsided social development.[68]

Globalization is not without its social costs, and they become more pronounced and get higher priority in the emerging market economies because of greater consideration for economic equity and social justice. In the emerging markets, a large destitute population without a social safety net require care and programs for those rejected by, and also those outside, the market mechanism. It is the absence of provision for a social safety net or programs for rehabilitation of the poor and destitute market rejects that has been the biggest failure of globalization. This has been the central and common theme of attack of the 3S, (Stiglitz, Sachs and Soros) against the 3W Model.

The market fundamentalists give the logic and arguments advocating abandonment of investment by public sector business enterprises through the Plans and replacement of this investment by private sector initiatives and investments. The promoter role, which the state assumed in creating public enterprises, will have to be gradually taken by private and foreign entrepreneurs and corporations. The entrepreneurship will have to be supplemented by technology as well as capital.

One of the primary reasons for investment in heavy industries by the public sector in India for more than three decades was the size of investment required, which was beyond the capacity of private sector investment. The public sector in India built the huge industrial base for the economy, exploiting its tremendous untapped natural resource endowment. The public sector's industrial structure encompassed oil exploration and refineries, iron and steel, non-ferrous metals, coal, fertilizers, heavy chemicals, power, telecoms, railways and airlines. Without the public sector, rapid development in these industries would have been difficult. The period of 1997 to 2002 witnessed a reversal of this trend. It brought about a decline in the investment rate. The private sector including the foreign multinational corporations were not yet able to fill the void in investment created by the policy of abandoning public sector investment. The volume as well as the rate of investment dipped. In several other countries, more particularly China, liberalization brought a dramatic surge in foreign direct investment, which has transformed the development process.

India has yet to see a significant jump in foreign direct investment. Although liberalization has accelerated the foreign direct investment from $6.1 billion in 2001–2002 to a record $15 billion in 2006–2007, it pales in comparison to foreign investment in China of $50 billion. If this investment hiatus in India is not bridged quickly and at a fast rate, the growth rate is unlikely to move into the higher orbit of 10 percent. A peculiar development in India, which has to some extent mitigated the hardship from lower public investment, is India's technical human capital which has played the lead role in the Information Technology industry, growing in the last few years at an extraordinarily high pace. India's endowment in human capital has enabled participating in global growth in the IT industry. With IT not being a very heavily capitalized industry, but more human capital intensive, India has been able to move in the post-liberalization era with much better composure due to the heavy expansion and high growth of the IT industry. IT has substituted the vacuum created by the decline or slow growth of old economy sectors adversely affected by liberalization.

The infrastructure sector, comprising Power, Telecoms, Transportation, Water and Irrigation, is the sector that is most favorably endowed as the engine of future growth in India. The current low per capita availability of these services and the large pent up demand for them warrants investment in this sector, which would be more potent and a stronger transmitter of growth in the economy. This sector has strong forward and backward linkages and has greater employment potential and a larger effect on income growth because of a low capital–output ratio. The requirements of the infrastructure have been estimated at $320 billion for the next decade. The infrastructure is the new harbinger and the most potent engine of growth in the coming decade. In addition to domestic private and foreign sectors, the Government and public sector can also participate in the infrastructure jointly, to accelerate the investment rate to achieve a 10 percent growth target. India's forex glut of $200 billion can be harnessed and exploited to part finance the massive capital formation in the infrastructure sector. This aspect is discussed in Chapter 14.

9 Indian economic gradualism

The basic hypothesis on which the economic philosophy of reforms rests is that the unfettered market mechanism is a better guide or signal for allocation of resources. It brings out greater efficiency in the process and pattern of allocation, and the use of financial and real resources. Higher efficiency means gains in productivity and higher rate of growth. The disturbing side effect of reform is that the process of transition or change in allocation is painful, and the greater the degree of regulation of market forces and the faster its reversal, the more dislocating is the change emerging from altered allocation of resources. Reforms have to cover several sectors of the economy, such as industry, agriculture, fiscal, banking, financial and capital market, trade and tariff, BoP and exchange rate. They could cover all sectors at one go with speedier implementation. Alternatively, they could be sequenced and implemented gradually in phases. Many economies have gone in for total reforms at one go, replacing all major economic regulations by the freer market mechanism. Others have taken a more secure route for dismantling controls and regulations in phases. This approach of gradualism has its advantages in mitigating the pains of reform in the initial phases. Pains of reform are reflected in higher unemployment, increasing inflation and growing inequality. Gains of reforms are higher growth, lower prices, better allocative efficiency, higher productivity and productivity-based gains in wages and salaries, and return on capital. Yet, the marketization of economy may not benefit those in the lower strata of society who are beyond the reach of the market economy. The reforms have also to ensure higher consumption especially among the lower strata of society to elevate their living standards through direct government action. This alone can guarantee the execution of reforms with a human face.

The economic reform process has been pursued in different emerging markets in differing patterns and pace. Several emerging market economies in Asia and Latin America adopted the path of faster reforms. India pursued the path of gradual sequencing of reforms. The central distinguishing feature of the process of economic reform in India has been gradualism.

Sequencing for synergistic development market reform first

Optimizing the sequencing and its pace in the economic reform process is an issue requiring skill, judgment and finesse in policy making and execution. There is no simple rule book to refer to. Countries differ in their political constitution and philosophy, historcial economic policy background and experience, nature of their economic, commercial and financial institutions and their social and political interests, geo-political status, trading and investment relations and status in the global economy. Hence, there cannot be any standard or uniform model. China built its model of reform within its own ideological set-up and perception in embracing the market-oriented philosophy. South Asian and the Latin American economies followed the faster model of reform with speedier liberalization for quicker economic results. The transitional economies of Eastern Europe, the erstwhile USSR and Russia, had mixed models. The crises in the fast reforming economies could have been averted with better surveillance and quicker adjustment policies. What was lacking was the time to pause and review maladjustments arising from the rapid economic growth, and judge their gravity. This view is corroborated by the fact that most of the countries that faced the crisis recovered quickly, regaining their composure and rejoining the earlier path of higher growth. Unfortunately, in the current international scenario, if a country cannot be forewarned by its own think tank on the impending crisis, no other international body rings the alarm bells. The global credit rating agencies do change ratings for countries courting a crisis but have so far not forewarned the crisis.

The Indian model of reform with gradualism received applause only after the realization of the Asian Crisis. A critical factor in the success or failure of economic reform is not only the speed of reform consistent with the ability and potential of market institutions to adapt to the pressure of market forces of demand and supply. The supply elasticities have to be very responsive for any reform to give the desired economic results. Reforms demand efficient market institutions with responsive elasticities to generate higher economic growth. Hence, in addition to the speed of reform it is imperative to ensure the most appropriate or optimum sequencing of reforms in several sectors of the economy. The philosophy of globalization underscores the need for the right speed and right sequencing for each country, in the context of its eco-political structure and place in the global economy, to secure synergistic economic growth and development.

In today's economic world, the economic philosophy of liberalization cannot be based on the theoretical model of a free market and *laissez faire* economy. Reforms towards a market mechanism, whether in agriculture, industry, commodity and forex markets, banking and financial services, capital market, and foreign trade, need to be qualified in line with the realities of several market imperfections and inefficiencies.

In many cases, looking to these market inefficiencies, liberalization can do exactly the opposite of what it was intended to do. The Asian Crisis of 1997 is a classic example of how faster and indiscriminate liberalization can hamper the realization of its goals and cause traumatic adjustments costs. Latin American economies also paid the price of full scale liberalization in the form of periodic exchange crises and economic chaos. It is, therefore, imperative to reform the market mechanism while liberalization is in progress. Market reforms should create a stable market structure resilient enough to withstand destabilizing tendencies and influences.

The market is an institution, and is built up and improved gradually. The policy changes provide stimulus for better, orderly and broader based functioning of the market. However, this is required to be assisted by simultaneous infrastructural improvements in the mechanism and operation of the market. The market mechanism, therefore, needs judicious tempering and careful and constructive supervision and regulation by either government or self regulatory organizations.

> The Washington Consensus policies were based on a simplistic model of the market economy, the competitive equilibrium model, in which Adam Smith's invisible hand works, and works perfectly ... . The market system requires competition and perfect information. But competition is limited and perfect information is far from perfect – and well functioning competitive markets can't be established overnight ... . Ideology ignores these matters; it says simply move quickly to a market economy as you can. But economic theory and history show how disastrous it can be to ignore sequencing.[69]

Gradualism in reforms in India has paid dividends due to the improvements in the market mechanism preceding or coinciding with gradual and not abrupt policy changes. The trauma states have been skipped or bypassed. It has worked in generating productivity gains and bringing about greater efficiency in the use and allocation of resources. The policy of gradual changes has enabled the supply side to respond to pent up demand in a smoother and more orderly fashion without causing much disruption and pressure on prices as well as existing production capacities and resources.

Industrial liberalization of 1980s

India pursued the path of gradual reform process, with industrial reforms of the price and output controls, in the 1980s. These were followed by BoP and exchange rate and fiscal reforms in 1991. The financial, foreign trade and tariff reforms were kicked off in the mid 1990s. This sequencing of reforms enabled India go step by step in different sectors of the economy in an orderly fashion without facing any bottlenecks and roadblocks. It also created results in each sector as it progressed in reform, benefiting the next sector and creating more synergistic development.

The first phase of reform, launched by Rajiv Gandhi in 1984, began by removing internal regulations and controls in the industrial economy. The industrial economy, which was also subject to licensing of capacities, and pricing and distribution controls needed to be decontrolled in order to create a more competitive environment. The Indian industry needed to face global competition from imports and also be globally competitive. The licensing of new industrial units and the expansion and diversification of existing units was removed. The price controls on many industrial products were abolished. For nearly more than four decades, Indian industry survived under the protective umbrella of tariffs and quotas. High tariffs enabled the large units to grow and quotas permitted even smaller units to survive due to excess demand situations. The removal of licensing restrictions for domestic industries allowed forces of competition within the domestic economy by allowing new units to enter and existing units to expand to achieve economies of scale.

The industrial reforms began in 1984 with two historic measures that totally changed the industrial scenario in India.

1   Industrial licensing was abolished for all projects, except in 18 industries of strategic or environment concern or of high import content. With this historic decision, 80 percent of the industrial sector became free for fresh investments and capacity expansions without licensing.
2   The monopoly and Restrictive Trade Practices Act was amended to enable corporates to expand or diversify and thereby gain economies of scale to become globally competitive.

The reforms allowed existing industrial companies to expand and diversify without licensing. Several new players also entered the industrial economy. So great was the demand for industrial investment that these measures of liberalization of the industrial sector received an immediate and very high response. This phase was characterized by unprecedented expansion and diversification by the Indian corporate sector, which brought a sharp growth in capital investment. There was considerable expansion in the capacities of several industries such as iron and steel, cement, aluminum, automobiles, two-wheelers, textiles, paper, fertilizers, chemicals, computers and consumer durable and non-durable goods. It raised investment spending as well as industrial growth. The spurt in investment was supported by the existence of tremendous pent up as well as potential demand from the fast growing consumer market. Corporates showed higher earnings growth, the stock market boomed and the capital market responded to mobilize more savings. Banks, financial institutions and mutual funds played their role in promoting capital formation and accelerating the growth process. The policy gave a big boost to investment with the rate of capital formation rising to a high of 23 percent GDP in the 1980s compared with an average rate of 15.5 percent during the 1970s. The industrial growth spurted and doubled to a double-digit level of 11.3 percent in the 1980s compared with 5.35 percent in the 1970s. This had an impact on the overall economic growth, which also doubled from 3.5 percent to 7.2 percent. India's shortage economy of the 1970s was transformed into the surplus economy in consumer goods and the industrial sector by the end of the 1980s.

Second phase of reforms, the 1990s

The success of liberalization of the industrial sector paved the way for the next phase in reforms. The removal of price, output and capacity controls on industry infused an adequate domestic competition in the industry and brought about a substantial growth in industrial capacities and output. The decade of the 1990s marked the second phase of reforms, with the focus on foreign trade and exchange rate policies and financial liberalization. The protective umbrella of high import tariffs and quotas had sustained the higher cost structure of many industries in international comparison. These tariffs and quotas needed to be very gradually and carefully lowered and removed, allowing industry to be globally competitive. Liberalization of foreign trade and exchange regulations also meant that the Indian industry had to have access to inputs such as power, and capital at international rates. The interest rates needed to be reduced in order to lower cost of capital. This was the task of financial deregulation, which had to be launched in sync with trade and forex liberalization. India's step-by-step or gradualist approach in economic reforms was working well. It gave minimum dislocations and trauma in the economy and gradually transformed the economy from the one regulated by discretionary pricing and controls to the one governed by the free pricing and market mechanism, which itself was to be made more competitive and efficient than the one prevailing under the control regime.

The stage was, therefore, set for external sector reforms to be also accompanied by financial sector reforms. Unfortunately, the oil crisis of 1990 brought a severe pressure on India's balance of payments and foreign exchange reserves. The breakneck pace of economic growth in the 1980s also exerted pressure on both interest rates as well as the external payments position. Interest rates reached very high levels, the BoP deficit grew and the rupee came under pressure. From a macro angle this situation can be viewed as one when the savings gap grew there was no requisite domestic policy initiative to raise savings or to raise foreign investment to sustain a higher trade deficit.

Foreign exchange crisis 1990

The process of reform received a set back when India faced a serious balance of payments problem in the late 1980s, culminating into a crisis in 1990.[70] For nearly a decade until 1990, India succeeded in tackling the foreign exchange imbalance. The stressful situation was diffused in the 1980s by resorting to the IMF loan, euro-currency borrowings and persistent depreciation of the rupee under the system of managed floating. Despite these developments, the balance of payments crisis was simmering in the second half of 1980s, primarily due to rising external debt servicing payment. The IMF Jumbo loan of SDRs 5 billion, out of which SDRs 3.9 billion were drawn in the first half of the 1980s, enabled India to tide over the crisis temporarily and gave adequate breathing time to carry out the structural adjustments to correct both the internal as well as external equilibria. But the commercial borrowings increased at a much faster rate. The outstanding euro-currency borrowings increased from Rs.2500 crores in 1983–84 to Rs.26,700 crores in 1990–91.[71] The total external debt (excluding short term debt and NRI deposits) rose from Rs.27,600 crores to Rs.99,450 crores, during the same period i.e. from 13 percent to 20 percent of GNP. This had an impact on the debt servicing obligations, which increased by 28 percent per annum during the 1980s compared with 7 percent per annum in the 1970s, with the debt servicing ratio as a percentage of export going up from 13 percent to 30 percent. Escalating external debt servicing and a decline in the fresh inflow of capital was beginning to bring pressure on the foreign exchange reserves. During 1984–85 the exchange reserves of Rs.6800 crores could finance five\ months' imports. The level declined in 1989–90 to Rs.5800 crores, only 2 months' imports and further to a record low of Rs.2150 in December 1990, equivalent to just 2.5 weeks' imports.

The economy entered one of the worst phases in its balance of payments history. The problem became acute because of dwindling foreign exchange reserves, and prolonged negotiations for the IMF loan, which finally required India swapping and pledging its gold holdings in the international financial markets, and with the Bank of England for raising foreign exchange to meet its international commitments. Although the trade deficit had risen from Rs.5400 crores in 1984–85 to Rs.10,640 crores in 1990–91, in relation to GNP it had fallen from 2.3 percent to 1.8 percent.

The forex crisis was precipitated by a number of factors.

First, the gulf crisis following the Kuwait war was the most severe setback that accelerated the exchange crisis. The oil import bill rose in 1990–91 by Rs.4500 crores, i.e. 72 percent. The loss in remittances from the gulf area was around Rs.490 crores, while that of exports was Rs.500 crores. In addition to this, non-realization of other export proceeds cost Rs.200 crores and the foreign exchange cost of emergency repatriation of Indians from the Kuwait war zone was Rs.360 crores. All this totaled a huge and unexpected burden, and a shock of Rs.5200 crores.

Second, the current account deficit reached the record high of Rs.15,500 crores, 3 percent of GNP in 1990–91, on account of the increasing pressure of debt servicing payments. External debt servicing enlarged to Rs.10,000 crores with the debt servicing ratio, which had already run into the danger zone, rising to 30 percent.

Third, while the capital requirements were increasing, the inflow of capital declined from the foreign capital markets as well as the international agencies, like the IMF. The decline in credit rating raised problems for India, raising commercial credit, and the prolonged negotiations on the IMF loan delayed the grant of quick assistance to meet the immediate balance of payment crisis.

Comparative analysis of BoP stress

The Foreign Exchange crisis of 1990 can be compared with the three earlier situations of balance of payments stress faced during 1965–66, 1974–75 and 1980–81. The degree of stress can be examined from four parameters.

1   Trade deficit as a percentage of GNP indicating the degree of imbalance in foreign trade.
2   Trade deficit as a percentage of exports showing the capacity of exports growth to bridge the trade gap.
3   Current account deficit as a percentage of GNP, reflecting the degree of a more fundamental disequilibrium.
4   Foreign exchange cover for imports giving the capacity of the country to finance imports.

The following observations can be made from the above analysis and the comparative data given in Table 9.1.

1   The degree of stress in 1964–65 faced by the trade account as well as the current account was high. The import financing level was also poor.
2   In comparison, the 1974–75 situation was not acute. Both trade and current account gaps did exist but were not alarming and the trade gap was only 36 percent of exports, compared with 75 percent in 1965–66. Nevertheless, foreign exchange reserves were low.
3   The crisis in 1980–81 was more acute since the trade gap had reached the record level of 4.3 percent of GNP and 87 percent of exports. Although the reserves position was little better, there was a fundamental disequilibrium.
4   In 1990–91, the trade disequilibrium showing a favorable score reduced to 1.8 percent of GNP and to the lowest level of 32 percent of exports. However, exchange reserves were weak, while the current account deficit position of 3 percent of GNP was alarming. This was primarily the result of high debt servicing of 30 percent of exports.

In order to resolve the crisis, India had to endeavor to close the trade gap and achieve trade surplus, as was attained in 1972–73 and 1976–77. Promotion of invisible inflows was also required to add to the export surplus for meeting the rising debt servicing.

Table 9.1 Balance of payments stress, comparative analysis

	1965–66	*1974–75*	*1980–81*	*1990–91*
i Trade deficit as % of GNP	2.5	1.7	4.3	1.8
ii Trade deficit as % of exports	75	36	87	32
iii Current account deficit as % of GNP	1.5	0.9	1.2	3
iv Foreign exchange cover for imports (months) average for year	2	2	3	2.5

Data Source: Economic Survey, Government of India.

Trade gap versus savings gap

The foreign exchange crisis can also be examined from the point of view of the savings gap. Although the trade gap seems to be more dominant than the savings gap in India, the latter also plays a role in enlarging the former. This view further strengthens the stand that any measure taken to reduce directly the trade gap is required to be supplemented by the broad macro-economic policy to reduce the absorption in the economy, which would tend to limit the saving gap.

Following the sharp increase in the savings rate in the 1970s, from 15 percent to the peak of 23 percent, the rate declined in the 1980s and fluctuated between 18.2 percent and 21.7 percent. While the investment rate rose from 15.6 percent to 22 percent during the 1970s, it further increased to 24.1 percent in the 1980s in the face of a declining saving rate. The savings gap, therefore, rose from 0.6 percent in the beginning of the 1970s to 2.4 percent in 1989–90. The counterpart of the savings gap is the current account deficit, and hence, if the former is reduced, the latter will automatically adjust with appropriate trade and exchange rate policies. It is, therefore, necessary to reduce the savings gap by promoting savings in the household, corporate as well as government sectors. Since the decline in the overall saving rate in the 1980s was caused entirely by the reduction in the government saving rate from 4.5 percent in 1981–82 to 1.7 percent in 1989–90, measures to cut the budgetary deficit were imperative to raise the rate and volume of savings.

Corrective measures

In order to avert further deepening of the crisis culminating into a situation of default, urgent and drastic measures were required. In light of the gravity of the problem, the Government initiated a series of measures to stall any payments default, improve the confidence of the international community in the rupee, and correct the rapidly deteriorating external payments situation.

Revaluation of gold

Since 1940, the gold stocks held by the Reserve Bank of India (RBI) were valued at Rs.53.50 per gram up to June 1966, when the valuation was increased to Rs.84.39 per gram following the first devaluation of rupee by 36.5 percent. In spite of a substantial increase in the price of gold in the international market, the RBI had not revalued its gold reserves. The gold stocks of RBI of 10.45 million ounces as on March 31, 1990 were valued at Rs.163 crores. With a view to enlarging the exchange reserves and improving the credit rating in the international market, by indicating the true value of the country's total exchange reserves, the gold stocks of RBI were revalued on October 17, 1990 at the international price of gold. This measure boosted the figure of gold reserves of RBI to Rs.6828 crores as on March 31, 1991. The overall exchange reserves, including the foreign currency assets of Rs.4388 crores, therefore rose to Rs.11,216 crores, equivalent to three months' imports. Gold revaluation improved the reserves position and gave an adequate buffer and breather to the economy to adopt hard measures to resolve the crisis and improve the country's image and credit rating in the international market.

Higher LC margin

In order to curtail the growth in imports by discouraging the building up of a large inventory of imported inputs and to defer payments for imports, the RBI enhanced the cash margin against all imports except the capital goods, from 50 percent to 133 percent in March 1991 and further to 200 percent in April 1991. While this measure was intended to slow down the import payments, in order to accelerate quick realization of export bills, the RBI also raised the interest rates on post shipment credit from 8.5 percent to 18 percent for 90 days to 6 months, and 25 percent beyond 6 months.

IMF borrowing

The response of the international community and institutions to the unprecedented and sudden calamity faced by India was slow, inadequate and disappointing. The multinational banks reduced the flow of euro currency lending and raised the spreads due to the lower credit rating caused by the deteriorating payment situation. The IMF reacted slowly to India's request for a large structural adjustment facility but, in turn, agreed to extend, initially under the Compensatory and Contingency Financing Facility and first credit tranche, only a sum of SDRs1268 million in January 1991. India's request for bigger assistance remained pending the agreement on the conditionality, which covered several macro/micro-economic policy issues, such as the reduction of the budgetary deficit, the reduction of Government non-plan expenditure, a cut in subsidies, liberalization of controls including financial and trade liberalization, devaluation of the rupee, privatization and openness to foreign private investment.

Gold pledge

To reduce the growing mismatch between external receipts and payments, which was constantly dwindling the reserves, in July 1991 the RBI, pledged 25 tonnes of gold with the Bank of England to raise US$300 to US$400 million. This was intended to keep the reserves at a respectable level and avert the payments default until the opening of the loan tap by the IMF. The RBI held 332 tonnes of gold in July 1991 and the RBI Act permits 15 percent of its gold holdings outside India. The government allowed the Reserve Bank of India to ship 47 tonnes of gold to the Bank of England in July, 1991 helping to raise $600 million more.

Rupee devaluation

The much talked about and debated measure of a large depreciation of the rupee was resorted to. On July 1, 1991 the Reserve Bank depreciated the rupee vis-à-vis the US dollar by 9.6 percent and against sterling by 8.8 percent. Another dose of depreciation of 12.3 percent against the US dollar and 11.8 percent against sterling was given on July 3. The two depreciations caused a 22 percent decline in rupee value against the basket of five major currencies.

Increase in bank rate

The RBI also raised the Bank Rate from 10 to 11 percent and hiked the bank deposit rates. The commercial bank lending rates were already freed from the ceiling to check the rapid growth in bank credit.

Removal of export subsidy

The cash subsidy for exports has been a perennial feature of India's trade policy, virtually amounting to the operation of multiple exchange rates and indirect depreciation of the rupee. With the two depreciations of the rupee the export subsidy became redundant and was removed. The new Export Import Policy announced in July abolished the cash subsidization of exports which imposed a burden on the worsening budgetary position of the Government.

Announcing further liberalization of industrial policy and foreign exchange regulations, the Government permitted foreign equity investment in the industrial sector up to 51 percent. This was intended to attract more foreign equity capital as against the borrowings that carry a larger debt servicing burden.

BoP reform

The forex crisis of 1990 rang an alarm bell for steps to bring out an orderly reform in the financial sector and an external account to raise savings in the economy and create a stable and sustainable balance of payments position. Following the two-step devaluation of the rupee, the capital account was partially opened up in 1994 by allowing Foreign Institutional Investors (FIIs) to invest in new issues and the stock market. A more liberal foreign direct investment policy was directed to bring in higher inflows of foreign capital. Opening up the capital account worked very quickly in redressing the savings-investment mismatch, bringing a downward pressure on interest rates by infusing fresh liquidity, improving the forex reserve position, raising export growth, giving adequate protection to import competing industries, and stabilizing the rupee in the forex market.

Liberalization of the gold import policy also played a critical role in promoting a viable and sustainable balance of payments pattern. Smuggling of gold had always created distortions in India's BoP situation. It deprived the economy of external resources, which could have been mobilized for development through official channels. The BoP reform, therefore, in addition to developing a sustainable BoP equilibrium also managed to bridge the domestic savings gap and eased pressure on domestic liquidity. The portfolio investments as well as the foreign direct investment were primarily guided by the signals from the stock market and capital market, unlike the earlier regime where the investments flowed into areas where industrial licenses were cleared.

The first two phases of reform, the opening up of the domestic industrial economy and the liberalization of foreign investment (both direct and portfolio), brought a tremendous growth impact on the economy. In the economy starved of resources and facing, supply scarcities in several industries, rapid growth in industrial investment brought the multiplier effect on industrial growth and employment.

Coinciding this phase, the financial sector also underwent a major reform process. Interest rate deregulation, lowering the Statutory Liquidity Ratio (SLR) and Cash Reserve Ratio (CRR) for banks, and the entry of private sector banks injected greater flexibility, dynamism, and competitive spirit in banking and the financial services industry. Financial liberalization and reform and their impact are considered in the next chapter.

10 Financial and capital market reform

The road to full convertibility passes through the pathway of domestic financial liberalization. Financial regulation before liberalization leant heavily on the administered interest rate regime. In the capital and credit short economy like India until the beginning of 1990s, the pressure on the interest rate was upward, and in order to make credit and capital available for investment at lower cost, a cap on interest rates was imposed. Inter-bank call money, bank deposit and lending, and long-term bond interest rates faced ceilings. In order to promote long-term investment in industry, the long-term bond or debenture rates were fixed at a lower level than the bank lending rates. The demand for bank credit always remained higher than funds available with banks due to pre-emption of a large share of banks' resources by the Reserve Bank of India (RBI) and the Government by way of high Cash Reserve Ratio (CRR) and Statutory Liquidity Ratio (SLR) requirements. The profitability rates of trade, business and industry were, however, much higher than the bank lending rates, and this continued to keep pressure on commercial credit availability from banks. The bank lending rates in 1991 were higher than the debenture interest rate by 4 to 5 percent. This compartmentalization of markets for short-term and long-term capital, and the Government pre-empting large resources for its long term borrowings from the banks, created a peculiar feature, which is unconventional in the financial theory. The yield curve, which usually slopes upward, was downward sloping and inverted in the Indian financial market for a very long period.

It was imperative to remove pricing controls and distortions arising there from in the financial markets before proceeding towards convertibility. The financial markets needed to be more market driven with greater competition and flexibility. The final test of liberalization lies in more efficient and transparent functioning of the market. While deregulation of the financial markets involved removal of administered controls on interest rates, it also necessitated other steps. First, the technological upgrading of the market to improve market efficiency and transparency was the primary prerequisite for all further improvements yielding right results. Secondly, a freer market presupposes prudential, proactive and effective regulation to avoid irregularities and manipulations as well as crisis situations. In fact, a proactive regulation relies more on an ongoing monitoring to prevent these occurrences.

Table 10.1 Structure of interest rates (percent per annum)

	Call money	G Sec 1 yr	Deposit Rate 3 yrs	Prime lending rate
1990–91	15.85		9	15
1991–92	19.57		12	19
1992–93	14.42		11	18
1993–94	6.99		10	16
1994–95	9.4		11	15
1995–96	17.73		12	17.5
1996–97	7.84	13.21	11	16.2
1997–98	8.69	9.86	10.5	13.3
1998–99	7.83	8.67	9	13.5
1999–2000	8.87	10.47	8.5	15
2000–01	9.15	9.38	8.5	14
2001–02	7.31	8.85	8	11.5
2002–03	5.5	6.32	6.3	11
2003–04	4.4	5.16	6.25	11
2004–05	4.8	5.61	6.25	10.5
2005–06	6.25	6.3	6.25	10.5
2006–07	7.2	7.44	9.5	11.5–14.5

Source: Economic Survey, Government of India.

During the 1990s, financial liberalization in India witnessed deregulation of the market along with its infrastructural improvement, and more prudential and healthy regulation. The ceiling on debenture interest rates was removed in 1992. This was also followed by the RBI gradually freeing deposit interest rates and lending rates so that by 1996 all interest rates in the banking sector and capital markets were free from any control. The pressure on short-term funds was also gradually reduced by the RBI lowering the CRR and SLR.

The behavior of financial markets under liberalization can be divided into two phases. The phase of rising interest rates from 1990 to 1996 and phase of declining interest rates thereafter (see Table 10.1). Both these phases were in harmony with the liberalization in other sectors of the economy, responses of the economy, and changing global economic and financial environment. The success of financial liberalization in India is again attributable to the ideology of Gradualism, the step-by-step approach, and right sequencing, which has avoided sharper jerks in policies and resultant dislocations, hardships and trauma across the financial sector and economy.

In the second phase of reform, the major thrust in the policy came in the Budget of Dr Manmohan Singh in 1991. It encompassed the industrial sector, foreign trade, fiscal policy, foreign exchange and the capital market. The major policy changes on the fiscal front, which provided great stimulus to the financial sector and capital market, were as follows.

1 The limit on foreign equity holding in priority industries was raised from 40 percent to 51 percent.
2 Income tax slabs were reduced from four to three with rates of tax 20 percent, 30 percent and 40 percent.
3 Long-term capital gains tax carried a flat tax rate of 20 percent and capital gains were adjusted with cost inflation index.
4 Wealth tax was abolished on financial assets such as shares, securities, bonds, and deposits.

The measures created a vibrant environment for the growth of the financial system, capital market and robust investment climate.

Banking reforms

The Indian financial system is one of the most vibrant sectors of the economy, contributing to the economy's high growth and balanced development. The rising savings rate, predominance of the household sector in the total savings and the fast development of the banking network and outlets have brought a rapid and sustained development of the financial system in the country. Bank deposits witnessed annual growth rate of 17 percent in the 1990s. In the new millennium, the growth was 15 percent but rose again to 18.1 percent in 2005–2006. The share of bank deposits in GNP, which was 29 percent in 1980–81, went up to 39 percent in 1990–91, and in the post-reform era to 40 percent in 1995–96, to 50 percent in 2002–2003 and to 86 percent in 2005–2006. All these indicators are a pointer to the growing financial deepening of the Indian economy and its progress and graduation into a mature financial system. The saving rate has gone up from 18.9 percent in 1980–81 to 23.1 percent in 1990–91, to 24 percent in 2001–2002 and to a record 28.1 percent in 2005–2006. The share of household sector in total national savings rose from 73 percent in 1980–81 to 83 percent in 1990–91, further to 93 percent in 2001–2002 and was 80 percent in 2005–2006. The growing influence of household savings on the savings flow in the country has been a factor adding strength, resiliency and vibrancy to the Indian financial system.

The banking system until 1991 was beset with administered interest rates, high interest rates, high CRR and SLR, higher NPAs, low capital adequacy and inadequate competition. Banking reforms were speeded up in the 1990s with a number of steps aimed to impart greater efficiency and strength to the banking system.

1 High SLR and CRR used to pre-empt a large portion of lendable resources of banks affecting their profitability. The statutory Liquidity ratio (SLR) on incremental demand and time deposits was gradually lowered from a high of 38.5 percent in 1991–92 to 25 percent in 1995–96. The incremental Cash Reserve Ratio (CRR) was abolished in 1992 and the average CRR lowered from 15 percent in 1992 to 8 percent in 2000 and further to 4.5 percent. These

measures left commercial banks with adequate liquidity for commercial credit at higher interest rates. It also helped banks improve their earnings base and increase their profitability.

2   Since 1992–93, banks were free to decide interest rates on deposits and lending. Free interest rates increased competition in the banking sector and lowered the spread between deposit and lending rates. Lower spread reflects a greater efficiency of the banking system, helping both depositors and lenders with better and competitive interest rates.

3   The public sector banks dominated and, therefore, virtually controlled the Indian banking system. In order to impart competition in the banking system and promote its broad-based development it was proposed to open up the banking sector to the private sector. Licenses were given to ten private sector banks to introduce greater competition and efficiency in the banking industry. New private sector banks accounted for 15 percent of total assets of all scheduled banks in 2006. The share of all private sector and foreign banks in the commercial banking system rose to 28 percent.

4   The bank rate was lowered gradually from 11 percent in 1991 to 7 percent in 2000 and later to 6 percent. The cost of credit was substantially reduced in the second half of the 1990s.

5   In addition to the recapitalization of the public sector banks through budgetary support, the banks were also permitted to make public issue to enhance their equity capital and list their shares on the stock market.

6   There was substantial improvement in the capital adequacy and NPAs of the commercial banking system. The capital adequacy of banks on the risk weighted basis improved to 12.3 percent of total assets in 2006 and the gross NPAs reduced 1.9 percent total assets.

7   The Indian commercial banking system remains geared and poised to comply with the Basel II norms.

Yield curve transformation

One of the most significant achievements of financial reform has been the correction of a falling yield curve in the Indian market into a rising one. The fundamental tenet of finance, the rising yield curve, indicating a premium for time in the use of funds or time value of money, was not fulfilled in the Indian capital market. The administered interest rate and its regulation, low rates of interest on Government securities, high SLR requirements forcing banks to hold Government securities despite low returns, and the basic liquidity gap both in the short term as well as long term markets – all worked in giving a downward sloping yield curve. The fundamental logic of the policy behind this was that since the economy was short of resources and needed growth through a high investment rate, long term interest rates needed to be kept lower to enable the Government and corporate sector to borrow at a lower rate and achieve a higher investment rate. Although a laudable objective, the policy does create distortions in the financial markets, financial flows, investment pattern and also productivity and

Table 10.2 Yield rates of Government of India securities (percent per annum)

Maturity in years	1996–97	1997–98	1998–99	1999–2000	2000–2001	2001–2002	2002–2003	2003–2004	2004–2005	2005–2006	2006–2007
1	13.21	9.86	8.67	10.47	9.38	8.85	6.32	5.16	6.19	6.59	7.44
2	13.36	10.29	9.86	10.81	9.43	8.92	6.33	5.15	6.18	6.59	7.46
3	13.51	11.16	10.47	10.99	9.58	9.15	6.49	5.54	6.09	6.89	7.46
4	13.65	11.65	10.8	11.17	9.74	9.29	6.57	5.68	6.54	7.11	7.48
5	13.79	12.14	11.06	11.31	9.83	9.4	6.73	5.9	6.09	6.51	7.5
6	13.91	12.36	11.43	11.44	9.97	9.6	6.89	5.75	6.57	7.06	7.52
7	14.03	12.55	11.55	11.61	10.05	9.72	7.09	5.87	6.71	7.22	7.55
8	14.13	12.66	11.68	11.79	10.17	9.85	7.3	5.97	6.87	7.22	7.57
9	14.01	12.76	11.8	11.84	10.29	9.99	7.37	6.07	6.63	7.25	7.59
10		12.87		11.89	10.37	10.08	7.39	5.71	6.4	7.26	7.61
11				11.97	10.48	10.18	7.45	6.05	6.44	7.34	7.61
12				12.05	10.53	10.49	7.63	6.04	6.68	7.38	7.62
13				12.12	10.58	10.6	7.71	6.06	6.78	7.36	7.62
14				12.2	10.61	10.48	7.78	6.11	6.78	7.46	7.63
15					10.65	10.56	7.47	6.09	6.7	7.41	7.64
16					10.68	10.52	7.81	6.06	6.52	7.36	7.65
17					10.69	10.41	7.97	6.16	7.25	7.54	7.66
18					10.7	10.51	7.92	6.17	6.94	7.49	7.67
19					10.71	10.6	7.87	6.16	6.97	7.49	7.68

Source: Economic Survey, Government of India.

efficiency of capital. A downward sloping yield curve, which prevailed in the Indian market until 1995, turned positive in 1996 (see Table 10.2).

The positive yield curve also coincided with the declining interest rate phase, which began in 1996. Yet another change in the yield curve, especially for the Government securities, has been that the yield curve was getting flatter than earlier, indicating a shorter spread between the securities of short and long maturities. The spread between the yield on 1-year and 10-year Government paper, which was 2.8 percent (10.6 percent and 13.4 percent) in 1996–97 narrowed to a mere 0.36 percent (5.62 percent and 6.08 percent) in 2002–2003 and further to 0.17 percent (7.44 percent and 7.61 percent) in 2006–2007. The spread between the risk-free rate of interest on Government securities and riskier private security also came down due to better availability of finance, which was in dearth earlier. Some top AAA corporates were able to borrow long term in the market at rates very close to the rates on Government paper.

The migration from the high interest rate regime to the low interest rate one has been very gradual and smooth, without causing any disruption in the financial system. This soft landing of the financial system has been truly remarkable. The interest rate on 10-year Government securities, which was 14 percent in 1996, halved to 7 percent in 2003 and then decreased to 5.4 percent in 2004.

The overall balance of payments position has also played a crucial role in the transformation in the Indian financial system. The perpetual liquidity crunch, which the system suffered from for so long, became history. Ever since 1996, India's balance of payments has been in a sizeable and increasing surplus. The accretion in the forex reserves every year since 1996–97, has been of the order of a low of $3.8 billion in 1998–99 and a high of $11.8 billion in 2001–2002. Capital account surplus from direct as well as portfolio investments has been the main contributory to this high liquidity flow from abroad. The growing current account surplus emanating from buoyant service exports of software and the declining trade deficit during 1998–2002 further added to the accretion in forex reserves, which has kept the liquidity situation easier. The continuation of a comfortable balance of payments in coming years is unlikely to exert any pressure on liquidity and hence on interest rates.

The banking sector has been the centre of transformation following the financial reforms. Increasing competition, deregulation of interest rates, lower CRR and SLR and the infusion of the latest technology have revitalized the banking sector. The higher efficiency of the sector can be seen from the declining spreads between lending and deposit rates, better, faster and cost efficient customer service, and higher employee productivity. Higher capital adequacy, lower and declining NPAs, better financial results and profitability of banks have given a boost to the valuation of shares in the stock markets.

Capital markets reform

The Indian stock market has emerged as one of the largest in the world, next only to the New York Stock Exchange considering the number of scrips listed, deals transacted and the size of retail investor participation in the market. It is also one of the oldest stock exchanges, and has grown and adapted with time. Liberalization of the financial system also necessitates participation of foreign investors in the stock market. In 1994, with the entry of FII, the Indian stock market was partially integrated into the global capital market. The stock market has witnessed buoyant growth during the 1990s after economic liberalization. Although the market did show weakness during intermittent periods, due to the bearish influence following the exuberance, the long-term trend in the market has been bullish and shows higher returns on risk capital compared with the returns on traditional and less risky financial assets. The Sensex, which was 1100 in 1990, touched 6000 in January 2004, giving an annual return of 32 percent. The market capitalization has gone up from Rs.110,000 crores to Rs.1,000,000 crores in 2004, and as a percentage of GNP from 22 percent to 44 percent during the same period.

The capital market plays a critical role in the process of financial reforms and its success. A number of steps were taken to reform the capital market. At the broad policy level, a number of changes were made to remove several restrictions in the operation of the capital market. They relate to the pricing of equity and debt issues, and foreign institutional investor participation in the capital market. They were the epoch making steps in the development of the capital market.

1   One of the major liberalization measures in the capital market was the abolition of the office of Controller of Capital Issues in 1991. With the introduction of market pricing of equities, companies were free to approach the capital market with the clearance of offer documents by the Securities Exchange Board of India (SEBI).
2   The ceiling on interest rates on debentures of Indian companies was removed and rates were left to the market forces.
3   Foreign Institutional Investors (FIIs) were allowed to invest in the capital market in 1994 on registration with SEBI. The initial limit for equity holdings in the Indian corporates by FIIs, which was 24 percent, was raised to 40 percent.

Prerequisites of an efficient market

Financial liberalization and openness is supposed to bring large foreign capital inflows into the economy. Deregulation also involves a greater play of market forces. Hence, an important prerequisite of successful financial liberalization is ensuring the elimination of market imperfections and the promotion of a healthy and proactive institutional framework of supervision. It also presupposes accounting and audit standards and practices comparable to international standards, transparency in disclosure of information and financial reporting, and healthy corporate governance.

The market imperfections may arise out of the very nature of the markets. It may be narrow with a small and limited number of players and dominated by a few large players. Encouraging the markets to develop a broader base with greater depth where a large number of players operate and no single player or group of players has any dominance, is the primary prerequisite of an efficient market. Apart from this technical nature of the market structure, the market imperfections may arise due to market functions and practices, infrastructure, and regulatory and governance procedures.

The market trading, settlement and payments systems needed to match international standards in the major markets, such as New York, London, Hong Kong, and Tokyo. In many emerging markets, this was the most primary requirement of reform based on the market system and mechanism. A faulty market mechanism can not only hinder the smoother progress of reforms but also cause misallocation of resources out of line with that occurring under a perfect market system and mechanism. The adoption of state-of-the-art hardware and software technology for markets has to ensure the efficiency of the market mechanism and functioning. Screen-based trading, dematerialization of securities, uniform trading and settlement cycles and procedures have homogenized the market in all the emerging economies. There have also to be improvements in regulatory and governance standards. These improvements cannot be expected over a short period, and weaknesses that generate market crises are the warning signals for action towards changes involving a greater streamlining of the control system, which has to be neither too rigid, stifling innovation and growth, nor too open, leaving loose ends ripe for market abuse or excesses.

As has been the experience for centuries in different countries, different systems and different environments, markets move in cycles, and the testing time for the market behavior is the transition from one cycle to another. The systemic, infrastructural, and regulatory weaknesses reveal themselves during the critical cyclical turns. Crisis or collapse necessitates action towards systemic and regulatory improvements.

In addition to the exchange rate rigidity of the pegged system, an important aspect, which many observers and researchers believe to have contributed to the Asian Crisis, is the financial vulnerability caused by the weak financial and corporate sector institutions.

> Growing vulnerability was the result of private sector decisions rather than public sector deficits. These private sector activities took place, however, in the context of government policies that did not do enough to discourage excessive risk taking, while providing too little regulatory control and insufficient transparency to allow markets to recognize and correct these problems. At the root of the problem were weak and poorly supervised financial sectors against the backdrop of large capital inflows. Equally, inadequate corporate governance and lack of transparency masked the poor quality and riskiness of investments. In addition, although macro-economic policies were generally sound, pegged exchange rates regimes and implicit guarantees tilted incentives towards excessive short term borrowings.[72]

The role of information needs to be emphasized more in the functioning, perfection and efficiency of a market. A market encompasses turnover, players, participants but also information and its quality. In increasingly information-based economies globally, the influence of information in the market has greatly compounded and become critical in price formation and movements.

Stock market reform

Routing investments through a capital market presupposes the efficient functioning of the capital market. In the latter half of 1990s, a number of measures have been taken to improve the infrastructure and efficiency of the stock markets in India.

1 The National Stock Exchange (NSE), formed in 1995, provided electronic trading in equity shares across the country. The screen-based computerized trading replaced the physical trading on the floor of the market. The operations of the NSE are spread over 353 cities all over India. The NSE developed a truly national electronic market and enabled investors throughout the country to participate in stock market investment. The Bombay Stock Exchange (BSE) also followed suit and adopted electronic trading systems. Both these exchanges, NSE and BSE, carry a daily turnover of Rs.10,000 crores and Rs.5000 crores respectively in 2007 and are ranked third and fifth in the world by the number of transactions.

2 To initiate and promote paperless trading it was necessary to have demateri-alization of shares and securities. Paper trading was a major handicap against the growth in trading volume and turnover. It hampered quick settlement and payments and prevented the introduction of shorter trading, settlement and payments cycles. Settlement cycles could not be lowered from T+15 due to paper load and bad delivery volumes. Bad deliveries were in large numbers and affected investor confidence and interest. The National Securities Depository Ltd (NSDL) was formed in 1997 in order to provide the services of dematerialization shares and securities, their custody and electronic transfers. NSDL enabled trading in demat shares. The majority of companies have now demated their shares and all transactions in the stock market are in demat shares. There are more than 400 Depository Participants, comprising banks, broking firms and other institutions whose braches are spread all over the country, providing demat service to investors. This has enabled swift transfers and payments and promoted participation of investors from all regions into trading in the national stock market. The volume jump in stock market turnover is reflective of this major transformation in share holding and transfer mechanism.

3 The switchover to demat trading has also permitted reducing the settlement period with a shorter cycle. The settlement period has been reduced from the earlier T+7 to T+2 and finally to T+1.

4 Electronic trading has enabled instant information on bid and offer prices of shares at any trading terminal across the country. This has helped in

improving the breadth as well as depth of the market, which has become truly national and broader based.

5 Due to the quick and widespread display of information on market quotes on the screen, the trading has become more transparent and the spread between bid and offer prices has narrowed considerably compared to the earlier practice of physical trading.

6 Dematerialization of shares has eliminated bad deliveries arising out of faulty transfers. The electronic transfer of dematerialized shares has also enabled quicker settlements and larger turnover.

7 The reduction of spreads in bid and offer prices, lower brokerage rates and demat transfers have considerably lowered the transaction cost for investors.

8 The emergence of a broader market with higher turnover providing the electronic trading, demat holdings and transfers, and shorter settlement period has also lowered the impact cost of trading in the market.

9 Infrastructural improvements have considerably improved the efficiency of the stock market, which is now on a par with any other international market.

10 With the introduction of stock and index futures and options, the futures and derivatives markets have shown rapid growth in turnover reflecting broad basing and the depth of the market.

The movement of the Bombay Stock Exchange Sensex and Dow Jones Industrial average over the last 15 years from 1991 to 2006 is shown in Table 10.3. Both the US and Indian stock markets have shown a distinctly bullish long-term

Table 10.3 Dow Jones industrial average and BSE Sensex

	Dow Jones		Sensex	
	(year end)	*% change*		*% of change*
1991	3168		1167	
1992	3301	1.33	4285	31.18
1993	3754	4.53	2280	−20.05
1994	3834	0.8	3778	14.98
1995	5117	12.83	3260	−5.18
1996	6448	13.31	3366	1.06
1997	7908	14.6	3360	−0.06
1998	9181	12.73	3892	5.32
1999	11,501	23.2	5001	11.09
2000	10,790	−7.11	3972	−10.29
2001	10,022	−7.68	3262	−7.1
2002	8348	−16.74	3377	1.15
2003	10,454	21.06	5839	24.62
2004	10,783	3.29	6602	7.63
2005	10,717	−0.66	9397	27.95
2006	12,459	17.42	13,786	43.89

Source: Dow Jones; Bombay Stock Exchange.

trend over 15 years. The compound annual rate of growth for Dow Jones works out to be 9.6 percent, compared with 17.9 percent for Sensex. The market capitalization of Indian equities has moved to $1 trillion, equal to India's annual GDP.

The role of foreign institutional investors

In addition to interest rate deregulation and banking reform, the opening up of the financial sector involved the gradual entry of foreign portfolio investment into the capital market. The Indian capital market needed to be gradually integrated into the global capital market. Except for Non-Resident Indians (NRIs), the Indian stock market did not give access to foreign investors. In 1994, the first step was taken by permitting Foreign Institutional Investors (FIIs) to invest up to 24 percent of equity of Indian corporates. This limit was later raised to 49 percent. However, the companies need to get the approval of shareholders in the general body to raise this limit to 49 percent. The Indian stock market offered lucrative returns on equity investments in international comparison. Low PE ratios of the Indian equities also made them attractive. Higher economic growth, large potential for absorption of growth in industrial investment and attractive returns on direct investment offered enormous prospects for sustained growth in the market capitalization of equities in India. The entry of Foreign Institutional Investors was imperative to meet the resource gap in a rapidly growing capital market in India.

The opening up of the equity window provided a number of advantages.

1   Entry of large professional institutional investors helped in improving the turnover in the stock market. This brought about a broader based development of the market.
2   The inflow of forex improved the foreign exchange resources of the country. FII investment increased from $3.5 billion in 1995–96 to $7.6 billion in 2003–2004 and a record $10.3 billion in 2004–2005 and $10 billion in 2006–2007. The outstanding FII investment at cost crossing of $50 billion has been a healthy addition to forex reserves. Although there may be ups and downs in FFI investments, looking to the long-term prospect for growth of the corporate sector in India, FII investment is likely to show a sustained rise in the future and cause a net accretion to the forex reserves.
3   The presence of equity ownership by foreign professional investment managers brought pressure on the corporates to be globally more efficient, competitive, and transparent in their operations and ensure good corporate governance.
4   Greater demand for several capital market related financial and other services, such as broking, merchant and investment banking, depository, and research promoted their growth.
5   Proportionate increase in equity values and higher trading caused a sharp growth in the market capitalization and turnover.
6   The market for primary issues of equities received a boost due to improvement in valuation of listed stocks. This contributed to higher corporate

investment and equity funding of several industrial projects, which traditionally looked to debt as a means of project finance.

7   Indian corporates, which were debt oriented during the 1980s, became
    equity oriented in the 1990s in financing their expansion. As a result of
    higher equity issues by the Indian corporates during the 1990s the debt-
    equity ratio of Indian corporates declined sharply.

8   Higher equity issues and rising market capitalization increased allocation of
    equity investment in the portfolio of financial asset holdings of households.
    Better returns on equity also improved returns to household investors.

9   The spread of equity cult also spurred the growth of mutual funds, which
    further reinforced broad-based trading and growth in the equity markets.

FIIs have now been a feature of the Indian capital market, with the outstanding
investment at cost crossing the $50 billion mark and annual investment of
around $10 billion in the last few years. They are not only going to be an integ-
ral part of the market but also a critical factor in the investment climate and
growth in the country. Growing Indian markets and vibrant corporate sector
growth in India offers a huge opportunity to foreign investors to capture value in
Indian equities in a wide range of industries. The global equity resources have to
flow to the Indian market to find its equilibrium in India's equity stocks, now
valued at over $1 trillion, equal to its annual GDP.

FII investment – boon or curse

The portfolio investment in the emerging markets has been subject to criticism
due to the dominance of the hedge funds and short term nature of their investment, looking only for opportunities for quick profit. The large FII inflows and
outflows are also criticized for creating boom–bust situations in the emerging
markets. We have seen a number of positives which FII investments have
achieved in India and which are also evident in other emerging markets.
Although both the possibilities of volatility of FII investments and their short-
term nature creating destabilization in the market cannot be ruled out, these
situations are likely to arise in the initial stages of the development of the
emerging markets. As the integration of the global capital market under globalization progresses faster, more and more resources are bound to flow to
the fundamentally strong and lucrative emerging markets. The emerging
markets with strong economic fundamentals, sustainable BoP position, flexible
exchange rate regime, buoyant investment environment, healthy corporate
performance and earnings growth are bound to attract higher volumes of portfolio investment. Although hedge funds are a part of the FIIs, investments by
mutual fund, pension funds and insurance companies tend to be equally large to
provide longer term investment tenure for the overall FII investment profile.
The FII investments also broad base the development of the stock and capital
markets in the emerging economies to provide a cushion to the fluctuations
arising out of capital flights. Nevertheless, as the global money, capital, forex

and stock markets are getting increasingly interlinked, it is unlikely that the ripples in the large developed markets would not reach the shores of the emerging market. In a globalized economy all the countries have to follow the rules of the global market and pursue policies that show positive trends. In such a competitive market-driven global economy, countries are competing in managing their economies to produce a sustainable growth climate. The wrong policies would be punished by the global economy in terms of its implications on the BoP by the foreign investors as well as traders. Hence, the FII investment also brings a strong pressure for sound economic management. More important is the pressure for sound management of the BoP and flexible exchange rate policies. All the crises that may have different fundamental underlying causes first erupt in the forex markets. This is amply demonstrated by the crises of last one and half decades. In a globalized world, BoP and exchange rate management assumes high importance to avert a crisis. We shall discuss the proactive exchange rate management and alarm system to be devised for a crisis-free environment in Chapter 13.

What rules can the emerging market economies follow to bring a positive economic contribution from the FII investments and avert their deleterious effects. The experience of India has been very positive and encouraging in this regard. India allowed the gradual opening of FII investment through registrations, screening and close monitoring. It has so far not allowed pure hedge funds to invest, although it may do soon after devising an appropriate guideline. What could be the guidelines for opening the capital markets for the emerging market economies? The Indian experience offers sound criteria.

1　The emerging markets should open the capital market to FII gradually after scrutinizing their credentials.
2　It essential to see that the domestic money, financial markets are free, competitive, broadbased and operate with the latest infrastructure. The market reforms need to precede the FII inflows.
3　Many small markets need to be careful in opening up gradually so that FII flows do not inundate the market and cause overheating.
4　The pure hedge funds can be kept out of the market until the market is fairly broadbased to handle the hot money movements of FIIs.
5　It has to pursue sustainable BoP management and proactive exchange rate policies to forestall any currency crisis. Apart from several fundamental causes, the major trigger for the Asian Crisis was the overvalued exchange rate arising from passive and not proactive exchange rate policy and management.

FDI versus FII

Keynes regarded capital investment as one of the most critical inputs in the growth momentum of a economy. Coupled with innovation, investment can further accelerate the pace of an economy's growth. The Keynesians, therefore, give greater importance to foreign direct investment (FDI) as a major driver to the recipient country's development. Foreign direct investment builds capital asset and starts the output and income generating cycle and thereby brings multiple increases in income, output and employment. It directly enhances the productive capacity of the economy. Foreign direct investment is also accompanied by technological support and upgradation and management inputs. The effect of all these is to improve the productivity and efficiency in the concerned industry and also generally. It is long-term investment and is not repatriable unless the stake is sold to the domestic investor. It has positive impact on the BoP and it draws on the BoP only after a lag when the dividends are paid.

In contrast to FDI, foreign institutional investment (FII) is a portfolio investment and unless it is made in new issues of equity, it does not create new investment but is acquired on the stock market from the existing stocks of equity or debt securities. Because of the portfolio nature of its investment, it can be withdrawn any time, nullifying the initial benefit to the BoP. Nevertheless, it has a lagged effect in promoting investment. The FII demand for equity has a bullish impact on the stock market of the recipient country, thereby encouraging corporates and entrepreneurs to raise more fresh equity capital for investment. This lagged effect on real investment is much stronger as it revitalizes the investment climate. In fact FDI and FII can complement each other in giving a strong push to the county's investment rate. Such a complementarity was archived in India in 2006–2007 when FDI rose sharply to $15 billion, while the FII was $10 billion.

Over the last few years there has been considerable opening up of foreign direct investment, with the cap raised in several sectors. The sectoral cap for FDI in Telecoms has been raised to 74 percent. The FDI and FII limit in Private Sector Banks has been increased to 74 percent. Non-banking Finance Companies have been allowed 100 percent FDI. Several other sectors where 100 percent FDI is permitted are, Development of Integrated Townships, Tea Plantations, Telecom Infrastructure, Petroleum Exploration, Refining and Marketing, Power, Drugs and Pharmaceuticals, Roads and Highways, Hotels and Tourism Services, Mining of Coal and Lignite, Gold, Silver and Precious Stones, Films, Mass Transit Systems, and Special Economic Zones (SEZs). Airports face a 74 percent cap. However, the cap on insurance continues to be at 26 percent. The other sectors in which FDI is permitted up to 49 percent are Domestic Airlines and TV Channel Broadcasting. With FDI being permitted in a broad range of industries and services, and especially the SEZs, the effect on the inflow is now visible. It is likely to cause a significant jump in the next few years from the figure of $15 billion in 2006–2007. That sets India on a 10 percent+ sustainable growth path.

Globalization has enabled India to build a vibrant and efficient financial system. Finance or capital is no longer in short supply for investment and capital formation. Lower interest rates and adequate availability finance, even for the household sector, which was, until liberalization, denied finance, shows the systemic development and change in the banking and financial structure and its approach. Retail finance for housing and education has emerged as a significant and new wealth creator in the economy. Better infrastructure, prudent and proactive regulation, and greater transparency have improved the efficiency of the financial system. Globalization has galvanized the Indian financial sector to play the role of an important catalyst for faster growth and development.

11 Post-reform BoP and rupee exchange rate

Record forex reserves build up

The Goddess of Wealth, Lakshmi, has been smiling on the Reserve Bank of India with the forex reserves crossing the $200 billion mark in April 2007, giving a coveted position that only a few countries in the world hold. A bumper agricultural harvest, revival of industrial growth, sustained export growth, a pick-up in bank credit expansion, were all signs of the booming phase of the economy. With inflation under control and interest rates still stable at lower levels, the outlook for the rise in industrial and infrastructure investment remained optimistic.

In contrast to the policy of gradualism in economic reforms and liberalization in India, the Asian neighbors were on the path of faster and quicker reforms, and had to face hiccups in their economies with temporary disruptions and agony. The Indian reform process has been smooth and steady, and is paying rich dividends. A drastic cut in import duties in 1997 did affect Indian industries adversely. Nevertheless, it set in process the restructuring, modernization, optimization, cost rationalization and qualitative excellence, which the Indian industries needed badly. As a result, we find Indian industry today much more vibrant and able not only to compete with imports but also capture overseas markets. This is true of both private as well as public sector enterprises. The Indian corporate sector is revitalized and is now becoming globally competitive. The weak units have gone under but the adaptive ones have grown stronger and bigger.

The corporate success stories are not isolated in a few sectors but are broad based in a wide cross-section of industries – be it the steel, metals, textiles, apparels, engineering, forging, two wheelers, cars, auto-ancillaries, telecoms, power, airlines, construction and, not to forget, software in which India has tremendous comparative advantage in cost and quality. Indian corporates from these sectors have significantly captured the export markets over the last few years. Indian industrial and corporate rejuvenation under reforms and liberalization has been truly remarkable.

The forex bounty again raised the issue of full convertibility of the rupee. India's approach of gradual capital account opening and its adroit exchange rate management has earned kudos even from the World Bank and IMF, which are now citing the Indian example as the role model for other developing nations. While, the Asian, Russian and Latin American experiences have left a bitter taste and memories, Indian policy has stood the test of time, and international policy makers now acclaim India's liberalization for emulation by others.

Liberalization has been a success story in India's balance of payments and forex fronts. In fact, the step-by-step approach and gradualism, and not a one-time fully fledged opening up of the economy, has been the key element of this success. Both current account and capital account have shown unprecedented flexibility in responding to the changes covering financial and forex liberalization, changing global economic conditions and trends, and India's domestic investment and growth management. The response has been good both within the economy as well as without. The global community and NRIs have also shown the agility and zeal in quickly reacting to the liberalization measures. All this is finally visible in the balance of payments and forex reserves numbers.

Both the exchange rate policy and rupee convertibility measures have acted in unison to bring about a healthy and positive impact on the balance of payments and forex reserves position. Coinciding with this has been the liberalization on the foreign trade front. With the removal of QRs on all imports and substantial scaling down of import tariffs, the average rate of customs duty on imports, which was 47 percent in 1990–91 came down to 24 percent in 2001–2002. The peak customs duty rate came down progressively from 150 percent in 1991 to 30 percent in 2002 and was further reduced to 12.5 percent in the Budget proposal for 2007–2008. Asian countries are to reduce the duty rate to 0 percent from 5 percent in next four years. The Average rate in developed countries is 3.8 percent.

The removal of quotas and the lowering of tariffs has not shown any major increase in imports but has helped the economy in many ways:

> Actual import of 300 sensitive items, monitored by the Inter Ministerial Group set up in the wake of removal of QRs on balance of payments basis revealed growth in dollar rates to only 2.9 percent in 2001–2002, the growth being almost entirely accounted for higher import of cotton.[73]

The domestic competitors of imports have reduced their prices. This has helped the consumers and has been one of the pertinent factors in keeping the rate of inflation low, ever since liberalization got its momentum in the mid-1990s. The domestic industry has also faced the pressure of competition and has vigorously followed its rationalization, restructuring, and modernization. These measures have helped the industry in becoming more cost effective, competitive, and efficient and more quality conscious. Not only have some industrial units achieved a global scale, but many have been in the international markets successfully facing tough competition. The industrial economy of India is being revitalized and rejuvenated in achieving more efficient utilization of resources.

The productivity levels have shown a drastic rise in the industry. The consumers have benefited with lower prices and better quality products and services.

What is significant to note is that this change has been brought about through a lower landed cost of imports without any substantial increase in the actual volume of imports. Hence, there has not been any significant forex outage following one of the most pervasive changes of the import tariff regime, influencing the domestic industry in the consumer goods, capital equipments, intermediates as well as services sectors, which had hitherto remained cozy under the protective umbrella of import tariffs and quotas for nearly four and half decades.

Structural change in India's BoP

Since 1990, when India faced one of the worst crises in its balance of payments history with reserves plummeting to a mere $2 billion, giving import cover of less than one month's imports, economic reforms have gradually lifted the Indian economy into the higher growth orbit. Consolidating from its crisis by the mid 1990s, it has grown steadily, building its balance of payments strength. When, in 1998, the Asian economies were gripped in the vortex of the forex crisis and were spreading it to their neighboring economies, India could repulse the Asian contagion effect and pilot the rupee in the forex market in a safe and stable zone. After the Asian crisis, India's balance of payments went from strength to strength, and its forex policy has won global commendation. India has now become a role model of reform among the emerging markets and more so in respect of its financial reform and policy on convertibility. With the opening up of the external sector of the economy, the structure of India's balance of payments has undergone a favorable structural change.

Strengthening of the current account

1   The current account of India's BoP has shown a sharp change and growth following the liberalization of foreign trade and investments. The share of imports and exports in GDP went up from 16 percent in 1990–91 to 35 percent in 2005–2006. The invisible account, representing the transactions in the services sector, factor receipts and payments and private transfers, which was showing a small negative balance in 1990–91 turned into a large surplus of 5 percent of GDP in 2005–2006. The broad basing of the current account has been one of the key features in strengthening India's BoP. Unlike many countries where capital account transactions have grown substantially compared with trade transactions after liberalization, India has shown healthy growth in current account transactions. The current account transactions have immediate and direct influence on the GNP, while capital movements bring indirect as well as lagged impact on GNP.

2   Exports have shown a buoyant growth from $18 billion in 1990–91 to $105 billion in 2005–2006, a compound annual growth of 12.3 percent. The share of exports in GNP also more than doubled from 6.6 percent to 14.3 percent.

The reforms have given a boost to India's manufactured goods in the world market. They accounted for 77 percent of exports in 2004–2005 compared with 73 percent in 1990–91 when reforms began. Reforms have, therefore, worked on enlarging the foreign trade segment of the economy. It is a clear signal of the Indian economy's greater participation and integration with the global economy, deriving greater national benefits from the gains in foreign trade.

3 Despite substantial scaling down of import duty rates consistently throughout the 1990s and also the scrapping of all import quotas, India's imports have not grown at a very fast rate. Hence, trade deficit as a percentage of GNP reduced to 2.9 percent by the end of the 1990s. A trade deficit of $9.4 billion (3.3 percent of GNP) in 1990–91 rose consistently to a high of $17.8 billion (4.4 percent of GNP) in 1999–2000 before falling to $12.7 billion (2.9 percent of GNP) in 2001–2002. It rose sharply to $51.8 billion in 2005–2006 (7 percent of GNP) primarily due to rising crude oil prices and higher imports on account of higher economic growth.

4 The oil import bill, which was 25 percent of total imports in 1990–91, had come down to 15.1 percent in 1998–99 owing to lower oil prices. A hike in oil prices brought the oil bill to 30 percent of total imports in 2005–2006. Despite the hike in oil prices, India has been able to curtail growth in its oil consumption and marginalize the pressure of the impact of an oil price hike on its overall balance of payments strength and growth momentum of the economy.

5 The invisible receipts have made a significant contribution to BoP. The software exports and inward remittances have been the major sources of surplus in the services sector in India and take care of the trade deficit. Inward remittances from migrant workers or non-residents working overseas have been a critical contributor to the BoP in many emerging market economies. In a labor surplus and skill-rich economy like India, inward remittances have traditionally been an important source of forex earnings. Over the last decade or so, there has been sustained growth in remittances contributing to BoP, and GNP and savings growth. Globalization has promoted the growth rate of the global economy and raised the demand for labor and skill rich personnel in several developed and oil exporting economies. Globalization has improved the labor mobility with the relaxation of visa and immigration restrictions in several countries. The inward remittances, which were a mere $2 billion in 1990–91 multiplied more than sixfold in a decade to reach $12.9 billion by 2000–2001 and further doubled to $24 billion in 2005–2006 surpassing China at $22.4 billion and Mexico at $21.7 billion. Continuing double-digit annual growth in inward remittances has given a great cushion to the current account in the face of pressure on the trade balance caused by the rising crude oil prices. India's inward remittances account for 3.5 percent of its GDP and are one of the main factors behind the rise in savings rate.[74]

6 One of the biggest success stories in India's technology, economy and BoP fronts has been the leapfrogging growth of the IT (Information Technology)

Table 11.1 India's imports ($ million)

	1990–91	1995–96	1998–99	2000–2001	2001–2002	2002–2003	2003–2004	2004–2005	2005–2006
Cereals	102	24	228	20	18	20	19	26	36
Petroleum oil	6028	7526	6398	15,650	14,000	15,650	20,569	29,844	43,963
Fertilizers	984	1683	1010	664	621	664	635	1135	1991
Total	24,075	36,678	42,389	50,536	51,413	59,639	69,444	109,173	149,166
Oil imports as a percentage of total	25.00	20.50	15.10%	31.00	27.20	26.20	29.60	27.30	30.00
Oil imports as a percentage of GNP	2.14	2.37	1.70	3.76	3.20	2.50	3.10	4.60	6.00

Source: Economic Survey, Government of India.

Note
The figures of imports given here are from DGCI&S and are from physical movement basis, and would not match with import figures of RBI given in other Tables which are on payments basis.

Table 11.2 India's balance of payments ($ billion)

	1990–91	1994–95	1996–97	1998–99	2000–2001	2001–2002	2002–2003	2003–2004	2004–2005	2005–2006
Imports	27.9	35.9	48.9	47.5	59.3	57.6	64.5	80	118.8	157
Exports	18.5	26.9	34.1	34.3	44.8	45	53.8	63.4	82.2	105.2
Trade balance	–9.5	–9.1	–14.8	–13.2	–14.4	–12.7	–10.7	–16.6	–36.6	–51.8
Invisible receipts	7.5	15.6	21.4	25.8	34.5	35.6	41.9	53.5	71.9	92.3
Invisibles (net)	–0.2	5.7	10.2	9.2	11.8	14.1	17	27.8	31.2	42.7
Current account (net)	–9.7	–3.4	–4.6	–4	–2.6	1.4	6.3	14.1	–5.4	–9.1
Capital account (net)	7.2	9.2	11.4	8.2	8.4	10.4	10.6	17.3	31.6	24.2
Overall balance (+ increase in reserves; – decrease in reserves)	–2.5	5.8	6.8	4.2	5.8	11.8	17	31.4	26.2	15.1

Source: Economic Survey, Government of India.

or software industry to meet the global demand. The IT sector has emerged as the most strategic and fastest growing sector, of $48 billion (6 percent of GDP) employing 1.6 million professionals. India's IT and BPO (Business Process Outsourcing) exports have grown steeply from $2 billion in 1990–91 to $24 billion in 2005–2006 and further to $32 billion in 2006–2007. IT exports account for 22 percent of total goods exports and 3.2 percent of GDP. Since nearly 35 percent to 45 percent of IT revenues are spent on compensation to employees, the multiplier effect of the IT industry on the overall growth quotient and momentum has been larger than in other industries. Further, as the export earnings of the industry account for 66 percent of its total revenue, the industry gives the dual beneficial effects on both growth and also BoP. Due to relatively low capital intensity of the industry having low capital-output multiples, the industry has been growing in India at a faster rate. By the year 2010, India's software exports are likely to touch $60 billion. This gives a tremendous underlying strength to India's BoP, forex reserves position and rupee.

7   The current account deficit of $9.7 billion (3.5 percent of GNP) in 1990–91 declined to $5.9 billion (1.9 percent of GNP) in 1995–96 and turned into a surplus of $14.1 billion (2.5 percent of GNP) by 2003–2004. The current account went into a deficit of $9.2 billion (1.2 percent of GNP) in 2005–2006. The current account surplus turning into a deficit reflects the drawing on the foreign trade sector in promoting a higher economic growth of 9 percent.

8   One of the reasons for the forex crisis among the Asian countries was that, during the period of reform and high foreign capital inflow, the current account in these economies did not get broad based to take care of debt servicing. The forex reserves were built up primarily from capital account and not current account strength. In contrast, India's current account has shown a healthy growth in line with the capital account expansion, which has to occur naturally following the reform. India's build up of reserves has a very stable and stronger base of current account and would, therefore, provide an enduring stability and strength to India's balance of payments, its build up of forex reserves and the exchange rate of the rupee.

Vibrant capital account

1   Unlike the Asian countries, which relied extensively on capital account transactions for growth, India's moderation in gradually opening up a capital account instead of making it a free for all saved her from the imminent crisis. Following liberalization, there has been a remarkable change in the structure of BoP transactions. This is in line with the global policy of enhancing the flow of private capital through the capital market instruments and its intermediaries and reducing the emphasis on both multilateral and bilateral loans and aid. This change has been caused by several factors. With the opening up of the country's capital market in 1994, the foreign portfolio investment in equity and debt securities has risen. Portfolio investment, which was

Table 11.3 India's balance of payment indicators

	1994–95	1997–98	2000–2001	2001–2002	2002–2003	2003–2004	2004–2005	2005–2006
Trade deficit as a percentage of GNP	3.1	4.2	3.4	2.9	2.3	2.5	5.8	6.4
Trade deficit as a percentage of exports	34	44	32	28	20	21	45	50
Current account deficit as a percentage of GNP	–1.2	–1.5	–0.6	0.8	1.4	2.5	–0.9	–1.1
Foreign exchange cover in months' imports	8.5	7.3	12	15	14	16	14	12
Debt servicing as a percentage of GNP	3	2.7	2.9	2.4	2.7	2.8	1.9	1.8
Short term debt as a percentage of forex Reserves	16.8	20.8	8.6	6.4	3.7	4.6	3.2	5
External debt as a percentage of GNP	27	24.3	22.4	20.9	21	21.3	19.4	15.8

Source: Economic Survey, Government of India.

$4.4 billion in 1994–95, rose to $11.96 billion in 2000–2001, and was $11.7 billion in 2005 and $10 billion 2006–2007. The net cumulative FII investment exceeded $50 billion in December 2006, accounting for 6.3 percent of market capitalization.

2   The foreign direct investment also received a boost with a liberal foreign direct investment policy opening several sectors of the economy and allowing 100 percent equity investment in some sectors and raising the limit to 49 percent and 74 percent in several others. Foreign direct investment, which was a mere $100 million in 1990–91, increased thereafter to $1.3 billion in 1994–95 and to $6.1 billion in 2004–2005 and to a record $15 billion in 2006–2007. Although this has been an impressive achievement, India has so far not been able to attract investment in the range of $25 billion which it intends achieving by 2010. This would give real thrust to the growth process, raising its growth rate from the current 9 percent level to the higher trajectory of 10 percent+.

3   Although the Non-Resident Deposits inflow has continued to show sustained growth, with net inflows rising from $1.5 billion in 1990–91 to $3.6 billion in 2003–2004, its relative share in total capital account transactions has reduced. The total NRI deposits stood at $33 billion in March 2005. It forms an important segment of India's balance of payments and should continue to show healthy growth due to the close cultural links of the NRIs with India.

4   Foreign investment, both direct and portfolio, which was less than 1 percent of total capital account transactions in 1990–91, accounted to 24 percent of capital account transaction in 2004–2005. Compared with a mere $133 million in 1991–92, foreign investment (direct and portfolio) grew steeply to a high of $6.1 billion in 1996–97 and stood at a record $15 billion in 2004–2005 and $25 billion in 2006–2007. Throughout this 14-year period, foreign investment totaled $80 billion and played a crucial role in building economic growth, lower inflation, and a stronger balance of payments position.

5   The importance of external assistance has fallen from 12 percent to 7 percent over the same period. It manifests the magnitude of change, which the liberalization has brought to the balance of payments. Capital flows now are also more market determined, which also requires more synchronous monetary policy. Interest rate differentials and differentials in returns on equity assets have been the prime movers behind the capital flows between nations and also in India.

Healthiest external debt profile

An aspect of India's external economy, which has shown a very positive development and is imparting strength to its balance of payments, is its external debt profile (Table 11.4). India resisted the temptation of opening up a capital account and allowing the flood of short term debt, which is what the Asian countries did. It avoided the debt trap and kept its BoP more stable. India's external

Table 11.4 India's external debt profile

	March end								
	1998	1999	2000	2001	2002	2003	2004	2005	2006
($ billion)									
Long term debt	88.5	92.6	94.5	97.5	95.7	100.3	107.3	115.8	117.7
Short term debt	5.1	4.3	3.9	3.6	2.8	4.7	4.4	7.5	8.7
Total external debt	93.6	96.9	98.2	100.7	98.5	105	111.7	123.3	126.4
(Ratio as percent)									
External debt to GDP	24.3	23.6	21.9	22.4	21.1	20.4	17.8	17.3	17
Short term debt to total external debt	5.4	4.4	4.6	3.6	2.8	4.5	4	6.1	7
Short term debt to forex reserves	19.4	14.5	11.2	9.2	5.4	3.7	4.6	3.2	5
Total external debt to forex reserves	312	298	248	236	182	140	100	87	83
Debt servicing to current receipts	19.5	18.9	16.1	15.4	13.8	16	16.3	6.2	10.2

Source: Economic Survey, Government of India.

debt of $126 billion at 17 percent of GNP is the lowest among the emerging markets. Its short-term debt as a percentage of total external debt remained at the low level of 7 percent in 2006. Short term debt as a percentage of forex reserves declined from 19.4 percent to 5 percent during 1998–2006. The debt servicing ratio is also in a healthy range, showing a decline from 16.3 percent in 2003 to 6.2 percent in 2005. This exemplary record of India's external debt profile offers a balanced and healthy structure to India's BoP and renders it an enduring strength. It is this feature of India's BoP that enabled it to repulse the Asian contagion in 1998 and will continue to provide positive support and remarkable resiliency to its BoP.

Rupee exchange rate policy

The exchange rate is a relative concept. In the floating exchange rate mechanism a country's exchange rate is influenced not only by its own balance of payments position but also by the behavior of the major currencies in which its rate is expressed. The concept of an equilibrium rate as discussed in theory is difficult to be translated into reality.

In the financial and commodity markets, the concept of equilibrium is subject to considerable criticism due to the prevalence of imperfect knowledge, information, and foresight, as also are the possibilities of destabilizing speculation, market rigging and intervention. Under these circumstances, the market price or exchange rate is not the equilibrium rate but the imperfect equilibrium rate, and cannot be relied upon as such for policy adjustment.[75] So long as the supply–demand match, the resultant rate or price is always the equilibrium rate or price, but it need not be the perfect equilibrium rate or price. Hence, when the exchange rates are regulated by monetary authorities or are moved by the forces of destabilizing speculation, they reflect the imperfect equilibrium rate.

Under the floating rates system, the rates, although free, can be and usually are managed by the central banks. Yet another aspect of the present structure of the exchange rates of major currencies is that the exchange rates are governed by not only trade flows but also capital movements. The experience of the US dollar during 1980–85 is a classic example of exchange rate movement contrary to trade behavior and against the forces of comparative cost advantage. The exchange rates are more amenable to control by the central banks through their monetary policies and interest rate changes. The perfect equilibrium exchange rate arising from considerations of current account balance has lost its significance for major countries. The capital movements caused by real interest differentials have become equally significant in the determination of exchange rates. In the light of this aspect of exchange rate determination, the perfect equilibrium rate of currencies of countries like India (which have to tag their currencies to one or a basket of major currencies) needs to be considered against the backdrop of the trend in the exchange rates of the major currencies.

In order to measure the general trend in a currency's exchange rates and also its real purchasing power vis-à-vis several other currencies, the concepts of the Nominal Effective Exchange Rate (NEER) and the Real Effective Exchange Rate (REER) are used. The method of the Nominal Effective Exchange Rate shows the weighted average nominal movement in the exchange rate, while the Real Effective Exchange Rate indicates the exchange rate movement based on the purchasing power parity. The disparity in NEER and REER indicates the degree of overvaluation or undervaluation of a currency on the basis of the purchasing power parity. This method, however, suffers from the following drawbacks.

1   The rate of inflation measured by consumer price indices or wholesale price indices, which are used in computing REER, includes all commodities, while, for the determination of exchange rates, one needs to consider only prices of traded goods.
2   If the exchange rate is more influenced by the capital movements, the NEER and RER would not indicate a correct direction and degree of exchange rate change. While the trade and current account balances may indicate the need for depreciation of currency, the NEER and REER indices may suggest the exactly opposite change in the exchange rate.
3   The indices are computed from the base year. Hence, it is assumed the exchange rate in the base year is the equilibrium rate of exchange. This need not be the case, and the indices would indicate only a change from the base year without touching the degree of disequilibrium in the base year.

Despite these handicaps, the NEER and REER are useful tools and indicators of the change in the external value of a currency. They should not be, however, indiscriminately used for exchange rate changes but considered as one of the essential inputs in decisions on exchange rate managements.

Basket peg or managed floating

In contrast to the system of pegged exchange rates pursued by the Asian countries, India followed the practice of managed floating, with the US dollar used as the intervention currency.

The IMF classifies the exchange rate arrangements of the members under the system of floating rates into three broad categories:

1   pegged to a single currency or a basket of currencies;
2   limited flexibility in terms of (a) a single currency, or (b) a group of currencies;
3   more flexible, (a) adjusted according to a set of indicators, or (b) other managed floating or (c) independently floating.

As a member of the IMF, India can pursue its exchange rate policy. It can also set the rupee freely floating, making it a convertible currency by removing major exchange regulations. India's exchange rate arrangement, popularly known and discussed as one pegged to a basket of currencies, was classified by the IMF as one of managed floating. Countries that had adopted a similar exchange arrangement include China, South Korea, Mexico, Indonesia, Portugal, Singapore, Sri Lanka and Pakistan. Out of 154 member countries of the IMF in 1990, 25 had pegged their currency to the US dollar, 14 to the French Franc, six to SDR and 35 to a basket of currencies. Twenty-five members adopted managed floating, while 25 members were floating their currencies independently.

When the rupee's link with sterling was snapped in 1975, despite managed floating it became necessary to choose an intervention currency and so sterling continued to be used as an intervention currency. Since the majority of trade and other transactions in foreign currencies are made in US dollars, there was a suggestion in 1975 for the use of the US dollar as an intervention currency.[76] Further, since the RBI was primarily monitoring the rupee–US dollar rate, it was operationally more convenient to make a change in exchange rates through the US dollar than to achieve the target rupee–US dollar rate through sterling. Through the US dollar route, the frequency of exchange rate adjustments as well as the volatility in exchange rates was lower. In September 1975, in a historic decision breaking the tradition it had been following since 1931, the Reserve Bank of India abandoned the pound sterling and adopted the US dollar as the intervention currency. The rupee was then pegged to a basket of currencies. Since March 1993, the RBI adopted the unified exchange rates system with managed floating for the rupee. In December 2001, 41 countries had independent floating exchange rate systems, 42 countries operated managed floats, 40 countries had conventional fixed pegged arrangements, eight countries had currency board arrangements, five countries had pegged exchange rates within horizontal bands, four countries had crawling pegs and six countries operated exchange rates within crawling bands.[77]

Rupee exchange rate 1991–2003

The forex crisis of 1990, reflecting the basic disequilibrium in India's balance of payments, was corrected by a large adjustment in exchange rate by way of a devaluation in the rupee. After a two-step devaluation of 9.6 percent and 12.8 percent in July 1991 against the US dollar, the rupee depreciated by 22 percent against a basket of five major currencies. The rupee–US dollar rate rose from Rs.17.94 to Rs.24.48. For a brief period of a year, India followed a dual exchange rate system, from March 1992 until March 1993. Under the dual rate system, 40 percent of current receipts were required to be invested with the RBI at the official exchange rate, while 60 percent could be sold at the market rates. The 40 percent portion was used for essential imports at the lower rate. Dual exchange rates worked well in absorbing the shock of a sudden rise in import costs of goods like crude oil, but are always used as a stopgap measure as they penalize exports and invisible earnings. This was quickly abandoned in favor of a unified exchange rate system.

Under the system of managed floating in the 1990s, the rupee has gradually depreciated against the US dollar and other major currencies. Since March 1993, until February 2003, the rupee-dollar rate depreciated by 35 percent from Rs.31.52 to Rs.48.73. It depreciated by 31.1 percent in NEER but the REER depreciated by only 2.2 percent. During these years, the rupee depreciated against the yen and pound sterling by 27 percent and 37 percent and against the euro by 6 percent.

Rupee tilted towards undervaluation?

India's exchange rate policy of managed floating has been remarkably success-ful throughout the period of liberalization in the 1990s, both on the banking and financial as well as foreign exchange fronts. The most significant aspect has been that India has been able to withstand the pressure of the neighboring Asian crisis. The contagion effect of the Asian crisis could not touch the Indian sub-continent – thanks to its stronger financial, forex and balance of payment struc-ture. This has earned the Indian policy rich compliments even from its earlier critics, who had urged India to go faster on financial and forex reforms, and adopt a one-step full convertibility of the rupee. In fact, the Indian policy has now become a role model after the experience of the Asian, Mexican and Russian crises, to be adopted in liberalization and reforms among the emerging market economies in the New Millennium.

Table 11.5 shows the exchange rate behavior of the rupee from 1990–91 through 2006–2007. The rupee–dollar exchange rate shows that following the major depreciation of the rupee effected in 1991–93, the rupee has not shown any further major fall in subsequent years. The double digit depreciation has been observed in 1993–94, 1995–96 and 1998–99. Apart from that, the rupee has only shown a minor annual depreciation. The REER shows the movement has been in line with NEER. The REER, which was 124.2 in 1990–91, fell to 95.5 in 1993–94 rose to 101.2 in 1994–95, and has more or less moved around

Table 11.5 Effective exchange rates of rupee and US dollar

	Rupee			US dollar	
	Exchange rate (Rs. per US$)	*NEER**	*RFER**	*NEER*	*REER*
			(1995 = 100)		
1990–91	17.94	200.7	129.2		
1991–92	24.47	143.9	105.9	107.4	111.6
1992–93	30.65	118.8	96.1	105.2	109.0
1993–94	31.37	110.2	95.5	108.4	111.1
1994–95	31.40	106.3	101.21	106.4	108.5
1995–96	33.45	97.6	98.0	100.0	100.0
1996–97	35.50	95.7	101.1	105.2	103.6
1997–98	37.17	95.1	105.2	113.8	109.5
1998–99	42.09	84.1	101.1	119.3	116.6
1999–2000	43.33	81.4	99.7	116.4	114.8
2000–2001	45.68	80.4	99.0	121.1	123.5
2001–2002	47.69	79.5	102.4	129.1	135.01
			(2000 = 100)		
2001–2002	47.69	98.5	103.4	106.4	107.0
2002–2003	48.40	93.1	100.9	104.8	105.2
2003–2004	45.90	92.1	103.1	99.0	98.9
2004–2005	44.90	90.8	103.5	94.0	93.3
2005–2006	45.70	93.5	106.8	92.0	92.4
2006–2007	44.30	91.3	109.1	91.3	92.6

Source: Economic Survey, Government of India, Bank for International Settlements.

Note
* 5 Country Index.

that level in the following years; moving to 102.4 in 2001–2002, and showing a marginal appreciation over the seven years.

The exchange rate policy, therefore, aimed at primarily keeping the purchasing power of rupee in the international market from eroding, did not substantially jeopardize the competitive edge to Indian exports in the international market. The rupee has not been over-depreciated and kept undervalued, as has been the policy of China, in order to generate higher exports growth.

In fact, the figures of the nominal and real effective exchange rate of the US dollar are revealing (Table 11.5). The NEER of the US dollar, which showed depreciation from 107.3 in 1991 to 100 in 1995, has since then persistently risen, to 129.1 in 2001, a 29 percent appreciation in the US dollar over the six years of period. In real effective terms the US dollar has gone up further, from 100 in 1995 to 135.1 in 2001, a 35 percent real effective appreciation. This has happened due to depreciation in the currencies of countries that are major trading partners of the US as well as the low inflation rate in the US.

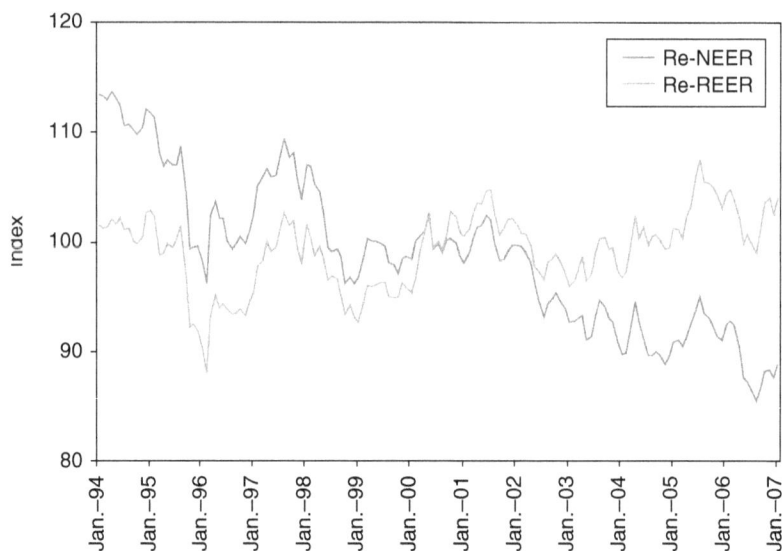

Figure 11.1 NEER and REER of the rupee (source: BIS).

The Indian exchange rate policy has to be seen in the context of this move-ment in the US dollar as well as the trend in India's balance of payments during this period. A comfortable current account balance position and steady accumu-lation of forex reserves did not require any large or persistent depreciation of the Indian rupee, such as the other Asian neighbors needed. India's overall balance of payment surplus, which was $5.8 billion in 2000–2001, rose to $11.8 billion in 2001–2002. A trend in reserves shows an indication of further improvement in both the current account surplus as well as net capital inflows. Naturally, the rupee had to show appreciation in order to neutralize the persistent accumulation of forex reserves. The rupee-dollar rate fell from Rs.48.14 in January 2003 to Rs.44.93 in March 2004, while forex reserves rose from $68 billion to $113 billion.

Rupee appreciation 2003–2007

The year 2003–2004 showed an extraordinary improvement in India's overall balance of payments and forex reserves. In spite of the higher trade deficit, current account surplus rose from $2.9 billion to $3.2 billion because of continu-ous and buoyant growth in software exports. However, it is the capital account that has been the center of rising inflows of dollars and bulging forex reserves. A bullish stock market and relatively undervalued Indian stocks attracted record FII investment in the market. New issues also remained buoyant primarily due to the PSU disinvestments programme offering blue chip equities in some of the best managed PSUs. FII investment in the disinvestments of PSUs was also high. The interest differential in favor of Indian gilts and corporate debt securities and the relatively stable rupee, which started appreciating in 2003, boosted NRI flows, and FII investment in debt. Things could not have been much better for equities and the debt market in India.

The record inflow of foreign funds into the country did pose a problem of money supply as well as exchange rate management. The net surplus on capital account was $17.1 billion in 2003–2004 compared with $12.1 billion in the earlier year. The forex reserves during 2003–2004 jumped by $35 billion to $113 billion, an increase of 49 percent. This alone would have caused a monetary expansion of Rs.160,000 crores in the money supply (M3) of Rs.1,725,222 crores on March 31, 2003, i.e. on increase of 9.3 percent. But the money supply actually grew by 14.6 percent in 2003–2004, compared with 15 percent in the earlier year. The RBI's policy of sterilization managed to curtail growth in the money supply caused by a spurt in forex reserves. The RBI performed a record sterilization of reserves by reducing its holdings of Government securities to the tune of Rs.87,541 crores, from Rs.114,998 crores to Rs.27,457 crores. In addition to this, the creeping rupee appreciation during the year itself slowed the growing inflow of funds. The rupee appreciated against the US dollar by 8.1 percent in 2003–2004. The RBI's policy of money supply and exchange rate management achieved the most judicious balance in the mix of targets for money supply growth, rupee appreciation and forex growth. Money supply growth created ample liquidity, avoided the periodic funds crunch, and lowered interest rates, without overheating the economy and pushing up the inflation rate. The inflation rate measured by CPI came down to 3.5 percent and measured by WPI to 4.5 percent. Interest rates during the year came down by 0.5 to 1 percent. Growth in forex reserves increased the balance of payments strength and resilience.

A factor, which needs an adequate reckoning during the period of rupee appreciation, is that the phase coincided with a sharp downward slide of the US dollar in the foreign exchange markets. Since the US dollar is used as an intervention currency, a stable rupee–dollar rate would have caused depreciation of the rupee along with the dollar against other major currencies such as the yen, D-mark, euro and sterling. Appreciation of the rupee against the dollar avoided such depreciation of the rupee. In fact, the data on the effective exchange rate of the rupee shows the Nominal Effective Exchange Rate depreciating by 2.2 percent and the Real Effective Exchange Rate appreciating by only 0.89 percent during 2003–2004 as against 8.1 percent appreciation against the US dollar alone. Since then, until 2006–2007 the rupee has depreciated marginally in nominal terms but appreciated in real effective terms (Figure 11.1).

Figures 11.2 and 11.3 show the behavior of the rupee with the dollar and yuan. It would be seen that since the dollar and yuan have fixed parity, the yuan has moved in line with the dollar in nominal and real terms. The US dollar appreciated from 1994 to 2002 and depreciated since then. Further, the nominal and real exchange rate movement in the dollar is in tandem and without much divergence. So is the behavior of the yuan. However if we consider the behavior

Figure 11.2 Nominal effective exchange rate indices – dollar, yuan, rupee (source: BIS).

of the rupee, the divergence between nominal and real rates, which was nominal until 2002, has been gradually widening until 2007, showing appreciation of the rupee in real purchasing power terms.

The phase of rupee–dollar appreciation caused a lurking apprehension that it might hurt exports. However, the figures for exports showing robust growth and beating the targets belie this hypothesis. It also supports the view that after the exchange rate has achieved the equilibrium range, a nominal change in exchange rate is not an important factor governing exports growth, but other factors – such as overall economic growth, saving growth, and pressure of foreign demand for goods and services – dominate the export behavior. Further, during this period, the international commodity prices went up very sharply. Experiencing a typical cyclical behavior, these prices had fallen to record low levels earlier. During the phase of low prices, the Indian industry operated and struggled to survive and grow under stiff international competition. A drop in import tariffs had compounded the problem of import competing industries. Nevertheless, the industry gained resiliency to work under a declining price cycle. The upswing in the price cycle provided much needed relief to the industry. In this context, the appreciation of rupee did not turn out to be a handicap to exports, which had earlier worked under worse conditions. The growth in exports has, therefore, not slowed down despite the appreciation of the rupee. Similarly, the import competing industry would also have to strive to work much better under an appreciating rupee since it went through tougher times earlier when tariffs were reduced. Indian industry has, therefore, become much more resilient to price changes and

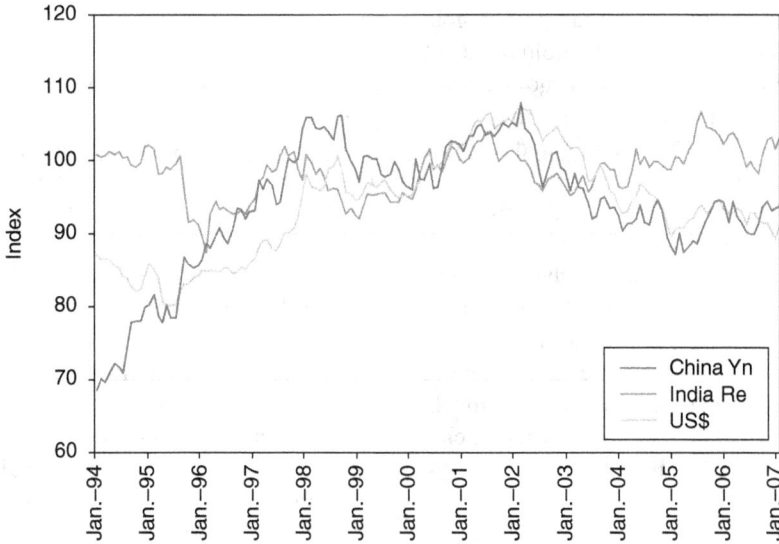

Figure 11.3 Real effective exchange rate indices – dollar, yuan, rupee (source: BIS).

worked for higher growth despite stiffer competition. High economic growth and a sustained increase in domestic demand have made the industry grow and strive for higher quality and efficiency levels.

Gold parity exchange rate

For centuries, gold formed the basis of determining the exchange rates between the currencies, until it was demonetized from the international monetary system in 1971. However, gold stocks have continued to constitute a large buffer in the exchange reserves of central banks. Gold has a special significance in India's balance of payments because of the strong propensity for the yellow metal by the Indian household savers. In retrospect, it seems the Indian instinct and fancy for gold accumulation make economic sense when gold is viewed as an inflation-hedging asset of the households. Over two decades, from 1970–71 to 1990–91, the international gold price increased ten times, even though, since 1980, the gold price declined and it stagnated in the late 1980s. The gold price in India over the same period rose 22 times, while wholesale prices increased nearly sixfold. Indian gold holders have, therefore, successfully hedged inflation in India at domestic as well as international gold price levels. Since 2001, the gold price has been rising from $270 to a high of $690 in April, 2007.

The disparity in the international and domestic prices of gold in the pre-reform period was earlier caused by the ban on gold imports. This disparity is an indicator of the unofficial exchange rate of the rupee as well as the possible equilibrium rate of exchange. The gold parity exchange rate can be derived by equating the international gold price with the domestic gold price.

Table 11.6 shows the gold parity exchange rate of the rupee, which is derived by dividing the Bombay price of gold in Rs. by the London price of gold in US$. This is compared with the official exchange rate of the rupee, and the degree of premium or overvaluation of the rupee is shown. It can be observed from Table 11.6 that from 1970–71 until August 1991, the gold parity exchange rate or implicit exchange rate of the rupee against the US dollar always remained higher than the official exchange rate, except for the year 1980–81 in which it was the reverse. This is primarily due to the domestic gold price increasing at a higher rate than its international price. Demand for gold in India is price insensitive and, except for 1980–81, the domestic gold price was increasing persistently and at a much higher rate than the international gold price. Hence, the gold parity exchange rate was higher than the official exchange rate. It indicates the degree of overvaluation and the unofficial exchange rate, which has to be a little lower than the gold parity rate to make the unofficial gold flows into the country profitable. The gold parity rate in the

Table 11.6 Gold parity exchange rate of rupee

	Gold price			Implicit exchange rate	Prevailing exchange rate	Degree of overvaluation %
	London	Bombay				
	An ounce	10 g		3/2		
	US$	US$	Rs.	Rs.–US$		
	(1)	(2)	(3)	(4)	(5)	(6)
1970–71	36.8	11.83	185	15.64	7.50	108.5
1971–72	43.0	13.83	200	9.58	7.59	26.2
1972–73	64.9	20.87	242	11.60	7.43	56.1
1974–75	166.4	53.51	519	9.70	8.38	15.8
1976–77	126.6	40.71	549	13.49	8.74	54.3
1979–80	405.4	130.35	1159	8.89	7.86	13.1
1980–81	584.9	188.07	1522	8.09	8.66	−6.6
1981–82	421.0	135.37	1719	12.70	9.46	34.3
1985–86	327.8	105.40	2126	20.17	12.61	60.0
1988–90	436.8	140.55	3160	22.50	16.22	38.7
1990–91	383.6	123.34	3455	28.01	17.96	56.0
1991–92	343.9	110.6	4255	38.47	24.47	57.2
1995–96	384.2	123.5	4799	38.85	33.45	16.1
1996–97	387.87	124.7	5191	41.82	35.5	17.8
2000–2001	271.04	87.15	4462	51.22	47.69	7.4
2003–2004	406.71	130.76	5701	43.6	45.95	5.4
2006–2007	650.4	209.11	9434	45.12	44.3	−1.8

Source: Consolidated Gold Fields, Annual Reports, Reserve Bank of India Bulletin, World Gold Council.

pre-reform period was an indicator of the free market rate of the rupee. This is confirmed by the statistics of gold smuggling into India.[78] The only year in which gold was smuggled out of India was 1980–81 and this is reflected in the gold parity rate of Rs.8.09 being lower than the official rate of Rs.8.66. It was the year when the international gold price reached the peak of $850 and averaged $584.

One of the factors governing the unofficial exchange rate of the rupee was the volume of gold smuggling. In view of the price inelasticity of demand for gold in India, in spite of persistent depreciation of the rupee, the unofficial premium continued to remain high. From 1970–71 until 1980–81, the official exchange rate was stable and moved between Rs.7.43 to Rs.8.96, the unofficial premium ranged between 13 percent in 1979–80 to 109 percent in 1970–71, with the exception of a negative premium of 6.6 percent in 1980–81. When the rupee depreciated gradually, from Rs.8.66 in 1980–81 to Rs.17.32 in 1990–91 and Rs.26.02 in August 1991, the premium on the dollar continued to range between 26 percent and 60 percent. The rise in the domestic price of gold was much stronger and kept the pressure on the unofficial exchange rate. Hence, the gold parity exchange rate is an important indicator that has to be monitored in order to judge the pressures on the balance of payment from the unofficial market. Despite depreciation of the rupee, the gold parity rate remained at a premium over the official rate due to the relative inelasticity of domestic demand for gold.[79] It has, however, remained marginal in the last few years due to open imports of gold.

The phenomenon of gold smuggling and the high premium on the dollar in unofficial exchange markets nearly disappeared after the reforms began and there was liberalization of the gold import policy, which permitted the free import of gold. The difference between the gold parity rate and unofficial exchange rate reduced progressively. The degree of overvaluation indicated by the gold parity rate reduced to a mere 5.4 percent in 2003–2004, from a high of 57.2 percent in 1991–92, and 1.8 percent in 2006–2007.

India's import of gold rose from 406 tonnes in 1995 to 660 tonnes in 1997. Although major imports were through the NRI import scheme, imports through unofficial channels still varied between 15 percent to 25 percent of total imports. In 1997, the import of gold was put on the Open General License (OGL) which resulted in a sharp reduction in the imports through the NRI route in the following years. India's total gold imports between 1998 and 2004 varied between 270 to 770 tonnes with unofficial imports accounting for only 8 percent to 15 percent.

India is not only, the world's largest consumer of gold, annually consuming nearly 20 percent of world gold consumption but India's private gold holdings are estimated to be the largest in the world. In addition to the official holdings of RBI of 10.45 million ounces of gold, the total private holdings in 1990 were estimated to be around 6500 tonnes. The gold stocks of the US Federal Reserve of 8086 tonnes are worth US$180 billion (at a gold price of $690 per ounce on April 20, 2007). In 2005, India's private holding of gold was estimated at 14,500 tonnes or $322 billion at a gold price of $690 an ounce. India's private gold holding is currently one and three quarter times the US Federal Reserve gold holdings. This constitutes a measure of tremendous strength to the rupee similar to the strength the gold stocks of Federal Reserves offers to the dollar, despite the fact that the US large gold holdings are in the public domain (with the Fed and not privately held), while in India it is in the private domain. Indian private gold holding is equivalent to Rs.1,450,000 crores, accounting for nearly 45 percent of India's GDP, 40 percent of Indian stock market capitalization and 60 percent of bank deposits. It is nearly three times the currency in circulation, and more than one and half times the country's forex reserves. The colossal size of private gold holdings in India offers the opportunity for the use of an imaginative means of mobilization of these stocks for national development.

12 Capital account convertibility
1997 report and after

The Indian financial system has been getting increasingly integrated with global financial markets. The move towards globalization has been steady, progressive and unblemished. India proved wise in not following financial reforms the whole way and simultaneously going ahead with full convertibility of the rupee. The step by step and gradualist approach in liberalizing the financial system, which had remained regulated for nearly four and half decades, was the right, most pragmatic and rational choice. However, the policy initially attracted lot of criticism from the champions of free markets and jet speed liberalization gurus both within India and abroad. Nevertheless, the course of events in the global economy and the currency crises in Mexico, South East Asia, and Russia in the 1990s gave a firm stamp of universal approval to India's policy of gradualism in moving towards full convertibility. These countries, after their forex crises, had to reintroduce capital controls in order to stop the currency speculation culminating into destabilization, dragging their currencies downward. The domino effect with which the crises erupted throughout the emerging economies needed a fresh look into the philosophy of financing growth in emerging economies through free foreign private capital flows and the unregulated play of market mechanism.

Markets have a peculiar behavior. They are not always rational. They tend to have trend-reinforcing dynamics caused by a herd instinct or mentality. Once they lose their competitive and rational character observed in theory, they tend to be destabilizing and disequilibrating. In this situation they swing from a destabilizing disequilibrium to imperfect equilibrium in successive spirals. In such a volatile market mechanism, the only salvation is healthy and prudential regulation to establish sustainable equilibrium. It is questionable whether the free, unfettered and unregulated market mechanism can establish sustainable equilibrium for growth. One of the staunch critics of the indiscriminate opening up of markets, more so the financial markets, and in particular, capital account convertibility, and a proponent of Transaction Tax (Tobin Tax), James Tobin observes,

> Those who rush emerging and transition economies into premature currency convertibility and free trade in financial instruments are not doing those countries a favor. After all, during 1947–72, the halcyon quarter century of economic growth, world trade, and international real investment, some

major capitalist democracies maintained controls on currency transactions and capital movements. These were not fully dismantled until the 1980s. Experience has not, not yet anyway, vindicated current orthodox confidence that free global financial markets are the keys to stable worldwide prosperity.[80]

This chapter gives the account of the gradual, systematic and step by step approach by India to move towards full convertibility. It is important to note how India moved, after it overcame the 1991 crisis, towards the forex bounty in 2007, coming closer to fuller convertibility. By the mid 1990s, when there was substantial improvement in India's balance of payments and forex reserves position, it was debated whether the rupee could float freely by providing full convertibility on the capital account. Several countries in Asia (Indonesia, Malaysia, Philippines, and South Korea) and Latin America (Mexico, Argentina, and Chile) had adopted full convertibility of their currencies in pursuing the policy of liberalization and reforms. It was time for India to work out its road map for moving towards full convertibility. In 1996, the Reserve Bank of India appointed a Committee on Capital Account Convertibility (CAC) to: (1) examine and indicate preconditions for full convertibility of the rupee; (2) recommend measures to achieve full convertibility; (3) specify the sequencing and the time frame for such measures; and (4) suggest domestic policy measures and changes in the institutional framework if necessary.

Signposts of full convertibility

The committee on CAC submitted its report in May 1997. It recommended several preconditions, or signposts or guideposts, to ensure a smooth transition towards capital account convertibility.

Fiscal consolidation

The heavy and increasing fiscal deficit of the government is not only an indicator of weak government finances but also undermines the healthy and balanced growth of the financial system and markets. The government pre-empting large resources from the financial system through its crowding out effect keeps pressure on interest rates and diverts resources, which could be available for private investment. Beyond a cautionary limit, fiscal deficit also bears an inflationary potential that is hazardous for financial stability. The Committee recommended adoption of a safe fiscal deficit at 3.5 percent of GDP. The Government fiscal deficit has been declining and was 3.6 percent in 2006–2007.

Mandated inflation rate

Inflation is a tax on money and tends to weaken the currency both domestically as well as internationally. Full convertibility with inflation higher than the international rate can only open the gates for disaster for a currency because of the potential of triggering high speculative capital flight and heavy currency depreciation. It has been a practice among several major central bankers to contain inflation within a predetermined mandated range. The inflation rate experienced by the OECD countries during 1991–96 was averaging 3 percent. In the light of M3 growth of 15 percent to 15.5 percent, the Committee recommended a mandated rate of inflation to be monitored by the RBI at an average of 3.5 percent. While average inflation remained below 5 percent in the 52 weeks ending on January, 2007, there was upward pressure on prices with the price rise going above 5 percent in early part of 2007.

Financial reforms

For consolidation of the financial sector in order to evolve the domestic financial sector, which is flexible, viable and transparent, the Committee recommended complete deregulation of interest rates, progressive reduction in CRR to 3 percent and NPAs of commercial banks to 5 percent.

Deregulation and reforms in the financial sector over the last few years achieved the major task of preparing for globalization and integration of the economy with the global financial markets without causing any dislocation in the domestic financial system. Interest rates are totally free and interest rates on deposits and lending by commercial banks were left totally to market forces. For many years under the administered interest rate regime, the Indian financial system faced the phenomenon of an inverted yield curve with call money and short-term interest rates being higher than the long-term interest rates. A gradual reduction in SLR and CRR improved liquidity and enabled the removal of interest rate ceilings. The yield curve turned positive and reflects the true value of longer maturity and risk. The, SLR came down from 38.5 percent in 1990 to 25 percent and the CRR was gradually reduced from 15 percent in 1992 to 4.5 percent, which is very close to the recommendation of 3 percent. The Net NPAs of commercial banks as a percentage of total assets came down from 2.94 percent in 1999–2000 to 0.7 percent in 2006–2007. Gross NPAs reduced from 5.95 percent to 1.9 percent during the same period. These developments conform to the Committee's recommendations and augur well for the move towards more freedom on capital account.

Exchange rate policy

Exchange rate management is critical to the success of full convertibility. A viable and pragmatic exchange rate policy can avoid undue pressures and volatility in the exchange rate and is, therefore, indispensable to initiate full convertibility. A persistent and excessive overvaluation of a currency can be hazardous in triggering capital flight and heavy depreciation under full convertibility. The Committee recommended the evolution of a system of monitoring the exchange rate band of ±5 percent around the real effective exchange rate (REER) and using corrections to avoid any volatility or speculative forces.

The exchange rate of the rupee performed phenomenally well in line with low domestic inflation and the interest rate differential, high economic growth, steady improvement in BoP situation and bulging foreign exchange reserves. It kept the right balance of attaining both the domestic economic as well as BoP objectives.

Balance of payments indicators

It is essential to limit the balance of payments deficit within prudent limits to move towards a convertible rupee. The Committee required the current account deficit ratio as a percentage of GDP to be below 2 percent and the debt servicing ratio to be below 20 percent.

The BoP indicators showed positive movements. The current account deficit, which was 1.2 percent of GDP in 1994–95, came down progressively and turned into a surplus of 0.3 percent in 2001–2002 but rose to 1.1 percent in 2005–2006. The debt servicing ratio fell from 19.5 percent in 1997–98 to 13.8 percent in 2001–2002, and was 10.2 percent in 2005–2006, well below the 20 percent mark considered as a safe level.

Adequacy of forex reserves

The strength of a currency in forex markets lies in the volume of forex reserves with the central bank, which serve as a cushion against any attack on the exchange rate. Volatility in capital flow does influence exchange rates in the forex markets, often bringing them out of line with the long run equilibrium rate. To ward off uneven, unhealthy and undesirable movements in exchange rates and preserve the viability of the currency, the central bank must be guarded with sufficient forex reserves. The committee recommended four main indicators of adequacy of reserves.

1 Reserves to be more than 6 months' imports.
2 Reserves should not be less than 3 months' imports plus 50 percent of annual debt servicing payments plus 1 month's exports and imports.
3 The short-term debt and portfolio stock should be lower than 60 percent of reserves. The ratio of incremental short-term debt and portfolio stock to reserves should not be more than the one.
4 The ratio of net foreign exchange assets to currency should not be less than 40 percent.

India has passed these tests very well. The forex reserves of $200 billion give 12 months' import cover and cover of currency in circulation by a whopping 160 percent, more than double the 60 percent recommended by the Committee.

Gold import policy

Despite its official demonetization from the international monetary system, by abandoning its link with the exchange rate of a currency through the expression of its gold content, gold still continues to occupy a major position and strategic holding of central banks of major nations. The RBI's gold holdings of 358 tonnes at \$4 billion make it one of the largest holders of gold. The Committee recommended free imports of gold to move towards full convertibility. Ever since, India permitted official imports of gold with low import duty, the pressure of balance of payments and exchange rate subsided because of the elimination of a major source of illegal forex transactions and market. It eliminated an unofficial market for the rupee and avoided a perennial drain of forex inflows and reserves. Nevertheless, due to the continuing fancy for the metal among Indian household as jewellery as well as a quasi-liquid financial asset, gold imports in India have continued to rise sharply.

Recommendations and action

The CAC Committee laid the roadmap for full convertibility by gradual relaxation of restrictions on capital movements after fulfillment of prudential norms. The Committee also made several recommendations regarding relaxation of capital account transactions before full convertibility.

The important recommendations, and their implementation until 2005, are outlined below.

1 Direct investment in ventures abroad by Indian corporate should be allowed up to US\$50 million at the level of authorized dealers in terms of transparent guidelines by RBI and beyond US\$50 million through the Special Committee. The restrictions on repatriation of dividend, etc. within a time period should be removed. Ventures abroad should not be confined to exporters/exchange earners. *This was implemented with the limit of \$50 million increased to \$100 million.*[81]

2 Corporates should be freely allowed to open offices abroad for promoting their business. *The corporates were given liberal permissions to open offices abroad.*

3 The External Commercial Borrowings (ECB) ceiling should not be applicable for loans with an average maturity of ten years and above, which in Phase II could be reduced to seven years and above. Restrictions on the end use of ECB for rupee expenditure should be removed. *The restrictions on the end use of ECB were removed and there is greater flexibility on the terms of ECB.*

4 Exporters/exchange earners may be allowed 100 percent retention of earnings in foreign currency accounts with complete flexibility in operation of the accounts for current and permitted transactions, and may be allowed a cheque writing facility in these accounts. *Exporters and forex earners were permitted to open foreign currency accounts in India.*

5 Foreign direct and portfolio investment and disinvestment should be governed by comprehensive and transparent guidelines, and prior RBI approval at various stages may be dispensed with subject to reporting by Authorised

Dealers. Direct portfolio investment may be open to all non-residents on par with NRIs and FIIs. *Although RBI permission for these foreign investments was dispensed with, the foreign individuals have not yet been allowed to make portfolio investments.*

6   Banks may be allowed to borrow from overseas markets and deploy their funds outside India. Borrowings (short and long term) may be subject to an overall limit of 50 percent of unimpaired Tier I capital in Phase I, 75 percent in Phase II and 100 percent in Phase III with a sub-limit for short term borrowing. Deployment of funds outside India should be permitted subject to the adherence to Section 25 of the Banking Regulation Act and prudential norms relating to open position and gap limits. *The commercial banks have been given greater flexibility in their overseas borrowings.*

7   SEBI registered Indian investors may be allowed to set up funds for investments overseas subject to an overall limit of US$500 million in Phase I, US$1 billion in Phase II and US$2 billion in Phase III. *SEBI and RBI gave permission for mutual funds to float overseas investment funds up to $500 million. However, a lackluster overseas equity market and lower returns on debt securities abroad make Indian equity and debt more attractive than the overseas markets. Returns on the Indian capital market appear more attractive. Hence, any overseas investment fund contemplated must show good promise and better return. Templeton launched a global equity fund of $50 million for Indian investors.*

8   Individuals may be allowed to invest in assets in financial markets abroad to the extent of US$25,000 in Phase I, US$50,000 on Phase II and US$100,000 in Phase III. Similar limits may be allowed for non-residents out of their non-repatriable assets in India. *In order to enable individuals to have wider diversification of financial assets by investment in foreign securities, the RBI permitted individual investments abroad up to $25,000.*

9   Residents may be allowed to have foreign currency denominated deposits with corporates and banks. *Banks were permitted to open foreign currency deposit accounts for the residents.*

10   Residents may be allowed to obtain loans from non-residents of US$250,000 on a repatriation basis with interest at LIBOR with no restrictions on the use of the funds. This would bring in a lot of funds as NRIs need lucrative investment outlets and a number of NRIs have friends and relations who need money and to whom they can lend. Lenders would benefit from better returns and borrowers would get a cheaper, easier, convenient, and more flexible source of funds. *Non-residents were allowed to lend money to close relatives for periods exceeding one year but without interest.*

11   All participants in spot markets should be allowed participation in forward markets. FIIs, non-residents, and foreign banks may be allowed forward cover to the extent of their assets in India. *The forward market was opened up with all participants in the spot market given access therein.*

12   Banks and financial institutions should be allowed to participate in gold

markets in India and abroad and deal in gold products. *The commercial banks were allowed to import gold and also offer gold and gold products to savers.*

By 2005, the majority of recommendations of the CAC Committee were implemented. With this, the rupee was nearly fully convertible for all practical purposes except that foreign nationals, corporations and banks have not been given unlimited access to Indian money and capital markets for investments. Prudential regulations on foreign short-term lendings and debt and equity investments in capital markets still exist. Similarly, Indian nationals and corporations also have not been given unlimited freedom to shift their assets outside India for the purpose of asset risk diversification, better returns, arbitrage or speculative profits. Short of these restrictions on capital account, the rupee was convertible for all practical purposes with very liberal forex allocations for travel, medical treatment, education, and even investment, which was up to $25,000 for individuals.

13   Towards fuller convertibility

India has traditionally been an export surplus nation. Its vast natural and agricultural resource base, finest labor and skills enabled it to be the world leader in exports of several commodities and enjoy overall export surplus, not only in the Middle Ages but also as late as in the eighteenth and nineteenth centuries. During 1879 and 1892, India enjoyed an export surplus ranging between Rs.25 crores and Rs.40 crores accounting for between one half to two thirds of imports. In current value terms it would mean an export surplus of US$30 billion to US$40 billion. India even imported gold worth Rs.450 crores to 55 years from 1835.[82] The global economy was more open in the eighteenth and nineteenth centuries than in the twentieth century. The winds of change set by the globalization are now making the economies more open now than ever before in recent history.

The process of economic liberalization, which began in India in the mid-1980s, has shown distinctly positive results on the economy. Sustained growth in industrial production has been the prime spur to the overall high economic growth. No doubt, a higher growth necessitated larger external capital, since the trade gap could not be reduced to take care of higher debt servicing. Industrial liberalization required a similar action on trade, payments and financial fronts to evoke a favorable response on the balance of payments. The industrial resurgence triggered by liberalization has built up capacities in India to enlarge its foreign trade sector by encouraging import substitution and exports. The handicap posed by the exchange rate was one of the important factors stifling the growth of the foreign trade sector. Rupee depreciation in 1991 has eliminated the constraint of competitive disadvantage created by an overvalued exchange rate. With the corrective measures taken by the Government, the economy is set to realize its basic, inherent, and natural disposition to achieve export surplus.

Over the last two decades, the Indian economy gained remarkable resiliency in facing and overcoming unforeseen economic difficulties. India came out of the foreign exchange crises triumphantly in 1965–66, 1973–74, 1980–81 and 1990–91, and strengthened its position. The corrective measures in 1991 and removal of the overvaluation of the rupee with the complementary trade policy support, which triggered a current account surplus, set perfect conditions for making the rupee a convertible currency. Free imports of gold have also stabilized the domestic gold prices at the international level and eliminated other leakages in external payments. The Indian rupee has been an acceptable currency, freely traded in the Middle East and South East Asia for centuries. A fundamental correction in India's balance of payments set in motion by the policy changes over the last decade and the trend of a surplus on the current account emerging in the last few years has opened the way for a convertible rupee.

Dealing with bulging forex reserves

Following the policy of major adjustment and reform in 1991, healthy growth in India's balance of payments under globalization gave rise to persistent accumulation of forex reserves of the RBI. Forex reserves of $55.6 billion in 2002 more than doubled in three years to $140 billion in 2005, and nearly quadrupled to $200 billion in April, 2007. In the light of a heavy build up of forex reserves, a number of options arose for dealing with this phenomenon.

i Rupee appreciation

The RBI may stop accumulating reserves and allow the rupee to appreciate until a level where the large inflows stop. The appreciation of the rupee will lower the inflows. During 2003–2004, despite the appreciation of the rupee rate vis-à-vis the US dollar, from Rs.47.55 to Rs 44.93 (5.8 percent), the forex reserves went up from $72 billion to $107 billion, a whopping rise of 49 percent. The policy of moderating the rise in reserves would have caused much higher appreciation of rupee than the 5.8 percent experienced in 2003–2004. The rupee–dollar rate would have moved below Rs.40 on its way toward Rs.35 if the RBI had not bought dollars in the forex market as aggressively as it did. However, this would not be the correct policy. India still needs more foreign direct investment to raise its economic growth to 10 percent, which has been achieved by China with a similar policy. China has avoided revaluation of the yuan in order to maintain the tempo of its exports growth and flow of foreign direct investment, which have been the driving force of its miracle economic growth. If the rupee revalues in the wake of high foreign direct investment, it would defeat the very purpose of promoting higher capital inflows and go against the top macro-economic goal of higher economic growth of 8 percent to 10 percent.

ii Sterilization of forex reserves

The RBI purchasing forex in the market and accumulating forex reserves raises reserve money in the system and causes multiplier expansion in M1 and M3. Expansion in money supply brings down interest rates, but depending on the position of supplies of goods and import prices, money supply expansion can carry inflationary potential. A price rise may be halted if investment and output also go up and supplies improve.

In order to contain money supply growth, the RBI can sterilize reserves by entering into open market operations. It would sell government securities and neutralize the effect of buying forex in the market on the reserve money level. This would neutralize the expansionary impact of forex reserves accumulation.

However, this has two costs. First, sterilization may interfere with and impede the normal government borrowing program. Second, with the RBI running out of the stock of Government securities, the Government may have to issue more paper to the RBI, which would be deficit financing. Third, it also involves loss of revenue by way of interest on Government securities held by the Reserve Bank, which is higher than interest on forex assets.

> On a very general plane it can be argued that sterilized intervention by the central bank to contain liquidity impact of capital flows often involves a trade–off between low return assets and high return assets as far as the central bank is concerned. Earning from deployment of foreign exchange is understandably lower than the interest loss on account of open market sale of government securities essentially due to interest rate differentials.[83]

During 2003–2004, the RBI's policy of sterilization managed to curtail growth in money supply caused by a spurt in forex reserves. The RBI performed a record sterilization of reserves, during the year, by reducing its holdings of Government securities to the tune of Rs.87,541 crores, from Rs.114,998 crores to Rs.27,457 crores. RBI also floated Market Stabilization Bonds for the purpose of sterilization of forex reserves.

Full convertibility and free floating rupee

Full convertibility of a currency and free floating exchange rates are not synonymous. They are both mutually exclusive concepts and matters of policy. They may have some relativity among them but this need not necessarily be. Full convertibility means that there are no restrictions on current and capital account transactions. It reflects unregulated BoP manifested in uncontrolled transactions on the credit and debit side of BoP, and on the demand and supply sides of foreign exchange. Free floating of a currency means that the central bank of the country does not intervene in the forex market to manage the exchange rate or use any of its tools of monetary control, like the bank rate and open market operations for the purpose of exchange rate management. Free market rates are determined by the demand and supply of foreign exchange, and are not the targets of influence for the central bank's monetary policy. Although the monetary policy measures of the central bank are directed for regulating the domestic economic variables of growth and inflation, they influence the demand for and supply of foreign exchange and thereby affect exchange rate movement is another matter. But monetary policy is not used to manage exchange rates. It is possible to have free convertibility without free floating exchange rates. The currencies of several developed nations are fully convertible but need not be free floating. Such a floating rates system is termed as *dirty floating* by Friedman. It is also possible to have a free floating currency without full convertibility.

The US dollar is fully convertible but may not be a free floating currency in times when monetary policy is used to manage dollar exchange rates in the global markets. It may be argued that dollar exchange rate movement is the effect of monetary action and not its cause. The motivation for monetary action can only be substantiated by the prevalent domestic and external economic situation at the time. Yet it would be difficult to pinpoint with precision the weight given to each domestic factor and exchange rate in the conduct of every monetary action. Hence, even the US dollar remains a managed currency. And exchange rates of major currencies become a duopolistic pricing game and policy parameter. Armed with the monetary targeting tool for controlling aggregate money supply rather than the interest rate, the Chairman of the Federal Reserve, Paul Volcker, charted a tight money policy in 1980 that strengthened the dollar in the forex markets. The index of effective exchange rates for the US dollar went up to 179 in December 1984 from 101 in January 1980 (December 1970 = 100). Volckerism restored the dollar to its earlier glory in the international financial markets.

Full convertibility with managed floating rates means that there are no restrictions on BoP transactions for either domestic residents or foreign residents but demand and supply of foreign currencies in the forex markets can be managed by the central bank. Through its purchases and sales of forex in the forex market, the central bank will maintain a desired level of exchange rate. An emerging market economy moving towards full convertibility can never afford to have a free floating exchange rate. The exchange rate has to be at the level at which it can gain maximum advantage in capital inflows, preserve competitive strength of domestic production of its goods and services in the global market and also thwart any possibility of capital outflow. Managed floating of the exchange rate has to continue with even a full convertibility of the rupee in India. An argument in favor of free floating is that when large capital inflows occur, the exchange rate appreciation and elimination of the interest rate differential would lower capital inflows so that the central bank does not have to buy forex in the market and accumulate reserves.

At over US$200 billion in 2007, forex reserves more than fulfilled all the parameters set by the CAC Committee in terms of adequacy of reserves *vis-à-vis* imports, debt servicing, short-term debt, portfolio investments and currency in circulation. India has a good enough cushion on all these parameters to meet the adverse situation of sudden outflow without causing any destabilizing speculation.

The basic question is not whether India is now eligible for full convertibility, which it is now, but whether India should, as a matter of policy, adopt full convertibility. We have the example of China with its much larger forex reserve level of $1 trillion and fixed exchange rates still not adopting even partial convertibility. Hong Kong, now a part of China as an autonomous region, also has $150 billion reserves but still has a fixed exchange rate at HK$8.33 for a US dollar. In comparison, India has convertibility for all practical purposes except that foreigners cannot make unrestricted loans, investments or remittances to

India without RBI permission, and Indians also cannot make unrestricted loans, investments, or remittances outside India.

Under the fully convertible regime, the RBI will have to initially face unrestricted flows of money, either into or out of India. This is a one-time correction, which would take place immediately after full convertibility, if it is done at one go. Fortunately, looking to the favorable trends in India's trade and payments and differentials in interest rates and in rates of return on risk capital, continuing accretion in forex reserves and appreciation of rupee, it is very likely that full convertibility would now bring in short-term flows exceeding US$30 billion to US$50 billion. This would be a one time adjustment after full convertibility, which would bring in funds waiting to come to India but for restrictions.

It would either bring an increase in forex reserves with the exchange rate remaining the same or cause the rupee to appreciate to an extent that would stall the impending inflow. It may also result in some reserve accretion and some appreciation in the rupee. If the exchange rate were not allowed to appreciate, the inflows would swell reserves, expand money supply, and bring further downward pressure on interest rates. The inflationary potential of monetary expansion has also to be seen. However, as investment increases, it would step up the economic growth rate and keep inflation in check.

In addition to these macro effects, the short-term funds flowing into banks and corporates need to be used productively or serviced without pressure. Hence, full convertibility is also likely to raise bank credit and corporate borrowings as has happened in the Asian countries. From the experience of Latin America and Asia, it is amply clear that excessive lending has a tendency to be unproductive, speculative and finally cause more defaults. India survived the Asian Crisis because of its very cautious and judicious policy of restraint on short term borrowings by both banks and corporates.

Rupee appreciation – a caution

Alternatively, if inflows are allowed to cause rupee appreciation, reserves accretion and monetary expansion and their after-effects would not occur. However, the economy and industry will have to be ready to face the balance of payments effects which rupee appreciation would bring.

The case against rupee appreciation on full convertibility has already been made. First, the purpose of full convertibility is to promote a large inflow of foreign capital and its more efficient use. This process cannot be short-circuited by currency appreciation. Second, free trade and capital accounts evolve a new trade structure that needs to be developed further under a relatively stable exchange rate until the initial gush of capital inflows adjusts to the differentials in the return on capital and complete one time correction of mismatch. If inflows are allowed to cause appreciation in the rupee, it would be a roadblock in growth in exports and the evolving of a new trade structure.

Large rupee appreciation, caused by the one-time effect of large capital inflows, would eliminate the natural protection available to the industry from a

Table 13.1 Forex reserves and money supply

	1974–75	1980–81	1990–91	1994–95	1997–98	2000–2001	2001–2002	2002–2003	2003–2004	2004–2005	2005–2006
Forex reserves as a percentage of currency	16	39	21	76	80	86	129	134	165	178	161
Forex reserves as a percentage of DD	18	58	29	90	98	117	179	179	198	216	193
Forex reserves as a percentage of M1	9	24	12	41	43	49	75	76	90	98	88
Forex reserves as a percentage of M3	5	10	4	15	14	13	20	21	26	28	26

Source for Data: Economic Survey, Reserve Bank of India Bulletin.

higher rupee – dollar exchange rate. It would adversely affect the profitability of a large cross-section of industry; thereby, it has a negative impact on the capital market. One of the reasons for the lack luster performance of the capital market in India in 1996 was the effect QRs and tariff reduction had on the Indian industry for the first time. The industry has since then restructured, renovated, become more cost effective, productive and cost conscious, and adopted a strategy to be globally competitive. The weak units have closed down and efficient and progressive ones have moved faster and become stronger. The industry is now ready to face the globalization of the Indian economy. However, full convertibility and appreciation of the rupee, which it may cause, runs the risk of jeopardizing the growth of Indian industry. A large industrial sector, an import competing sector covering almost all industries, would be adversely affected by appreciation due to undesirable price competition from imports. It would also undermine the competitive strength of Indian exports including software exports, which are enjoying high and sustained growth.

Lower industrial growth would reduce the overall economic growth rate. Slower growth in exports and a rise in imports would raise the trade deficit and bring pressure on the balance of payments. This would have an effect on the forex market, and the trend in the exchange rate may reverse towards depreciation or capital flight, finally reducing forex reserves. Hence, the currency appreciation caused by the capital inflows but not warranted by the comparative cost advantage and current account fundamentals would not be conducive to the sustainable equilibrium in the overall balance of payments. It would definitely impede the economy's momentum to reach and sustain the target of 10 percent growth. It is, therefore, imperative for this reason to ensure stability of the rupee in the forex market in the wake of full convertibility of the rupee.

Road map of full convertibility

Looking to both these eventualities emanating from the initial positive movement of inflows and its impact in producing too much reserves or liquidity in the system, or unwarranted appreciation in currency, it seems desirable to chalk out a road map with an action plan giving options for further relaxation of restrictions on capital account relating to foreigners, non-residents, and residents on lending, investment, and remittances to reach the goal of full convertibility. It could be one step towards full convertibility, or progressive, or a step-by-step approach.

Before going into the policy options available to adopt full convertibility, it is worthwhile having a look at the major critical elements and items on the capital account that would be free from controls, limits, caps, ceilings, and also gauge their magnitude and impact, and the manner in which they can be relaxed.

i Short term capital inflows

1   Call Money and T bills
2   Loans to Banks and NBFCs

3   Trade Finance
4   Commercial Papers and Short-term Loans to Corporates
5   NRI Loans

ii   Long term capital inflows

1   Debt Portfolio

     i   G Securities
     ii   Banks and Corporates – Bonds and Loans
     iii   NRI Deposits

2   Equity Portfolio

iii   Capital outflows

1   Short-term Deposits and Loans in foreign currencies and Open Forex Positions
2   NRI repatriation
3   Investment in Foreign Equity and Debt Securities
4   Gifts by Residents

Short-term capital inflows

Restrictions on short-term capital inflows from foreign banks and non-residents may be relaxed further. The CAC Committee already recommended loans from NRIs, and higher limits on short term loans from foreign banks. These may be implemented.

A cap may be fixed on overall annual short-term inflows to avoid an unwarranted liquidity gush and preclude the possibility of destabilizing outflows later. The annual cap would also avoid undue pressure on debt servicing. India's external debt presents a very healthy trend and record on short term debt due to its restriction. The overall annual cap needs to be fixed in light of its impact on the rupee exchange rate or on the overall liquidity situation in the economy, its repercussion on interest rates and its inflationary potential. Hence, the overall ceiling on the short-term inflows becomes a function of the overall liquidity gap in the system, which can be filled by the sudden gush of external inflows and the system's absorption capacity.

How much a system can absorb is determined by three fundamental macro economic policy parameters, namely, the policy on the 3Rs (rates) – exchange rate, interest rate and inflation rate. Experience of two years' of cap would give a cue to its removal and gradually pave the way to full convertibility.

The liquidity gap in the system, which the short-term flows would fill, depends on the desired level of interest rates, which in turn would rest on the targeted economic growth and inflation rates. If the objective is to bring the current interest rates structure in line with the global rates structure, it would indicate the liquidity gap in the system and the amount of inflow that would take place.

The capital adequacy norms of the banking system would determine its absorption capacity of the banking system. The net inflow of short-term capital in 2005–2006 was around $1 billion. An inflow of $10 billion would inject liquidity of about Rs.45,000 crores. Two safeguards need to be built up in order to avoid a repeat of the Asian crisis. First, the banks need to restrain from using short-term funding for long-term loans and avoid the maturity mismatch. Second, they have to remain cautious in avoiding riskier lending, especially in securities and real estate markets. A free gateway to borrowing through short-term loans should not mean an open license for indiscriminate lending jeopardizing the norms of prudent banking.

Targets of economic growth rate of 8–10 percent, inflation rate of 4 percent and stable exchange rates would give a figure of liquidity growth that can be sustained by opening up the short-term capital route. Experience of the first year of the caps would give a cue to its removal and pave the way for full convertibility.

Treasury bills and government securities market

Under the current conditions of India's BoP status, rupee exchange rate movement, forex reserves position, and outlook on economic growth and inflation, the full opening up of a capital account would cause an influx of foreign capital, primarily debt and largely short term. It would also bring long-term debt and equity flows. Nevertheless, an immediate influx or gush would be dominated by short-term capital. The magnitude of this flow is determined by the interest rate differentials between India and abroad and the premium on the forward rupee. At the short end of the market with the call money rate hovering between 5 to 5.5 percent and three month Libor at 5.1 percent, there is not a big arbitrage opportunity for inflow of dollars. One-hundred-and-eighty days T bill is 5.57 percent vis-à-vis 5.19 percent on six month Libor. The current yield on the ten year G Sec in India is 7.2 percent vis-à-vis 5 percent on similar US G Sec. The premium on the six month forward cover for the US dollar of 1 percent to 1.5 percent, leaves a very low margin of 0.7 percent to 1.2 percent for arbitrage operations. Hence, the opening up of the short-term money market – call money and T bills markets – may not result in a large capital inflow. Similarly, in the G Sec market, the interest rate differential is not large enough to give a wide arbitrage margin after covering the forward cover cost. The recent hike by Fed Chairman Bernanke to raise the Fed Funds rate to 5 percent has further reduced the interest rate differential between the US and India.

One of the reasons for the Asian crisis, for was that the interest differential between the domestic and foreign rates was too large, nearly 4 percent to 5 percent, which led to the large inflows and accumulation of short-term debt, which ranged between 60 to 170 percent of forex reserves. This compounded with a high external debt servicing ratio left the currencies in a precarious balance against the onslaught of capital flight, causing a sudden drain of reserves and finally a huge depreciation of currencies.

Fortunately for India, the increases in interest rates by the Fed in the US over the last two years have substantially narrowed the interest differentials between the US and India. In the risk free securities market (T bills and G Secs) a huge inflow of funds is unlikely. In view of this, the current ceiling of $3.5 billion on debt portfolio of FIIs can either be removed or increased. Large inflows can be expected in a riskier debt and loan portfolio, especially in banks, NBFCs and corporate debt securities. The spread on riskier debt will be higher and that alone will give higher arbitrage over and above the forex cover cost.

NRI deposits

NRIs are given a special status by offering them special interest rates on their deposits in India. Total NRI deposits outstanding were US$38 billion in 2006. The interest rates offered to NRI are subject to a ceiling of 2.5 percent over Libor. Full convertibility would require dispensing with the distinction between the NRIs and non-NRI foreign depositors. While the NRIs would continue to keep deposits with the Indian banks, it would not be possible to discriminate against the other foreign depositors. Both the Indian and foreign banks could decide rates on their own liquidity situation, mismatch and gap, and ability to offer competitive rates.

Foreign currency deposits by foreign residents

Foreign banks, finance companies and corporates can be permitted to keep foreign currency as well as repatriable rupee deposits in India. These deposits could be kept at market rates. This would also develop Mibor (Mumbai Inter Bank Offer Rate) to be more popularly used as a reference rate for deposit and loan transactions. As and when foreign individuals are permitted to hold foreign currency and rupee deposits, the special rates for NRIs may cease to exist.

Short-term corporate borrowings

Full convertibility would enable Indian corporates to raise working capital and trade finance in foreign currencies. Indian corporates would also issue foreign currency denominated Commercial Papers for working capital. Short-term trade finance for India's imports is currently restricted and is given with the permission of the RBI. Low-interest foreign currency finance for imports is a big business opportunity for the foreign banks. Indian industry would also get cheaper mode of finance. Free or liberal trade financing would, however, increase India's short term debt and debt servicing. However, it would also remove pressure on the domestic liquidity situation, which would be much easier. With the current level of imports of US$200 billion, there could be a demand for US$15 billion to US$20 billion for import finance. This would replace the current rupee finance from Indian banks and would bring downward pressure on the lending rates of commercial banks.

Investment in debt securities

The annual ceiling for the investment in debt securities was recently raised to US$2 billion for Government securities and T bills and to US$1.5 billion for coprporate debt. In view of the tightening liquidity situation with the commercial banks due to rising growth in credit uptake, slower deposit growth, it may be the right time to remove the ceiling on FII investment in G Secs and T bills. The current yield on the ten year G Sec in India is 7.2 percent vis-à-vis 5 percent on similar US G Sec. The premium on the six month forward cover for US dollar of 1 to 1.5 percent leaves a very low margin of 0.7 to 1.2 percent for arbitrage operations. This opens up the opportunity for removing the ceiling on FII investment in G Secs and T bills. Removal of the ceiling on corporate debt is related to the overall ceiling on External Commercial Borrowings (ECBs). The same may be liberalized or dispensed with. If the overall ceiling on ECBs is removed, it may be necessary to cap Indian corporate's external borrowing related to its total borrowing and its net worth. This cap may not be applicable to corporates in sectors such as infrastructures and others that require a heavier debt-equity ratio.

Investment in Indian equity

Currently, only registered FIIs in addition to NRIs are permitted to invest in listed stocks and new issues of equity. Overall, the FII limit varies from 49 percent to 74 percent of equity capital subject to the sectoral limit and shareholders approval. This policy may continue. However, in order to broaden the base of foreign participants in the equity, foreign individuals may be permitted to invest in the equity through the registered broking houses. This would add yet another investor group with a different profile of risk, return, cash flow needs and tenure of investment. Individual investors are longer term investors in many countries and these investors balance the profile of overall foreign investors. Such a profile would be less volatility inducing than the profile of pure FIIs. The Indian stock market would be much broader based and less volatile. The foreign individual investment may come within the overall FII limit which may now be called FI (Foreign Investment) limit. This would also enable individual investors across the world to enjoy the benefits of equity investment in India and make the Indian stock and capital market truly global.

Overseas investment by residents

The residents may be permitted to hold a portfolio of foreign mutual funds, equities, and bonds more liberally. This would enable them to diversify their asset holdings across foreign currencies and markets. The current annual limit of $25,000 may be raised to $500,000 lifetime limit. Looking to the rates of return on debt as well as equity in India, the relaxation on this front is unlikely to cause much outflow. Within the overall investment limit, the residents may also be permitted to buy real estate abroad. Mutual funds should also be free to invest in the overseas securities. There may not be any cap on such investments. These outlets would, to some extent, neutralize the effects of a large influx of short-term capital on the opening up of the capital account.

Foreign corporate issues in India

Foreign companies may be permitted to make GDR issues in India and get them listed here. They may also be allowed to make rupee based issues of equity and debt, and get them listed on the Indian bourses. These may invite a ceiling or may be free, depending upon what convertibility option is adopted.

Short-term foreign currency deposits and loans and open forex positions

Resident individuals can currently hold foreign currency deposits, within the current overall limit, to invest in overseas securities, of $25,000. This may be relaxed. Individuals may be permitted to hold short-term foreign currency deposits within the overall lifetime limit of $500,000. Under normal circumstances, due to lower interest rates on foreign currency deposits, this would not cause a large outflow. However, it would be a cause for alarm in the event of currency weakness and speculation of depreciation of the currency. Speculation of about 5 percent to 10 percent deprecation of the rupee can cause a large shift from rupee deposits to foreign currency deposits. Although individuals may not be large players in this game, the large corporates, banks and NBFCs would play this card and also keep large overbought positions in foreign currencies to be covered after deprecation. Forex positions unrelated to the BoP transactions may not be permitted beyond a ceiling.

In order to stem destabilizing speculation in the wake of a weakening of the rupee, a cap could also be fixed on the outstanding speculative positions or outflows which the banks, corporate and individuals can take or effect during a critical period. These are the safeguards necessary to avoid a currency attack or panic. They would act as safety valves against currency pressures and could be withdrawn on normal or satisfactory behavior of exchange rates and reimposed on exigencies.

Foreign corporate acquisitions by Indian companies

In its bid to have a global presence, achieve greater economies of scale and technology, and be globally competitive with the dominant presence, Indian companies have been very quick in 2006–2007 to acquire foreign companies. The initial limit for foreign acquisitions may be set at $3 billion, to be raised to $5 billion, and may be free from any cap later. These are large limits because the majority of large acquisitions are made by Indian corporates from foreign currency funding.

Repatriation by NRIs and OBCs

Although the NRIs and OBCs are currently given full repatriation benefits, in the case of investments in real estate they are not permitted to repatriate the profits from the sale of real estate. Similarly, loans by NRIs have to be interest free. The reasoning behind these restrictions is that the absence of such restrictions would result in the dilution of forex reserves and an increase in the debt servicing burden. So long as the real estate sale is from a genuine market transaction, the repatriation may be permitted. Similarly, NRIs may be permitted to charge Libor-related interest on their loans to residents.

Another aspect of NRI repatriation relates to the rupee assets of NRIs. The status of inherited and gifted properties and assets of NRIs in addition to those purchased from NRO accounts or rupee resources which do not carry repatriation benefits needs to be considered. With full convertibility, NRIs may be permitted to repatriate sale proceeds of rupee assets comprising deposits, securities, properties, real estate and other assets such as gold, jewellery and other precious assets. There could either be full freedom on this repatriation or there may be a $1 million lifetime limit for NRIs, which may be raised to $5 million gradually.

BoP stressors

A proactive exchange rate policy, an indispensable lever for sustainable full convertibility, would ward off any currency speculation and also the resultant capital flight. In the unfortunate event of a currency crisis, the reimposition of controls on capital outflow becomes inevitable. When the rupee is fully convertible, what BoP stressors could trigger a currency crisis? These can be divided into external and internal stressors.

External stressors

1   Oil crisis
2   Global recession
3   Strengthening dollar

Internal stressor

1   Inflation rate
2   Fiscal deficit

Oil crisis

A persistent increase in oil prices has been a global phenomenon for the last few years. A further increase in oil prices is definitely going to erode and weaken the BoP of oil importing nations. A rise in oil prices has been an important factor turning India's current account surplus into deficit in 2005–2006. Nevertheless, looking to the magnitude of the current account deficit, which is relatively small, there isn't a big danger that, considering the overall BoP situation, it would trigger currency speculation. Further, an oil crisis affects all economies, and currencies of all countries get proportionately adjusted.

Global recession

Global recession is less likely to affect India than China and other Asian countries, which are more dependent on exports for their growth. The Indian economy is much more domestic centric, like the US, and would, therefore, be more resilient and less susceptible to global changes.

Strengthening dollar

A strengthening dollar ignited the Asian crisis. Pegged exchange rates were a disaster due to the absence of downward adjustments in exchange rates in the wake of the strengthening dollar. India's exchange rate policy has won kudos in international circles, especially after the Mexican, Asian and Russian currency crises. A sharp strengthening US dollar is less likely in the near future unless Fed chief Bernanke goes the Volker or mini-Volker way in raising interest rates. Even in that event, India's adroit exchange rate policy is capable of handling the strong dollar without the BoP damage.

Inflation

The real test of a strong convertible rupee lies in the rupee's internal strength. A check on the price rise and fiscal deficit keeps the currency internally healthy and its convertibility sustainable. A price rise weakens the currency externally if it is higher than the rate of inflation in major global economies. Inflation in line with the global trends keeps the currency stable in the exchange markets and obviates the fire fighting needed to manage the currency crisis. Inflation below 4 percent is the right recipe for a strong rupee in the fuly convertible era.

Fiscal deficit

Fiscal deficit not only manifests dissaving but also tends to enlarge the BoP deficit. A manageable fiscal deficit of 3.5 percent of GDP gives a positive outlook for healthy BoP and currency strength in the international market. India shares a good record of persistently lowering the fiscal deficit towards 3.5 percent and is, therefore, a worthy candidate for full convertibility. A fiscal deficit for 2005–2006 was 4.1 percent and came down further to 3.6 percent in 2006–2007. It must, however, be reckoned that for a growing economy like India, with a huge requirement for infrastructure investment, the 3.5 percent figure is not sacrosanct and to be strictly adhered to. Higher deficit financing for building productive assets in the infrastructure sector is most welcome.

All the BoP stressors, both external as well as internal, are currently in soft mode and are also unlikely have a strong influence on India's BoP in the near future so as to pose any threat to currency stability in the forex market. This provides a very stable environment for the rupee to be convertible and offers a much wider choice of policy options to full convertibility. A little hostile domestic or global economy and uncertain financial environment would have narrowed the choice of options available for action on full convertibility.

Policy options for full convertibility

There are three options available in moving towards full convertibility.

1   Full Convertibility – Fast Track (within one year, by 2008).
2   Full Convertibility – Progressive Track (over two to three years, by 2010).
3   Full Convertibility – Step by Step Track (over five years, by 2011).

Fast track convertibility

On several parameters of economic, monetary and BoP status and policies, India is ready to make the rupee fully convertible. The advantage of doing so at one go is to reap benefits instantly. It would bring a multiplier effect on investment and output in a very conducive current environment. With economic growth of 9 percent+, industrial growth in the double digit range, agriculture showing extraordinary gains, the services sector expanding fast and infrastructure playing a catalytic role, there couldn't be a better time for full convertibility. A growth-inducing current account deficit, rising forex reserves, a stable rupee, and low inflation keep the macro financials robust. A remarkably buoyant capital market with record new issues, mobilizations by mutual funds, an uptrend in stock prices supported by a superb corporate performance catapult the economy into a higher growth trajectory of 10 percent. Full convertibility in a year's time can elevate the economy into the 10 percent growth orbit. The merit of fast track convertibility is its multiplier effect which it can put to work on the economy which is already in a progressive growth path. It will accelerate the growth process further and bring in the benefit of an inflow of $40 to $50 billion. This inflow would be about one quarter the current forex reserves and 4 percent to 5 percent of GDP. Economic growth of 10 percent needs a higher investment rate and with a capital–output ratio of 4, a $50 billion inflow would raise the growth rate from near 9 percent to 10 percent by 2008. Foreign direct investment guidelines have paved a clear way for investment directions and inflow will move in those productive channels. A large amount of $50 billion would be short-term debt funding. However, it would be productive and would also spur foreign direct investment and also domestic corporate investment. An incremental rise in the debt servicing ratio would not be a heavy price to pay for higher growth. With a history of healthy and safe debt servicing margins, full convertibility would not substantially alter these low risk margins.

The entire credit side of India's capital account, which constitutes capital inflows will be fully open. The ceiling on FII investment in debt portfolio, comprising both G Sec and corporate debt of $3.5 billion, will be removed.

> It is interesting to note that the yield on 10 year Treasury bills in the US had risen to about 4.4 percent as compared with 5.6 percent on Government bonds of similar maturity in India at the end of July 2003. Taking into account the forward premia on dollars and yield fluctuations, except for brief period, there is likely to be little incentive to send large amounts of capital to India merely to take advantage of the interest differential.[84]

The current yield rate for US Treasury bill for 10 years is 5 percent, it is 7.2 percent for 10-year G Sec in India and the forward premium on the dollar is 1 percent to 1.5 percent. The call money rate in India is hovering between 5 percent to 5.5 percent vis-à-vis the Fed funds rate in the US of 4.85 percent. The interest rate differential is narrow. The recent hike in Fed Funds rate to 5 percent has further reduced this differential.

All the above capital account inflows would collectively bring in a total inflow of $50 billion to $70 billion a year. An inflow of this magnitude, when capital account convertibility is announced in 2008, will not cause any problem for monetary and forex management. During 2004–2005, India's capital account surplus grew to $28 billion from $17 billion in the earlier year. The Indian financial system and economy has absorbed large accretions in forex reserves. Increases in forex reserves have been $17 billion in 2002–2003, $31 billion in 2003–2004, and $26 billion in 2004–2005. The rise in forex reserves in 2005–2006 has been lower at $15 billion. With this record of absorption net foreign inflows, it would not seem difficult to accept fresh inflows from full convertibility of around $50 to $70 billion.

Further, in the present scenario of a current account deficit, such an inflow would be much more welcome and cause less inflationary impact on domestic liquidity and prices. It would also bring downward pressure on interest rates that have been going up due to tightening of liquidity. The current low level of short-term and total foreign debt, and debt servicing, will keep them in safe limits even after convertibility. The RBI should announce prudential norms for foreign short-term and long-term debt for banks, NBFCs and corporates, so that the opening up of this window does not lead to banks and coporates overborrowing, which happened in Asian countries, causing the currency panic later. RBI should also monitor the short-term and long-term borrowings to ensure that the prudent norms are not violated.

Full convertibility is expected to raise the forex reserves, crossing $260 to $280 billion. At this level it would provide enough cushion for any sudden capital flight whose magnitude could not be larger than $30 to $50 billion. The volatile portion of foreign investments in India concerns the FII investments and NRI Deposits. With cumulative FII investment of $50 billion and NRI deposits outstanding of $38 billion, total repatriable investment comes to about $90 billion.

Even in the worst case scenario, not more than 50 percent would be repatriated, requiring $45 billion of reserves to be used for this purpose.

Exchange rate management is very crucial after full convertibility, much more critical than it is currently. Rupee exchange rates will have to be more flexible and their management more vigilant and proactive. With full convertibility, India would have an overhang of about $100 billion of foreign capital, comprising short-term debt, NRI deposits, and FII investments, which could seek an exit in the event of any currency destabilization. Even the maximum capital flight range of 50 percent (of $100 billion) in the worst case scenario, would be manageable with the forex reserves of $260–$280 billion. Proactive exchange rate management could pre-empt any large capital flight and consequent currency destabilization, minimize the damage and sustain the level of forex reserves and BoP equilibrium.

The most critical aspect of full convertibility is how much freedom can the residents (individuals, banks, corporates) be given for acquiring overseas assets. Resident individuals can be given full freedom to invest in debt and equities abroad. Even with the limit of $25,000 for overseas investment not many individuals have used the facility. The reasons are obvious. The return on Indian equities is far superior to the one on foreign equities. Overseas interest rates are much lower than in India. The rupee appreciated from Rs.48.40/$ in 2002–2003 to Rs.44.27 in 2005–2006, an appreciation of 9 percent. It appreciated a further 7 percent to Rs.41 by May 2007. Currency depreciation offers gains on foreign currency holdings. Immediately on the announcement of full convertibility, the rupee would strengthen due to the expectation of a large inflow. In the event of a persistent deficit in the BoP, there would be shift of deposits by residents to foreign currencies. It would, therefore, be prudent to keep a limit on the foreign currency deposits by the residents. A limit of $100,000 could be fixed for foreign currency deposits by individuals. This could be within the overall limit of $500,000 for all overseas investments, including real estate. The limit of $100,000 for foreign currency deposits and $500,000 for all overseas investment would be lifetime limits. A similar limit could also be determined for remittance of a gift by resident individuals to relatives abroad.

Indian corporates could be given the freedom to acquire companies abroad or invest in equities or joint ventures without limit. There would not be major outflow from this source as large acquisitions are funded by overseas foreign currency resources. Restrictions or ceilings will have to be imposed on foreign currency deposits and lendings by banks, corporates, and NBFCs. Spot and forward forex positions unrelated to current and capital account transactions need to be monitored and regulated. Corporates may be permitted such speculative positions only up to $1 million each, with a total limit of $1 billion. Such dispensation is essential to watch the experience of full convertibility, especially during periods of stress, if they appear at all. The danger of giving total freedom to banks, NBFCs and corporates to keep short-term foreign currency deposits or give short term loans abroad in foreign currencies is that this sector is the most active one in triggering capital flight following the currency weakness. It would be prudent to watch the behavior of the BoP and exchange rate for some time before freeing this transaction from regulation. On judging the actual experience, these restrictions can be gradually removed later.

The biggest advantage of fast track convertibility is the trigger it can give to the financial system and investment climate. There is an imperative need to bridge the widening resource gap and step up the investment rate. The enormity of investment requirements for infrastructure is such that it would crowd out the traditional outlets of investment, such as agriculture, trade and industry for resources. A sudden injection of resources of $50 billion following full convertibility would catapult the economy into a higher growth orbit by stepping up the investment rate. The economy and financial system has ably demonstrated its absorption capacity in the past. Once the higher investment rate gets momentum, the very pressure of the enormous backlog the economy has, especially in infrastructure, would keep investment rate moving forward. Fast track convertibility will have a catalytic impact on the investment climate and pave the way for 10 percent growth. It will also send a positive signal to the global investment community about India's commitment to economic reforms and the speed of its implementation. The concern on the capital outflow can be handled with prudential limits on the outflows emanating from the residents without jeopardizing the freedom to withdraw money by foreign residents and NRIs. The RBI's prudent skillful management of liquidity, yield rates and the exchange rate will ensure fast track convertibility is a smooth and swift affair.

Progressive convertibility

The hallmark of India's economic reform process, which has earned kudos in the international community and become a model for adoption by the other emerging market economies, is its gradualism. A step-by-step and gradual unfolding of liberalization has enabled India to skip the trauma and market disruptions that other economies, with fast liberalization, had to undergo and suffer. The last 15 years of financial and capital market reforms have enabled India to adopt full convertibility on current account and partially convertibility on capital account of BoP. It is now on the last phase of its goal of full convertibility.

Progressive convertibility is also consistent with India's philosophy of reform. It is a more secure path. In an uncertain and complex international economic and monetary environment, the gradual approach to full convertibility has the advantage of learning and adapting in implementing the plan. The drawback of this option is that it will regulate the tap that brings capital inflow. The tap will be opened gradually in three steps. In contrast, a fast track would bring in foreign capital with a gush. This would have an instant impact on stepping up the investment rate and tempo. The progressive option would cause the investment rate to go up gradually.

Phase 1 – 2008

In the first phase of full convertibility in 2008, the ceiling on short-term capital inflows and debt securities can be fixed at $10 billion. This should cover investments in T bills, G Secs and corporate securities, including commercial papers and also short borrowings by the banks. Restrictions on NRI loans to residents may be permitted with Libor-based interests. Investment in equities by foreign resident individuals may also be permitted with overall cap fixed for FIIs related to the individual company's equity. Residents may be permitted more liberal investments abroad (deposits, securities and real estate) up to $100,000. Trade financing may be restricted to $5 billion. The limt for ECBs and foreign bonds may be $10 billion. A limit of $5 billion may be determined for overseas acquisitions and mergers by the Indian corporates. Speculative open positions, short-term bank deposits and loans may not be permitted beyond over $1 million, with an overall limit of $2.5 billion.

Phase 2 – 2009

On the basis of the experience of relaxations and limits in 2007, the second phase in 2008 would involve raising the limits by 50 percent to 100 percent. If the limits are not reached, the second phase may involve full-scale convertibility, with all inflows to enter without limits, but prudential higher limits may imposed on outflows by the residents.

Phase 3 – 2010

The third phase would involve gauging the experience of higher limits. A healthy experience of relaxations would pave the way for full convertibility in 2010. Capital inflows could be totally free but need to be guided by the prudential limits on both short-term and long-term borrowings by the banks, corporates and NBFCs. It would avoid the external debt trap and unproductive deployment of funds increasing the NPAs. The freedom of residents to invest or remit funds abroad beyond a discretionary ceiling needs to be regulated through the RBI permission. Individuals may be permitted to invest up to a lifetime ceiling of $500,000. Long-term investments by corporates may be totally free. Corporate Investments beyond $500 million may require RBI approval.

Speedier mode

Since the BoP is influenced by a series of domestic and international factors, in the experience of progressive convertibility in Phase 1 or 2, the capital account liberalization could made speedier. Positive developments in the economy and global markets would send quicker and better responses to the BoP. Convertibility can then be shifted in a speedier mode.

Step-by-step convertibility

This option involves a much slower move towards full convertibility. It would involve three phases: 2008, 2009 and 2011.

Phase 1 – 2008

The first phase would involve increasing the ceiling on investment in debt securities from the current $3.5 billion to $10 billion by 2008. For encouraging short-term borrowings by banks and corporates – comprising short-term loans and bank deposits, trade finance, commercial papers – another ceiling of $5 billion may be imposed. Foreign individuals may be permitted to invest in equities or debt through broking houses up to an exclusive ceiling of $1 billion.

Resident individuals may be permitted to invest abroad in bank deposits, securities, mutual funds and real estate within the lifetime ceiling of $100,000. They may also be permitted to give loans to relatives, friends or corporates at Libor-based rates within this overall ceiling of $100,000. Indian corporates may be permitted to acquire companies abroad with the overall limit of $3 billion. Banks, NBFCs and corporates may be permitted to make short-term deposits, loans or keep open speculative forward forex positions not related to the current or capital account within the overall limit of $2.5 billion.

Phase 2 – 2009

If the experience of relaxations of inflows and outflows in Phase 1 is favorable, the limits may be relaxed further.

The debt ceiling for FII investment may be raised to $20 billion. The short-term debt ceiling may be raised to $5 billion. The investment limit for foreign individual investments may be increased to $2 billion. Resident individuals may be permitted to invest abroad up to $200,000. The ceiling on Indian corporate acquisitions abroad may be raised to $5 billion. Short-term loans, deposits and forward forex positions abroad may be subject to a ceiling of $5 billion.

Phase 3 – 2011

Sustaining of a healthy BoP, in spite of the above capital account relaxations would be a signal for adopting full convertibility without any restrictions. By 2011 there would be a full convertibility of a rupee with no regulations, except that for the sake of exigency, it would be desirable to monitor short-term outflows of banks, corporates and NBFCs and keep prudential limits on their borrowings and forward forex exposures.

Implications for RBI's monetary, forex and exchange rate management

Full convertibility will add one more variable in RBI's monetary policy. Short term capital inflows, T bills and G Sec investments would influence call money rates, T bills and G Sec yields. This would be a new external factor affecting the short-term liquidity in the market. Buying and selling of T bills and G Secs by FIIs and other foreign investors could upset the RBI targets of yield rates and liquidity. It may have to take this in its stride or engage an open market operation countering these movements.

The exchange rate would be subject to greater volatility. Exchange rate and forex reserves are related. If the rupee depreciates due to a large capital outflow, future outflow would be less and so would be the reserves loss. If the rupee appreciates due to a large inflow, future inflow would be less and so would be the reserve gain. Reserves money and M3 get affected by fluctuations in forex reserves. If the capital flows are taken care of by rupee exchange rate movements, monetary policy and operations need not be tempered. A free floating exchange rate policy would leave a greater autonomy in monetary policy.

Managed floating implies dilution of the monetary policy. It would mean using the monetary policy tools to manage the capital account of BoP, similar to what the Fed is doing to keep the dollar stable in the international market. Although Milton Friedman abhors this diluted form of managed floating, which he calls *dirty floating*, the reality of exchange rate management in the forex markets, whether it is US dollar or Indian rupee, shows the split goals of monetary management – economic growth and inflation control on the one hand and exchange rate surveillance and proactive management on the other.

Free floating exchange rates with full autonomy for monetary policy for domestic economic goals have not yet been fully acceptable to policy makers the world over. The exchange rate, and its movements, is an important variable having an influence on domestic economic goals through the BoP. Free floaters like Friedman compartmentalize domestic and external economies. They advocate monetary policy to be exclusively devoted to the domestic economy and exchange rate policy to take care of the BoP alone, with the belief that this kind of segregation of two economic polices to exclusively manage two segments of the economy would maximize economic welfare.

This philosophy is undermined by several practical imperfections, deficiencies and limitations. First, foreign exchange markets are usually perfectly competitive for large economies but may not be so for many medium-size economies and emerging market economies. Even for the large markets, such as pound sterling or yen, there may be phases in the market behavior that do not resemble the perfectly competitive market. Often, short-term equilibrium rate movements or the volatility dictated by irrationality, herd instinct, the unreasonable fear of financial loss, are not in line with the long-term equilibrium rate. If the exchange rate is allowed to be swayed by these short-term imperfect equilibrium or disequilibrium rates, it could culminate into a destabilizing equilibrium.

Such free market behavior is not in the interest of either the long term BoP equilibrium or the domestic economic goals. Hence, a discretionary exchange rate intervention is an essential feature of the exchange rate policy to attain a sustainable BoP equilibrium compatible with domestic economic goals.

Second, Friedman regards the BoP equilibrium and domestic economic goals as mutually exclusive. BoP balance or imbalance, like the external economy, has an influence and is also influenced by growth and inflation, the domestic economic goals. In the era of Keynesianism and recession-proof economic policies, the exchange rate policy, even under floating rates, needs to be harmonized with monetary and fiscal policies, and cannot be left in isolation to be determined solely by the free market.

Matrix of policy parameters

As has been highlighted earlier, the conduct of monetary and exchange rate policies takes a much more complex route after full convertibility than before. How much inflow the financial system can absorb is determined by three fundamental macro-economic policy parameters, namely the policy on the 3Rs (rates) – exchange rate, interest rate and inflation rate.

Inflows and outflows of capital can be largely checked by exchange rate management. Appreciation would curb inflow of capital, while depreciation would check the capital flight. With stable exchange rates, inflows and outflows of capital would directly affect forex reserves, M3 and later interest rates, rate of inflation and debt servicing. The latter parameters need to be watched carefully to ensure sustainable domestic economic and BoP equilibria. RBI can also, through its open market operations, directly counteract the impact of these capital flows on M3 and also interest rates. Hence, exchange rate policy and open market operations of RBI become the focal points of monetary management on full convertibility.

Tables 13.2 and 13.3 give an alternative scenario of the impact of capital inflows and outflows of different estimated volumes with a stable exchange rate and the appreciation/depreciation of the rupee by different degrees. The impact is examined on M3, interest rates, the inflation rate and debt servicing.

Exchange rate surveillance and proactive management

Managing a currency in the international market is like managing a central bank or a commercial bank. No central bank or commercial bank is always 100 percent liquid. Nor is it required to be so. The system of central banking or commercial banking rests on the principle of a safe liquidity ratio or on dilution of liquidity to a safe level. However another most important principle or pillar of banking is the confidence in the currency or commercial bank. Lack of confidence in a bank or a currency can cause banking failure or hyper-inflation. In the international currency markets, a lack of confidence in the currency can cause a currency crisis. Sound management of a currency in the international market would pre-empt any lack of confidence in a currency.

Table 13.2 Matrix of policy parameters on full convertibility (capital inflow case)

Exchange rate		Inflow of capital	M3 impact	Interest rate impact	Inflation impact	Debt service impact
Stable rupee	Rs.45	$30 bn	5.20%	−0.75%	0.4%	1.1%
		$40 bn	7%	−1%	0.5%	1.4%
		$50 bn	8.80%	−1.50%	0.7%	1.8%
5% appreciation	Rs.42.75	$20 bn	3.50%	−0.50%	0.25%	0.7%
		$25 bn	4.40%	−0.62%	0.3%	0.9%
		$35 bn	5.30%	−0.75%	0.45%	1.2%
10% appreciation	Rs.40	$15 bn	2.70%	−0.37%	0.2%	0.5%
		$20 bn	3.50%	−0.50%	0.25%	0.7%
		$25 bn	4.40%	−0.62%	0.3%	0.9%
15% appreciation	Rs.38.25	$10 bn	1.80%	−0.25%	0.15%	0.4%
		$15 bn	2.70%	−0.37%	0.2%	0.5%
		$20 bn	3.50%	−0.50%	0.25%	0.7%

Table 13.3 Matrix of policy parameters on full convertibility (capital outflow case)

Exchange rate		Outflow of capital	M3 impact	Interest rate impact
Stable rupee	Rs.45	$20 bn	−3.5%	0.75%
		$30 bn	−5.2%	1.12%
		$40 bn	−7%	1.5%
10% depreciation	Rs.49.5	$15 bn	−2.7%	0.55%
		$22 bn	−3%	0.8%
		$30 bn	7%	1.2%
15% depreciation	Rs.51.75	$10 bn	−1.8%	0.37%
		$15 bn	−2.7%	0.55%
		$20 bn	−3.5%	0.75%
20% depreciation	Rs.54	$5 bn	−0.9%	0.19%
		$7 bn	−1.3%	0.28%
		$10 bn	−1.8%	0.37%

This brings us to two critical factors in sound currency management: active vigil on balance of payments and exchange rate trends, and proactive policy on their management. Half the battle is won with the acceptability of a flexible exchange rates policy. Exchange rate rigidity is an open invitation for currency crisis. A BoP surplus economy, such as China, can afford to do this due to its capacity to accumulate and absorb dollars and US T bills, and also keep the inflation rate manageable. The policy is similar to that which West Germany and Japan followed in the 1970s and 1980s, and thereby emerged as the super-growth economies. BoP deficit economies are trading on a more slippery path and have to go along with flexible exchange rates, something which Asean countries failed to do and so invited the currency crisis.

Adverse balance of payments trends, to a large extent, can be taken care of by a cushion of adequate exchange rate adjustments. More persistent trends in balance of payments may need broader monetary and fiscal adjustments. Once fully convertible, returning to capital account controls is an option that should never be used. The 3Rs – Rate of Exchange, Rate of Interest and Rate of Inflation – have to be used and managed to preserve and sustain the currency convertibility in the long run. In a rapidly growing continental economy such as India, management of these broad policy parameters, namely 3Rs, should sustain confidence in the convertible rupee.

Forex reserves are always a cushion to meet marginal adjustments in BoP or extreme situations of a crisis. Crisis prevention through proactive exchange rate management is the best strategy under full convertibility. With full convertibility, India will graduate into the club of mature economies and financial systems, and its monetary management will have a much wider implications than earlier. The monetary policy exercise will be of wider interest to international money managers due to their greater involvement in the Indian financial system.

Building alarm systems and a real-time database

Information – right information and timely information – is the crux of all decision making, and more so for strategic decisions. International currency crises have always caught out central banking authorities, Governments of countries and international agencies, be it the Latin American debt crisis in 1980, or the Mexican crisis of 1994, the Asian crisis of 1997, or the Russian rouble crisis of 1999.

International agencies with their powerful information base and intelligence have also not been able to ring alarm bells before the crises. There needs to be an alert of a systemic failure well before its onset in order to thwart the crisis. The importance of right and quick information cannot be more emphasized in this context. The risk of systemic failure needs to be averted by an intelligent, reliable and real-time information system that rings warning bells significantly in advance of the imminent crisis. In this context, adoption of full convertibility needs to be preceded by the establishment of an efficient alarm system that gives a constant flow of data regarding all parameters that have an influence on the price situation, liquidity, interest rates, BoP and exchange rate.

Table 13.4 gives parameters critical to BoP and the exchange rate, which needs to be watched on an ongoing basis. It gives the range of change for each parameter to be watched on a daily, weekly, monthly and quarterly basis. The range of change in each parameter is one considered to be potentially unsafe and risky, and the frequency of monitoring is decided on the speed of influence of each parameter. This surveillance is imperative for proactive management of money and forex markets. The parameters need to be monitored closely for an

Table 13.4 Alarm system for full convertibility operation

	Daily	*Weekly*	*Monthly*	*Quarterly*
Exchange rate				
Spot rate	>±0.5%	>±1%	>±1.5%	>±2%
Forward rate	>±0.5%	>±1%	>±1.5%	>±2%
Forex reserves	>±$0.5 bn	>±$1 bn	>±$2 bn	>±$2 bn
Reserve roney		>+0.4%	>+1.5%	>+4%
M3		>+0.35%	>+1.5%	>+4.5%
Bank deposits		<+0.3%	<+1%	<+3%
Call money rates	>5%	>5%	>5%	>5%
Yield rate on Gsecs	>±0.25%	>±0.5%	>±0.5%	>±0.5%
Consumer prices		>+0.1%	>+0.4%	>+1%
Debt servicing ratio			>+0.5%	>+1%
Imports			>+1%	>+3%
Exports			<+0.5%	<+1%
Inward remittances			<+0.5%	<+1%
FII sales	>$50 mn	>$500 mn	>$1 bn	>$2 bn
FII purchases	>$50 mn	>$500 mn	>$1 bn	>+$2 bn

Note
All figures of percentage changes are changes for the variable during the concerned period except for call money, which is the actual call money rate.

alert about the onset of an unfavorable trend. The persistence of a negative trend would ring alarm bells, warranting prompt action.

Summary and conclusions

On several parameters of economic, financial, BoP and exchange rate prudence and security, the Indian economy and financial system is poised to make an entry into the final phase of its reforms and the process of integration into the global financial system. The policy options of Fast Track Convertibility and Progressive Convertibility are available with different implications of their effects on liquidity and M3 growth, interest rates, investment rate, forex reserves and BoP. The biggest advantage of fast track convertibility is the trigger it can give to the financial system and investment climate. Fast track convertibility will have a catalytic impact on the investment climate for 10 percent economic growth. It will also send a positive signal to the global investment community about India's commitment to economic reforms and the speed of its implementation.

Implications of full convertibility for monetary and exchange rate policies are analyzed, identifying the possible BoP stressors and also underscoring the importance of greater vigilance and proactiveness than before in their conduct. Building up the Alarm System is imperative for prompt, efficient and effective control of potentially damaging unfavorable trends to ensure the stability and sustainability of the financial system.

14 Fuller convertibility report and future scenario

The foregoing chapter is a part of a 'Convertibility Report' submitted in march 2006 to the Committee appointed by the Reserve Bank of India (RBI) to examine the issue of moving towards fuller convertibility. As discussed earlier, a number of recommendations of the 1997 committee have been implemented, moving India forward in this area. Yet the onset of the Asian currency crisis in 1997 put a brake on the process of capital account convertibility in the emerging market economies. India was able to ward off any currency instability and uncertainty, when some stronger emerging markets reeled under the pressure of foreign exchange turmoil, due to its cautious approach and step-by-step liberalization of the BoP under the philosophy of gradualism. There was a consensus amongst even hard-line reformists toeing the line of a gradual move towards convertibility. India's BoP situation continued to show substantial improvement and forex reserves remained buoyant in the new Millennium. This called for reviewing the process of capital account convertibility. The Prime Minister, Dr. Manmohan Singh, in a speech at the Reserve Bank of India, in Mumbai, on March 18, 2006 referred to the need to revisit the subject of capital account convertibility.

> Given the changes that have taken place over the last two decades, there is merit in moving towards fuller capital account convertibility within a transparent framework … I will therefore request the Finance Minister and the Reserve Bank to revisit the subject and come out with a roadmap based on current realities.

The Reserve Bank of India (RBI) issued a Memorandum on March 20, 2006.

> Economic reforms in India have accelerated growth, enhanced stability and strengthened both external and financial sectors. Our trade as well as financial sector is already considerably integrated with the global economy. India's cautious approach towards opening of the capital account and viewing capital account liberalization as a process contingent upon certain preconditions has stood us in good stead. However, given the changes that have taken place over the last two decades, there is merit in moving towards

fuller capital account convertibility within a transparent framework. There is a need to revisit the subject and come out with a roadmap towards fuller Capital Account Convertibility based on current realities.[85]

The RBI appointed a Committee to set out the framework for Fuller Capital Account Convertibility (FCAC) and give a medium-term framework, with sequencing and timing, for fuller capital account convertibility. The Committee submitted its report on July 31, 2006.

Broad framework for timing, phasing and sequencing of measures

As highlighted earlier and in the Convertibility Report, there were three options available to proceed with the fuller convertibility. The first option was the Fast Track Convertibility, which implied a quicker opening up of the capital account restrictions both on the inflow as well as outflow sides. It also meant much larger limits for several transactions with a view to adopting full convertibility by the end of 2007. The second option was to be a little slower, with lower limits to achieve full convertibility by 2009. And the third option was to move towards fuller convertibility step by step, spanning into 2011. The Committee did not adopt the options of Full Convertibility on Fast Track or Progressive Track, but chose the Step-by-Step Track, which was in line with the progress of liberalization of the capital account of the BoP and also India's successful policy of gradualism in reforms and step-by-step approach in economic liberalization. The Committee adopted the approach of gradual relaxation of capital account controls in three phases over a 5-year period until 2011.

> On a review of existing controls, a broad time frame of a five year period in three phases, 2006–2007 (Phase I), 2007–2008 and 2008–2009 (Phase II) and 2009–2010 and 2010–2011 (Phase III) has been considered appropriate by the Committee. This enables the authorities to undertake a stock taking after each Phase before moving on to the next Phase. The roadmap should be considered as a broad time-path for measures and the pace of actual implementation would no doubt be determined by the authorities' assessment of overall macroeconomic developments as also specific problems as they unfold. There is a need to break out of the 'control' mindset and the substantive items subject to capital controls should be separated from the procedural issues. This will enable a better monitoring of the capital controls and enable a more meaningful calibration of the liberalization process.[86]

Progress on preconditions/signposts

The Committee noted the significant progress made in the economic, fiscal, monetary, BoP and exchange rate management in India over the period of ten years since the 1997 Committee's report. The gross fiscal deficit of the Central

Government was 3.6 percent of GDP in 2006–2007 as against the recommendation of the Committee of 3.5 percent. The average rate of inflation for 3 years in 2005–2006 was 4.6 percent against the recommended range of 3 to 5 percent. Financial sector gross NPAs were 3.3 percent of total advances in 2005–2006 compared with the 5 percent recommendation. Average CRR (Cash Reserve Ratio) was 5 percent in 2005–2006 against 3 percent.

> The 1997 Committee indicated that with the then Current Receipts (CR)/GDP ratio of 15 percent, the economy could sustain a Current Account Deficit/GDP ratio at 2.0 percent. The 1997 Committee envisaged that the authorities should endeavor through external sector policies to increase the CR/GDP ratio such that the debt service ratio (DSR) comes down from 25 percent to 20 percent. The CR/GDP ratio in 2005–2006 was 24.5 percent. The debt service ratio for 2005–2006 is placed at 10.2 percent (including repayments under the India Millennium Deposit Scheme); the debt service ratio for 2004–2005 was only 6.2 percent. Clearly, there have been significant improvements in the external sector, much beyond that envisioned by the 1997 Committee Report.[87]

Four pillars of fuller convertibility

The Committee reiterated the need for four strong pillars to move towards fuller capital account convertibility. Vibrant fiscal consolidation, a broad-based and strong banking system, sustainable current account deficit and appropriate maintenance of forex reserves adequacy form the four pillars on which the superstructure of fuller convertibility can be built, developed and maintained with efficiency.

Rupee exchange rate management

In respect of exchange rate management, however, the RBI's policy has been more proactive than market oriented, as recommended by the Committee.

> The 1997 Committee had recommended that there should be a more transparent exchange rate policy with a Monitoring Band of ±5.0 percent around the neutral Real Effective Exchange Rate (REER) and that the RBI should ordinarily not intervene within the band. The RBI has not accepted this recommendation.[88]

The exchange rate intervention is a central banking prerogative. Most central banks do have their own formulae for intervention and which cannot be disclosed. Hence, the free floating snake in the tunnel (exchange rate moving freely in the narrow predetermined band) is a good theoretical tool but remains impractical in reality due to the need for quick central bank intervention, which is often more proactive than reactive and has to be secretive. The RBI's exchange rate management, despite the Committee's observation, has yielded positive results and been commendable. The Committee II continued to endorse the 1997 Committee's recommendation for the RBI to monitor the ±5 percent band around the neutral REER (Real Effective Exchange Rate) with RBI non-intervention within the band, except when warranted by the need to obviate speculative forces and unwarranted volatility. A periodic review of neutral REER for a change as warranted by the fundamentals was also suggested. The base year and country composition of the six-country and 36-country indices have been periodically altered. In the light of rapid growth of the services sector and its increasing contribution in exports, REER needs to be refined to incorporate this sector. The committee recommends a review of the exchange rate policy if the current account deficit (CAD) persists beyond the currently sustainable limit, 3 percent of GDP.

Non-resident Indians

With fuller convertibility, all non-residents, whether Indian, of Indian origin or other non-Indian foreign (individuals as well as corporates), will have to be given equal and non-discriminatory treatment. The current regime gives special benefits to the Non-Resident Indians (NRIs) in terms of higher interest rates on their deposits as well as tax concessions.

> The Committee recommended that the present tax benefit for these special deposit schemes for NRIs, [NR(E)RA and FCNR(B)], should be reviewed by the government. The existing concessions date back to an era when Indian tax rates were much higher; now they are comparable to the rest of the world. Moreover, in the interim years, India has entered into Double Taxation Avoidance (DTA) agreements with various countries which permit taxes levied in one country to be allowed as a tax credit in the other. These changes warrant a review of the current tax provisions. Non-residents, other than NRIs, should be allowed to open FCNR (B) and NR (E) RA accounts without tax benefits. In the case of the present NRI schemes for various types of investments, other than deposits, there are a number of procedural impediments and these should be examined by the Government and the RBI.[89]

The Committee recommended the opening of foreign currency accounts and repatriable rupee accounts by the foreigners.

Double taxation treaties

The Government of India has double taxation treaties with a number of countries to eliminate double or multiple taxation of income and capital gains of non-residents on their investments or earnings. The purpose of these tax treaties is to encourage investment and income flows by avoiding higher taxation. However, such treaties become discriminatory because they are limited to only a few countries. The Indo-Mauritius double taxation treaty has been very popular among foreign investors but has also become a ground for controversial litigation.

> As India progressively moves on the path of FCAC, the issue of investments being channeled through a particular country so as to obtain tax benefits would come to the fore as investments through other channels get discriminated against. Such discriminatory tax treaties are not consistent with an increasing liberalization of the capital account as distortions inevitably emerge, possibly raising the cost of capital to the host country. With global integration of capital markets, tax policies should be harmonized. It would, therefore, be desirable that the government undertakes a review of tax policies and tax treaties.[90]

The recommendations of the Committee in respect of relaxations of limits of transactions in different segments of capital account are given below.

Capital inflows

1 Short term capital inflows

The Committee expressed the view that even in the environment of FCAC, prudential limits may have to be considered for foreign investment in CPs and CDs. The Committee did not favor unlimited opening of short-term capital flows. It advocated prudential limits on foreign investments in CPs, CDs, T bills and G secs. This would mean that India is unlikely to witness any large influx of short-term capital inflow if the Committee's recommendations are accepted. This would keep interest rates higher and avert the downward pressure on interest rates.

2 Trade financing

The Committee showed concerns about the volume of trade credit as there could be sudden changes in the availability of such credit and also that data about the volume of credit were not fully captured, even while noting that suppliers' credit of less than 180 days was excluded from these data. Currently, short-term trade credit for all permissible imports up to $20 million for less than one year is permitted per transaction. Import credit is also available for capital goods up to $20 million per transaction for maturity between one to three years. The Committee wanted this scheme with a per transaction limit of US$20 million to be reviewed and revamped to avoid unlimited borrowing.

3 External borrowings by commercial banks

The banks' borrowing facilities are at present restrictive, although there are various special facilities that are outside the ceiling. Loans and borrowings by resident banks from overseas banks and correspondents were limited to 25 percent of unimpaired Tier I Capital; these limits amounted to US$2.7 billion as of March 31, 2006. The 1997 Committee had recommended significantly higher limits. The data regarding the extent of such borrowing was not readily available. The 2006 Committee recommended that the limits for borrowing overseas should be linked to paid-up capital and free reserves, and not to unimpaired Tier I capital, as at present, and raised substantially to 50 percent in Phase I, 75 percent in Phase II and 100 percent in Phase III. Ultimately, all types of external liabilities of banks should be within an overall limit.

4 FII investment in G Secs

The current limit on FII investment in G secs of $2 billion works out to be 4.8 percent of gross issuance of G Secs (Center and States). The Committeee recommended that instead of the *ad hoc* fixating of a limit or ceiling on the total amount, the ceiling should be determined as percentage of annual gross issuance of government debt and the ceiling should be raised gradually.

> The limit for FII investment in G-secs is recommended at 6 percent of total gross issuances by the Centre and States during 2006–2007 and to be gradually raised to 8 percent of gross issuance between 2007–2008 and 2008–2009, and to 10 percent between 2009–2010 and 2010–2011. The limits could be linked to the gross issuance in the previous year to which the limit relates.[91]

5 External commercial borrowings by the corporates

The overall annual limit on External Commercial Borrowing (ECB) is currently US$18 billion and ECBs up to US$500 million per year are under the automatic route. The Committee recommended that the overall ECB ceiling and the ceiling for automatic approval should be gradually raised. Rupee denominated ECB (payable in foreign currency) should be outside the ECB ceiling. ECBs of over ten-year maturity in Phase I and over seven-year maturity in Phase II should be outside the ceiling. End-use restriction should be removed in Phase I.

6 Investments in corporate bonds

The present FIIs' limit for investment in corporate bonds of US$1.50 billion works out to be an estimated 11 percent of the gross issuance in 2004–2005. The Committee felt that the present limits allowed for corporate debt to be far more liberal than the limits allowed for G-secs and the present absolute limit could be retained for 2006–2007; thereafter, the limit could be fixed as a percentage of gross issuance in the previous year. The Committee recommended retaining the present limit for 2006–2007 to be raised to 15 percent of fresh issuance between 2007–2008 and 2008–2009 and to 25 percent between 2009–2010 and 2010–2011.

7 Foreign corporate investment in equities

The Committee recommended that non-resident corporates should be allowed to invest in the Indian stock markets through registered entities, including mutual funds and Portfolio Management Schemes, who will be individually responsible for fulfilling KYC and FATF norms. The money should come through bank accounts in India.

8 Participatory notes of FIIs

In the case of Participatory Notes (PNs), the nature of the beneficial ownership or the identity is not known, unlike in the case of FIIs. These PNs are freely transferable, and trading of these instruments makes it all the more difficult to know the identity of the owner. It is also not possible to prevent trading in PNs as the entities subscribing to the PNs cannot be restrained from issuing securities on the strength of the PNs held by them. The Committee is, therefore, of the view that FIIs should be prohibited from investing fresh money raised through PNs. Existing PN-holders may be provided with an exit route and phased out completely within one year.

9 Foreign individual bank accounts

At present, only NRIs are allowed to maintain FCNR(B) and NR(E)RA deposits. The Committee recommended that non-residents (other than NRIs) should also be allowed access to these deposit schemes. Since NRIs enjoy tax concessions on FCNR(B) and NR(E)RA deposits, it is necessary to provide FCNR(B)/NR(E)RA deposit facilities as separate and distinct schemes for non-residents (other than NRIs) without tax benefits. In Phase I, the NRs (other than NRIs) could be first provided with the FCNR(B) deposit facility, without tax benefits. In Phase II, the NR(E)RA deposit scheme, with cheque writing facility, could be provided to NRs (other than NRIs). The committee also recommended the government review the present tax regulations on FCNR(B) and NR(E)RA deposits for NRIs.

10 NRI investment in equities

At present, only NRIs are allowed to invest in companies on the Indian stock exchanges subject to certain stipulations. Foreign individuals are not permitted to invest in Indian equities. Only the registered FIIs are allowed to invest in equities within then overall limit, varying from 24 percent of a company's equities to 71 percent depending on the limits fixed by the RBI for different sectors and approved by the shareholders at the General Body Meeting. The Committee recommended that all individual non-residents should be allowed to invest in the Indian stock market though registered entities, including mutual funds and Portfolio Management Schemes and the money should come through bank accounts in India.

Capital outflows

1 Investments/remittances by residents

Resident individuals are permitted to remit abroad up to US$25,000 per year for current or capital account transactions or a combination of both. This can be used to open foreign currency accounts abroad. The total remittances under this facility for 2004 and 2005 were US$28.3 million and an additional US$1.9 million was remitted for immovable property. This means that nearly 1200 individuals used this facility, which is not a very large number. The Committee recommended that this annual limit be successively raised to US$50,000 in Phase I, US$100,000 in Phase II and US$200,000 in Phase III. Difficulties in operating this scheme should be reviewed. Since this facility straddles the current and capital accounts, the Committee recommends that where current account transactions are restricted, i.e. gifts, donations and travel, these should be raised to an overall ceiling of US$25,000 without any sub-limit.[92] Residents are also permitted at present to invest, without any limit, directly in such overseas companies as have a shareholding of at least 10 percent in an Indian company. For portfolio investments by resident individuals up to November 2005 the total remittance was US$13.7 million. The bulk of these remittances were in 2004–2005 and a trickle in 2005–2006. This facility is cumbersome to operate and in the context of the proposed large increase in limits for individuals indicated earlier, the Committee recommended abolition of this facility.

2 Outflows by Indian corporates and partnership firms

Indian resident corporates were permitted to make financial capital transfers abroad within a limit of 25 percent of their net worth. In 2003–2004 a total amount of US$11.13 million was remitted abroad. The later data are not available. Investment overseas by Indian companies/registered partnership firms up to 200 percent of their net worth was permitted. The outflows in 2005–2006 were reported to be US$3.1 billion.

3 NRI outward remittances

NRIs holding non-repatriable assets [including Non-resident Ordinary (NRO) Accounts] are permitted to repatriate up to US$ 1 million per calendar year out of balances held in NRO Accounts/sales proceeds of assets/assets acquired by way of inheritance. This is a major relaxation but the Committee was unable to obtain data on outflows under this scheme.[93]

This was a major relaxation, and since the Committee was unable to get the data on the outflows under this scheme it recommended the RBI collect and monitor data in respect of this scheme in view of the larger limit.

4 Indian corporate investment abroad

Recognizing that Indian industry is successfully building up its presence abroad, there is a strong case for liberalizing the present limits for corporate investment abroad. The Committee recommended that the limits for such outflows should be raised in phases from 200 percent of net worth to 400 percent of net worth. As part of a rationalization, these limits should also subsume a number of other categories; furthermore, for non-corporate businesses, it is recommended that the limits should be aligned with those for corporates.[94]

5 Foreign corporate bond issues

At present, only multilateral institutions are allowed to raise rupee bonds in India. To encourage, selectively, the raising of rupee denominated bonds, the Committee recommended that other institutions/corporates should be allowed to raise rupee bonds (with an option to convert into foreign exchange) subject to an overall ceiling, which should be gradually raised.

6 Foreign investment by mutual funds and foreign mutual funds

At present, only mutual funds are permitted to invest overseas, subject to stipulations for each fund. The Committee recommended that the various stipulations on individual fund limits and the proportion in relation to NAV should be abolished. The overall ceilings should be raised from the present level of US$2 billion to US$3 billion in Phase I, to US$4 billion in Phase II and to US$5 billion in Phase III. The Committee further recommends that these facilities should be available, apart from Mutual Funds, to SEBI-registered portfolio management schemes.

7 Forward contracts in the forex market

On the issue of forward contracts in the foreign exchange market, the 1997 Committee had recommended that participation should be allowed without any underlying exposure. The hedging of economic exposures was also recommended but not permitted. The basic principle underlying the 1997 Committee's recommendation has not been accepted by the RBI.[95]

Implementation of recommendations of fuller convertibility report

With the continuance of healthy growth in forex reserves and a robust economic environment, the Reserve Bank initiated moves towards fuller convertibility by quickly adopting several recommendations of the committee. Some of the important recommendations are highlighted below.

1   In order to provide greater flexibility to Indian companies for investments in Joint Ventures and Wholly Owned subsidiaries abroad, the overseas investment limit of 200 percent of their net worth was increased to 300 percent of net worth

2   The listed Indian companies had a separate limit of 25 percent of net worth for portfolio investment abroad in listed overseas companies. This limit was enhanced to 35 percent of net worth.

3   To give greater access to mutual funds for investment overseas the aggregate ceiling on overseas investment by mutual funds of US$3 billion was raised to US$4 billion.

4   The corporates were allowed prepayment of external commercial borrowings (ECBs) up to US$400 million as against the earlier limit of US$300 million without prior approval of the Reserve Bank.

5   Under the Liberalized Remittance Scheme for individuals they were permitted to remit up to US$50,000 per year under a current or a capital account transaction or a combination of both. This limit was raised to US$100,000.

6   The importers and exporters were given greater flexibility and freedom in booking forward currency contracts. The resident individuals were also given permission to book forward currency contracts up to US$100,000.

On the journey to fuller convertibility

The step-by-step approach to fuller convertibility is in line with India's gradualist reform strategy. Following the recommendation of the committee, a number of restrictions on capital account transactions have been further relaxed, liberalized, and caps raised. The progress on capital account liberalization will continue. And in this process capital account management will have to be less an exercise by the exchange control department and more a function of monetary and exchange rate policies. When one looks into the brave new world of full convertibility, one needs to take a wider, more holistic and synergistic view, going beyond the narrow confines of nuts and bolts of foreign exchange management and break away from the mindset of licenses and limits. Yet, several important accounting identities in the BoP have a crucial significance for a sustainable BoP equilibrium and will have to be screened and scanned for their sensitivity to important economic variables. A strong and real-time database, and a surveillance and alarm system suggested in the earlier chapter have to be in place. Full convertibility is a move towards a free foreign exchange market uncontrolled by the limits and bans of the exchange control department of RBI. While the progress is slow, we have to move in that direction. A number of discretionary and prudential controls on short-term inflows and outflows by the residents may continue for a longer period than anticipated and desired. There is more international recognition or acceptance for such prudential and discretionary controls now in the wake of several currency crises in the last decade or so.

A number of favorable and positive policy-induced developments have brightened the scenario on the economic, and BoP and forex fronts in India. The economic growth at 9.2 percent is nudging the 10 percent target to be achieved for the next five years. With the appreciation of the rupee by about 10 percent during Jan–April, 2007 the GDP figure has crossed US$1 trillion. Buoyancy in exports growth has continued, with exports touching the US$125 billion mark in 2006–2007. The larger trade deficit caused by the higher crude oil prices and growth momentum is counterbalanced by the higher growth in services exports and inward remittances. The foreign direct investments reached a record high of US$15 billion and was targeted to be US$25 billion by 2010. The FII portfolio investments continue to be strong at US$10 billion. The forex reserves have crossed US$200 billion, accounting for 13 months' imports and 20 percent of GDP. The industrial growth continues to be 10 percent+. With deregulation and reforms the telecoms industry in India has emerged as not only the fastest growing industry in the country but in the world, with India requiring 100 million mobile handsets in 2008 and another 400 million by 2010 to reach 650 million telephone connections.

The stock market is buoyant with the leading index Sensex growing by 102 percent in the two years ending may 2007. The market capitalization of Indian equities has reached US$950 million accounting for 95 percent of GDP. The Indian Industry has shown resilience in competing with the international giants in the liberalized environment. It has captured export markets, established a global presence and acquired overseas companies in the industries in which they have core competence, and comparative cost and skill advantage. The Indian steel giant, Tisco, recently acquired Corus in a US$13.2 billion deal. Vodafone acquired the Indian mobile telecoms company Hutchison Essar for US$11 billion. These trends are indicative of India responding to globalization with success.

India is not only the world's largest democracy but is also the most diverse and heterogeneous society in terms of language, culture, customs, beliefs, and even attire and eating habits. Further, Indian democracy is a multi-party system that has it own peculiarities affecting the political leadership that rules the country. From time to time, the country has swung from single-party rule to coalition politics, reflecting the complexity of factors determining the leadership and the shape and thrust which its economic policies will take. Hence, economic development in India is not just a matter of putting the financial equations and economic matrix in place. The econ-financial mathematics is governed and molded by the political process and reflects the common will of the people. In this electoral arithmetic, the political alignment in the multiparty system is very much analogous to the game theory in economics. Reviewing Indian society and its economic development, Amartya Sen, the distinguished Nobel prize winning economist and social scientist, has gone into the historical roots of the Indian society and its tradition of public reasoning and tolerance of intellectual hetero-doxy.[96] The modern and western concept of democracy, according to him, has only reinforced this ancient way of executing the societal changes in India with prior debate and discussion. Despite this very complex electoral arithmetic and political diversity, India has shown continuity in economic policies. The economic policies once adopted have their own momentum in bringing about a lasting change and development. This has been the very positive trait of the political leadership that has contributed to its sustained economic development. What has changed is the nature of change and the degree of thrust in the economic policies.

India is now on the threshold of a revolution triggered by the infrastructure and service industries. The agriculture and traditional industries would continue to grow at a much faster pace but the leading drivers of the revolution would be the infrastructure and services sectors. Both sectors would draw very little from the BoP but would be the major contributories to it. The infrastructure as well as services sectors have very low import intensity, but the positive BoP sensitivity of these sectors on the capital inflows and exports sides is large. As these sectors grow faster they would contribute to and strengthen the BoP through investments and exports. The stronger and broader-based BoP would pave the way for faster progress towards sustainable fuller convertibility.

15 Infrastructure development fund

Monetization of forex reserves for capital formation in infrastructure

Infrastructure is a sector in which India needs immense investment and its development would be one of the major factors governing the overall rate of growth of the economy as well as the manpower absorption in the economy. The requirements of the infrastructure are estimated to be of the order of US$320 billion for the next ten years. Hence, the source of large-scale finance for the infrastructure has been a constraint, which has handicapped its faster development in India. Bulging forex reserves offers a welcome opportunity for financing infrastructure projects.

During India's early stages of development, the central bank, RBI, played a positive, constructive, and developmental role in promoting both agricultural as well as industrial development. The RBI set up NABARD (National Bank for Agricultural Development) and IDBI (Industrial Development Bank of India), and subscribed to their initial capital and extended long-term capital, in order to promote agricultural and industrial development. The growth and development of NABARD and IDBI over more than three decades demonstrates the contribution these institutions have made to the agricultural and industrial sectors. Without these institutions, the growth of these sectors would have been seriously jeopardized. The RBI's proactive developmental role in NABARD and IDBI set a successful model for emulation by many other developing nations.

Having captured the take-off stage in the agricultural and industrial sectors, the Indian economy is now on the threshold of major growth in the infrastructural sector. Leaving the growth of these sectors entirely to the initiatives of the private sector or foreign enterprises would not only delay the speedier development of this sector but also limit its growth rate. The initial thrust needed in this sector has to come from the budgetary financing of large projects, which are beyond the ambit of the private sector.

In the US, funding for the Hoover Dam, one of the most ambitious irrigation and power projects, and the National Highway Network, which built arterial lines for the US economy, came from the Federal Budget. It is imperative now to initiate in India development of large infrastructure projects from the budgetary funding.

It would not be out of place for RBI also to play a major role in accelerating the slow pace of infrastructural development. RBI can create an Infrastructure Development Fund (IDF) by initially earmarking US$5 billion (Rs. 22,500 crores) of forex reserves for financing high priority infrastructure projects. The author suggested this in 2003. Lawrence H. Summers, President of Harvard University and former US Secretary of Treasury during his visit to India in March, 2006, strongly advocated the use of forex reserves for infrastructure financing and development, and recommended US$20 billion for this purpose. He also recommended heavy forex reserves guzzlers of Asia to shift away from liquid and safe US T Bills to more aggressive investments. He said:

> it's an irony of our times that the majority of the world's poorest people now live in countries with vast international financial reserves ... It is appropriate that some part of the focus of the international financial architecture move towards the challenge of deploying their large reserves as effectively as possible.[97]

Before waiting for international action to take place on this issue of excess forex reserves, we start following a new path and initiate the reform process. In India, Montek Singh Ahluwalia, Deputy Chairman, Planning Commission, has been an ardent advocate of what he called monetization of forex reserves for financing infrastructure projects through Special Purpose Vehicle (SPV) in Public Private Partnership (PPP).

Forex financing of infrastructure would have several advantages over the conventional modes of financing. The rationale for the use of forex reserves for financing infrastructural development is as follows.

1 The forex reserves have reached US$200 billion and are at a comfortable level from the point of view of import cover, debt servicing, short-term indebtedness, currency in circulation and broad money supply. The reserves earn 2 percent to 4 percent return on gilt and other investments abroad. Since the majority of reserves are held in US dollars, the depreciation of the US dollar is reducing the purchasing power of reserves in real terms. Instead of keeping these reserves in foreign financial assets, the situation of excess forex liquidity is a welcome opportunity for building national assets and raising capital formation and thereby driving the growth rate not only in the immediate future but in the long run, due to tremendous productivity gains arising from the new capital assets and the multiplier and accelerator effects they bring in successive years. Infrastructural assets would give much better economic and social returns.

2 Monetization of forex reserves would not raise Government rupee borrowing and affect the normal Government borrowing programme. It would not have the additional crowding out effect.

3 The Government would not have to enter the international market for borrowing. It would not have go through the regular due diligence exercise of

credit rating agencies and other formalities with global investment bankers. It would not increase Government external indebtedness.

4 Foreign currency borrowing by the Government in the international market would increase external debt and bring pressure on a spread for future private as well as Government external borrowings.

5 As a substitute to external borrowing, monetization of forex reserves would also avoid further accretion in reserves and its monetary expansionary effect.

6 Monetization of forex reserves for infrastructure financing would reduce the level of forex reserves of RBI.

7 Lowering of forex reserves would have an immediate contractionary effect on money supply.

8 The monetary expansionary effect of monetization of reserves would be delayed until rupee balances in the Infrastructural Development Fund are spent by the Government on projects.

9 Deficit financing or monetization for capital formation is less inflationary in the long run. Adequate supplies of inputs, mainly steel and cement, would avoid inflationary impact on their prices.

10 The higher employment potential of infrastructure projects would create more jobs and stimulate demand for consumer goods and help in raising the overall economic growth rate. The backward and forward linkages of infrastructure spending have larger employment generating effects.

11 The longer term impact of this infrastructure financing would be to permanently raise the growth rates in agriculture, industry and services sectors through their backward and forward linkages.

Infrastructure development fund (IDF) versus foreign direct investment (FDI)

12 Compared to Foreign Direct Investment (FDI), the use of forex reserves for creation of Infrastructure Development Fund (IDF) investments in the infrastructure has several advantages.

    i Foreign direct investment would initially inflate forex reserves due to the inflow of foreign currency funds. Compared to this, the use of forex reserves through the Infrastructure Development Fund (IDF) would reduce the level of reserves and pre-empt any monetary expansion.

    ii The import intensity of infrastructure investments is expected to be very low due to the use of domestic equipment, materials and resources. In highly sophisticated projects such as airport and seaport modernization, there would be imports whose intensity is not likely to be very high. A rise in consumption imports due to a growth in disposable incomes is also not likely to be high due to a relatively low import propensity of Indian consumers. Despite the heavy reduction in tariffs on consumer goods, the imports have not gone up substantially due to the availability of competitive domestic products. Hence, the claim that foreign direct investment would reduce forex reserves by causing a growth in imports is not tenable due to the fact that Indian industry largely provides a wide range of consumer and capital goods at globally competitive prices, quality and technology. India's import dependence is only on highly advanced technical equipment, which would not have much import intensity in infrastructure projects.

iii   Compared to FDI (foreign direct investment), the forex financing through IDF would keep the control of these projects in Indian hands.

iv   Forex financing through IDF could be used as a supplementary quasi-financing cushion to large projects with FDI (foreign direct investment). Hence, a model would evolve of joint venture and joint financing under PPP, which would give a greater degree of confidence to foreign investors for quicker financial closures and execution of projects.

v   The IDF could also be used to provide supplementary financing to Indian private investments in such projects.

Modalities of monetization of forex reserves

The modalities of monetisation of forex reserves are as follows.

1   The Government issues Infrastructure Development Bonds (IDB) (denominated in US dollars) of US$5 billion.

2   The IDBs will have ten-year tenure and carry a libor minus rate payable quarterly or half yearly. The rate could also be a fixed rate.

3   The RBI would subscribe to the bonds and transfer dollar balances to the Government Account, called the Infrastructure Development Fund.

4   The RBI would sell forex in the Fund and create rupee balances for the Government whenever the Government has to draw rupee resources for project funding

5   The sale of forex in the market would reduce the money supply.

6   The money supply would increase when the Government spends rupee balances out of the Fund for projects.

7   In order to provide the Indian paper and dollar instrument from the Government in the global financial market, the RBI could later, if required, offer these bonds in the international market in limited lots. The bonds could be listed and freely tradable.

8   The Government would create an amortization fund for the repayment of the bonds over a ten year period.

Economic wisdom, and political vision and pragmatism

Economic wisdom is very difficult to define. What was economic wisdom in the nineteenth century became 'conventional wisdom' in Galbraith's terms in the depression years. Contemporary economic wisdom cannot remain as such if it is unable to grapple with the new economic realities, and then it becomes 'conventional wisdom'. Conventional wisdom can be dangerous for politicians and policy makers. Global economic history is full of critical moments when a failure to jettison conventional wisdom and adopt new paths unleashed economic disasters. A balanced budget was an anachronism in the 1930s. Roosevelt was the first and biggest Keynesian who shed the conventional wisdom of a balanced budget and, with the New Deal, changed the course of US as well as global economic history. Keynesianism became global and economic depression became history ever since. The once-forgotten seventeenth century economist, Adam Smith, became the hero of the wave of liberalization and globalization since the 1980s, after being politically resurrected by Thatcher in the UK and Reagan in the US. Friedman's monetarism elbowed Keynesianism out of political caucus when stagflation and its dark economic fallout shook the ruling political system. The Laffer curve and supply side economics ruled in the era of an increasing budget deficit reaching a record level in the Reagan era. Volcker's dear money policy restored the strength of the US dollar in the international market but only at the cost of record high interest and a sharp recession in the US. Cheap money, soft dollar, trade deficit and a buoyant stock market guided Greenspan's monetary management in the 1990s. Economic theories developed in response to the imperative need to view and analyze pressing economic problems or phenomena differently and with new glasses due to the inadequacy of the existing body of knowledge and theories to grasp them.

India's infrastructural needs stretch across road and highway transportation, railways, ports, airports, power, water, communication and also education and health. When the economy is in such a fortuitous state, if we do not capitalize now on our forex reserves and its growth, we may have missed the opportunity forever. When the US built its highway system it was most ambitious programme in US history. On June 29, 1956, President Eisenhower signed the Federal-Aid Highway Act to create the Interstate Highway System – the greatest public works programme in history, financing US$33.5 billion over a 13 year period. The system created a network of road transportation throughout the US that became the lifeline and growth pad for the US economy, and also a part of American culture and its way of life.[98]

India and China: different models – IDF, fuller convertibility and floating exchange rate versus FDI, exchange control and fixed exchange rate

It is possible to get bogged down by conventional wisdom again, which becomes one of the biggest handicaps at the turning points in any nation's history. We have to seize this most opportune and precious time in Indian's history and catapult the economy into the 10 percent growth orbit. Along with full convertibility, the creation and execution of IDF would give India a lead over the FDI route and usher a new development model compared with China, which relied only on FDI, exchange controls and fixed exchange rates. Instead, India will have IDF, fuller convertibility and a floating rupee as the focal points of its model. The conventional wisdom of 3.5 percent fiscal deficit applies more to the mature economies. A revenue deficit is a more important concern and needs to be eliminated quickly. India is now in a stage of infrastructure shortage. Liberalization has transformed the commodity shortage economy into a commodity surplus economy. In the second phase of reform now, it has to resolve the problem of a huge infrastructure gap that is widening fast under the pressure of a fast growing economy. The growing imbalance between private goods and public goods is a top priority problem.

It is coincidental that India is now in the state the US was in, in the mid 1950s. Galbraith made a brilliant analysis of this malaise faced by the American economy then, in his most popular and ground breaking book, *The Affluent Society*, portraying the paradox of private affluence and public squalor.[99] The Indian economy has graduated from the gains of reform to the next phase of reform, with the biggest challenge from the rapidly increasing shortage of public goods and infrastructure. India now suffers from the Galbraithian paradox. It needs a Galbraithian remedy. After the publication of *The General Theory* by Keynes, it was the US and not the UK that implemented it, by increasing Government spending and turning the balanced budget into deficit to cure unemployment. A balanced budget was the conventional wisdom then, which nobody wanted to violate. History is testimony to the success of this policy, in banishing economic depression from the face of the earth in the twentieth century. At this time in history, when the economy is facing one of the biggest infrastructural gaps, no conventional remedy will tackle this gigantic task. A 3.5 percent fiscal deficit norm is not sacrosanct for India. It will handicap its investment growth. The Economy is now geared to embrace full convertibility and bridge the last mile in the resources gap that alone can tackle the gigantic infrastructure issue.

The foregoing unconventional proposal has now been accepted by the Government. After great deliberation in the Reserve Bank of India, the Planning Commission and the Ministry of Finance, the Finance Minister, P. Chidambaram – one of the chief architects of reform and who also spearheaded the second phase of liberalization – in his Budget speech in February, 2007, announced the setting up of a Special Purpose Vehicle (SPV) of US\$5 billion from the forex reserves for the purpose of financing infrastructure projects. The funds will be used for capital imports and co-financing foreign borrowings for infrastructure projects. The government will also guarantee return on of more than 3.5 percent to the central bank on the funds borrowed. The success of this initial enterprise should pave the way for larger mobilization of forex reserves to meet a much bigger infrastructural gap.

Summary and conclusions

There is growing consensus on the use of excess forex reserves of the BoP surplus emerging market economies for more productive purposes. In 2003, the author recommended the use of India's forex reserves of US$5 billion in creating of Infrastructure Development Fund (IDF) to finance large infrastructure projects in highways, airports, power, irrigation, ports and other areas, both in public, private and joint sectors. The SPV, of US$5 billion, has now been set up for the purpose. Larry Summers recently advocated India using US$20 billion for this purpose. India's infrastructure needs to expand fast to keep up with pressure of demand from the surplus commodity sector, which has developed fast with liberalization and reforms. The Galbraithian paradox of the affluent society, reflecting the growing imbalance between public and private goods (expanding the infrastructure gap), needs to be corrected speedily to avoid serious roadblocks to moving towards a 10 percent growth path. In fact the policy to resolve this imbalance through the IDF mechanism itself would, with a big investment push, accelerate the momentum of the economy, and also remove bottlenecks to the higher growth of industry, agriculture, foreign trade and most dominant services sectors – which will have multiplier benefits from a bigger and better infrastructure. Conventional wisdom and a 3.5 percent+ fiscal deficit need to be given a back seat for catalytic economic change.

Notes

1 Galbraith, John Kenneth, *The Affluent Society*, Houghton Mifflin Company, New York, 1998.
2 Faveryear, A. E. *The Power of Sterling*, 1931. (Gold prices in 1934, 1980, 2005 and 2006 are given by the author).

Table N1 Gold price, 1257–2006

Year	Price per fine troy ounce		Percentage change per annum over the previous year	
	in shillings	in dollars		
1257	17/09			
1351	26/10		0.56	
1465	40/03		0.47	
1546	60/00		0.62	
1611	74/08		0.36	
1632	80/11		0.38	
1717	84/12	20.67	0.06	
1934		35.00	0.32	
1980		850.00		50.60
2005		450.00		−1.18
2006		650.00		55.55

3 Galbraith, John Kenneth, *Money – Whence It Came, Where It Went*, Bantam Books, 1976, pp. 190–91, 203.
4 Galbraith, John Kenneth, Ibid. pp. 202–3.
5 Ibid. p. 203.
6 Galbraith, John Kenneth, *The Great Crash*, Penguin Books, 1975.
7 Stewart, Michael, *Keynes and After*, Penguin Books, 1967.
8 Galbraith, *Money*, p. 203.
9 Bernanke, Ben, *Essays on The Great Depression*, Princeton University Press, 2007, pp. 70–107.
10 Stewart, pp. 76–7.
11 For an excellent account of criticism of Keynesian prescription of deficit financing in Britain and the US refer to the works of Galbraith (*Money*, Chapter xvi, *The Coming of J. M, Keynes*, pp. 263–84) and Stewart (*Slaves of Defunct Economists*, pp. 72–7).
12 For detailed account of the policy of 'benign neglect' and its adverse effects on the

global economy and monetary system when it outlived its utility, refer to the author's book. Nayak, S. S., 'Global Monetary Experience and India', Kedien, Mumbai, 1991, pp. 32–45.

13 Brahmanada, P. R. *Gold Money Rift*, Vora Publications, 1969. Professer Brahmanada saw the imminent collapse of the gold-dollar standard in 1969 when he analyzed the problem of US external liquid liabilities exceeding the value of its gold stock at the price of $35 an ounce of gold, and its implications for the instability of the global monetary system and international market price of gold.

14 Agtmael, Antoine van, *The Emerging Markets Century: How A New Breed of World-Class Companies is Overtaking the World*, Simon & Schuster, New York, 2007.

15 Bernstein, Peter L., *Against the Gods – The Remarkable Story of Risk*, John Wiley & Sons, 1996, pp. 247–83. Bernstein gives an excellent account of how theories of risk, probability and game by Markowitz, von Neumann, Arrow and Sharp in their effort to measure and quantify the Risk-Reward Matrix in portfolio selection and allocation, revolutionized the profession of investment management.

16 John Williamson coined the term Washington Consensus, giving articulation to the new reform policy in the emerging markets. See *Latin American Adjustment: How Much has Happened*, edited by John Williamson, Institute for International Economics, 1990.

17 Stiglitz, Joseph, *Globalization and its Contents*, Penguin Books, 2002, p. 215.

18 Soros, George, On globalization, *Public Affairs*, 2002.

19 Sen, Amartya, *Argumentative Indian*, Penguin Books, 2005, pp. 341–2. The words in brackets are added.

20 Galbraith, John Kenneth, *The Affluent Society*, Houghton Mifflin Company, New York, 1998. The concept of conventional wisdom and its impact on economic policies was first developed by Galbraith in this book, first published in 1958. This has had a tremendous impact on the interaction between new economic thought and policy making by the political leadership.

21 Myrdal, Gunnar, '*Asian Drama – An Inquiry into the Poverty of Nations*', Vintage Books, 1972, p. 120.

22 Myrdal, Gunnar, *Asian Drama*, p. 110.

23 Ibid. p. 122.

24 Sachs, Jeffrey, *Making the Brady Plan Work, Foreign Affairs*, 68 (3) (Summer, 1989), p. 91.

25 Lamfalussy, Alexander, *Financial Crisis in Emerging Markets*, Universities Press, 2002, p. 70.

26 Bernstein, Peter L., *Against the Gods – The Remarkable Story of Risk*, John Wiley & Sons, 1996, pp. 247–55. It gives an excellent account of the application and impact of Markowitz's theory and tools of measuring risk on fund and investment management in the US during the period.

27 Raghuram G. Rajan and Luigi Zingales, *Saving Capitalism from the Capitalists – Unleashing the Power of Financial markets to Create Wealth and Spread Opportunity*, Crown Business, New York, 2003, p. 70.

28 Ibid.

29 Agtmael, van Antoine.

30 Roger G. Ibbotson and Gary P. Brinson, *Global Investing*, McGraw Hill, 1993, p. 61.

31 Ibid.

32 Source: Zephyr Style Advisor: SsgA Advisor Consulting Services Research. The MSCI Emerging Markets Index comprises 26 countries and targets to capture 85 percent of free float-adjusted companies within each industry group in every country, 2004.

33 Singal, Vijay, *Beyond the Random Walk*, Oxford University Press, NY, 2004, p. 238.

34 Singal, Vijay, pp. 238–9.

35 Houthhakker and Magee, *Income and price elasticities in world trade*, *Review of Economic Statistics*, LI, (2) May 1969, pp. 111–25.

Table N2 Income elasticities in world trade (annual data in 1951–66)

	Income elasticity of demand for imports	Rest of the world income elasticity for country's exports
USA	1.51	0.99
UK	1.66	0.86
Japan	1.23	3.55
Italy	2.19	2.95
France	1.66	1.53
Canada	1.20	1.41
West Germany	1.80	2.08

Source: Houthakker and Magee (1969, p. 113).

36 IMF, *World Economic Outlook – Spillovers and Cycles in the Global Economy*, Chapter 3, Exchange Rates and the Adjustment of External Imbalances, Table 3.2, April, 2007.
37 Nayak, S. S., *op. cit.* For a review of the dual gap approach in analyzing BoP problem, pp. 67–78.
38 *Globalization, Growth, and Poverty – Building an Inclusive World Economy*, World Bank and Oxford University Press, 2002, pp. 31–2.
39 Refer to the following for a theoretical treatment of US dollar policy in the 1960s. Haberler, G. and Willet, T., *A Strategy for US Balance of Payments*, American Enterprise Institute, Washington, 1971. Klause, L. B., *A Passive Balance of Payments Strategy for the US*, Brookings Papers on Economic Analysis, No 2, Washington, 1970.
40 Meade, James, *The Balance of Payments*, Oxford University Press, London, 1951.
41 Botta, Joseph, *The Federal Reserve Bank of New York's Experience of Managing Cross-border Migration of US dollar banknotes*, BIS Papers No 15. The paper gives an excellent account of analysis and measurement of US dollar notes abroad and their costs and benefits.
42 Bernanke, Ben, Chairman, The Federal Reserve Board, The speech on *'Globalization and Monetary Policy'* given at the Fourth Economic Summit, Stanford Institute for Economic Policy Research, Stanford, California, March 2, 2007.
43 Botta, Joseph, *op. cit.*
44 Skidelsky, Robert, *John Maynard Keynes – Fighting for Freedom – 1937–1946*, Volume Three, Penguin Books, 2000, pp. 205–32. The most comprehensive and extensively researched and documented biography of Keynes published in Three Volumes, is a masterpiece and an eloquent account of the ins and outs of Keynes' life, writings and the world around him.
45 Cohen, Benjamin, in *The Future of The Dollar, Global Currency Rivalry: Can the Euro Ever Challenge the Dollar?*, ICFAI Books, The ICFAI University Press, India, 2006, pp. 1–30.
46 Woodward, Bob, *Maestro – Greenspan's Fed and the American Boom*, Simon & Schuster, New York, 2000, pp. 27–8.
47 Woodward, Bob *'Maestro – Greenspan's Fed and the American Boom'*, Simon & Schuster, 2000, pp. 221–22.
48 Galbraith, John Kenneth, *The Affluent Society*, Mentor Book, 1963, pp. 183–4.
49 Keynes, John Maynard, *The General Theory of Employment, Interest and Money*, Macmillan & Co Ltd, London (First published in 1936, Reprint 1961), pp. 316–17.

50 Keynes, John Maynard, pp. 321–2.
51 Ibid., pp. 315–16.
52 Ibid., pp. 322–23.
53 Ibid., pp. 322.
54 Bogle, John C. *Commonsense on Mutual Funds*, John Wiley & Sons, 1999.
55 Schumpeter, Joseph A., *Capitalism, Socialism and Democracy*, Harper, New York (first published in 1942), 1975, pp. 82–4.
56 Keynes, John Maynard, *op. cit.*, p. 319.
57 Stiglitz, Joseph, *Globalization and its Discontents*, Penguin Books, 2002, p. 48.
58 *Financial Markets Tick by Tick-Insight in Financial Markets Microstructure*, Ed. by Lequeux, Pierre, John Wiley & Sons, 1999.
59 Pierre Richard Agenor, Marcus Miller, David Vines and Axel Weber, *The Asian Financial Crisis – Causes, Consequences and Consequences*, World Bank Institute, pp. 11–12.
60 Lamfalussy, Alexander, *Financial Crisis in Emerging Markets – An Essay on Financial Globalization and Fragility*, Universities Press, 2002, p. 112.
61 Alba, Pedro, Bhattacharya, Amar and others, 'The Role of Macroeconomic and Financial Sector Linkages in East Asia's Financial Crisis', in *The Asian Financial Crisis: Causes, Contagion and Consequences*, Ed by Pierre-Richard Agenor, Marcus Miller, David Vines and Axel Weber, World Bank Institute, 2001, p. 13.
62 Sebastian Edward, On Crisis Prevention: Lessons from Mexico and East Asia, in *'Financial Markets and Development – The Crisis in Emerging Markets'*, Ed. by Alison Harwood and others, 2001, pp. 277–8.
63 Bhattacharya, Amar and Miller, Marcus, Coping with crisis: is there a 'silver bullet'?, in *The Asian Financial Crisis: Causes, Contagion and Consequences*, Ed by Pierre-Richard Agenor, Marcus Miller, David Vines and Axel Weber, World Bank Institute, 2001, pp 364–5.
64 *The Asian Financial Crises – Causes, Contagion and Consequences*, p. 59.
65 Lamfalussy, Alexander, *Financial Crisis in Emerging Markets*, Universities Press, 2002, pp. 166–7.
66 Jagdish Bhagwati, *In Defense of Globalization*, Oxford University Press, 2004, pp. 199–207. Bhagawati gives logical and cogent reasoning behind the fallacy of premature capital account convertibility with unregulated capital flows in the emerging markets.
67 Galbraith, John Kenneth, *The New Industrial State*, Houghton Mifflin Company, Boston, 1967, pp. 22–45.
68 Soros, George, pp. 6–7.
69 Stiglitz Joseph, p. 74.
70 This section followed by sections an titled Comparative Analysis of the BoP Stress, Savings Gap – Capital Consumption, and Corrective measures are reproduced/adapted from the author's earlier book, *Global Monetary Experience and India,* Ibid., pp. 138–47.
71 A crore in India is ten million. Rs.2500 crores (crs.) are Rs.25,000 million or Rs.25 billion.
72 *The Asian Financial Crisis – Causes, Contagion and Consequences*, Ed by Pierre-Richard Agenor and others, World Bank Institute, 2002, p. 10.
73 Indian Economic Survey 2002–2003, Government of India, January 2003, pp. 105–6.
74 For an analysis of India's remittances growth refer to, Chisti, Muzaffar, *The Rise in Remittances to India – A Closer Look*, Migration Policy Institute, February, 2007. www.migrationinformation.org.
75 Hicks, John R., *Value and Capital – An enquiry into some Fundamental Principles of Economic Theory*, Oxford University Press, 1939, pp. 30–5.
76 Nayak, S. S., *Exchange rate policy under the regime of floating rates – a critique of Indian experience,* Economic and Political Weekly, XII (3), January 1977, pp. 55–66.

77 Sections on rupee Exchange Rate Policy and basket peg or managed floating are adapted and updated from Nayak, S. S., *op. cit.* pp. 147–50.
78 Consolidated Gold Fields, UK, Annual Reports.
79 This section is adapted and updated for latest figures and data from Nayak, S. S., pp. 150–3.
80 Tobin, James, Global capital flows: should they be regulated?, in *World Finance and Economic Stability – Selected Essays of James Tobin*, Edward Elgar, UK, 2003, p. 38.
81 Draft in italics gives progress in respect of the recommendation.
82 This chapter is a part of the Report on titled *Convertibility Report* submitted to The Reserve Bank of India and the Committee on Fuller Convertibility in May, 2006 for their consideration for Policy Towards Full Convertibility of Rupee. Ranade, M. G., *Present State of Indian Manufacturers and Outlook of the Same*, Thackers & Co., 1898, pp. 50–1, 57.
83 Reddy, Y. V., *India's foreign exchange reserves: policy, status and issues Economic and Political Weekly*, May 18, 2002, p. 1911.
84 Jalan, Bimal, *Exchange Rate Management: An Emerging Consensus?*, Speech delivered by the Former Governor, Reserve Bank of India at National Assembly of Forex Association of India, on August 14, 2003.
85 Report of the Committee on Fuller Convertibility of Capital Account Convertibility, Reserve Bank of India, pp. 1–2, 158–9.
86 Ibid., p. 13.
87 Ibid., p. 18.
88 Ibid., p. 18.
89 Ibid., p. 11.
90 Ibid., p. 12.
91 Ibid., p. 43.
92 Ibid., p. 146.
93 Ibid., pp. 19–20.
94 Ibid., pp. 144–5.
95 Ibid.
96 Sen, Amartya, pp. 12–16.
97 *The Wall Street Journal, March 25, 2006. p. B5.* 'Reflections on Global Account Imbalances and Emerging Markets Reserve Accumulation', *L. K. Jha Memorial Lecture by Lawrence H. Summers, Reserve Bank of India, Mumbai, India, March 24, 2006.*
98 US Department of Transportation, Federal Highway Administration, has created a website on the 50th Anniversary of the Eisenhower Interstate Highway System giving its history and other details, www.fhwa.dot.gov/interstate/homepage.cfm.
99 John Kenneth Galbraith, *The Affluent Society*, Houghton Miffin Company, Boston, New York, 1958.

Bibliography

Book and articles

Agenor, Pierre-Richard, Miller, Marcus, Vines, David, and Weber, Axel, (Eds), *The Asian Financial Crisis – Causes, Consequences and Consequences*, World Bank Institute, 2001.

Agtmael, Antoine van, *The Emerging Markets Century: How A New Breed of World-Class Companies is Overtaking the World*, Simon & Schuster, New York, 2007.

Ahluwalia, Montek Singh, Reddy, Y. V. and Tarapore, S. S., *Macroeconomics and Monetary Policy: Issues for a Reforming India*, Oxford University Press, 2002.

Aluwalia, Isher Judge, and Little, I. M. D., (Eds). *Indian Economic Reforms and Development – Essays for Manmohan Singh*, Oxford University, India, 1998.

Basu, Kaushik (Ed.) *India's Emerging Economy, Performance and Prospects in 1990s and Beyond*, Oxford University Press, 2005.

Bernanke, Ben, Chairman, The Federal Reserve Board, The speech on *Globalization and Monetary Policy* given at the Fourth Economic Summit, Stanford Institute for Economic Policy Research, Stanford, California, March 2, 2007.

Bernanke, Ben, *Essays on The Great Depression*, Princeton University Press, 2007.

Bernstein, Peter L., *Against the Gods – The Remarkable Story of Risk*, John Wiley & Sons, 1996.

Bhagwati, Jagdish, *In Defense of Globalization*, Oxford University Press, 2004.

Bogle, John C., *Commonsense on Mutual Funds*, John Wiley & Sons, 1999.

Botta, Joseph, *The Federal Reserve Bank of New York's Experience of Managing Cross-border Migration of US Dollar Banknotes*, BIS Papers No 15.

Brahmanada, P. R., *Gold Money Rift*, Vora Publications, 1969.

Brandt, Willy, *North-South: A Program for Survival – The Report of the Independent Commission on International Development Issues*, Pan Books, 1980.

Cohen, Benjamin, *The Future of The Dollar, Global Currency Rivalry: Can the Euro Ever Challenge the Dollar?*, ICFAI Books, The ICFAI University Press, India, 2006.

Chisti, Muzaffar, *The Rise in Remittances to India – A Closer Look*, Migration Policy Institute, Washington D C, February, 2007.

Faveryear, A. E., *The Power of Sterling*, 1931.

Galbraith, John Kenneth, *The Affluent Society*, Houghton Mifflin Company, Boston (First published, 1958), Mentor Books, New York, 1963.

Galbraith, John Kenneth, *The New Industrial State*, Houghton Mifflin Company, Boston, 1967.

Galbraith, John Kenneth, *The Great Crash*, Penguin Books, 1975.

Galbraith, John Kenneth, *Money – Whence It Came, Where It Went*, Bantam Books, 1976.

Galbraith, John Kenneth, *The Culture of Contentment*, Houghton Mifflin Company, Boston, 1992.

Galbraith, John Kenneth, *A Short History of Financial Euphoria*, Viking, New York, 1993.

Gilder, George, *Telecosm – How Infinite Bandwidth Will Revolutionize Our World*, The Free Press, New York, 2000.

Gross, Daniel, *Bull Run: Wall Street, the Democrats, and the New Politics of Personal Finance*, Public Affairs, New York, 2000.

Haberler, G. and Willet, T., *A Strategy for US Balance of Payments*, American Enterprise Institute, Washington, 1971.

Harwood, Alison, Litan, Robert E. and Pome-leano, Michael, (Eds), *Financial Markets and Development – The Crisis in Emerging Markets*, 2001.

Hicks, John R., *Value and Capital – An Enquiry into some Fundamental Principles of Economic Theory*, Oxford University Press, 1939.

Houthhakker, Hendrir S. and Magee, Stephen P., *Income and Price Elasticities in World Trade, Review of Economic Statistics*, LI (2), May 1969.

Ibbotson, Roger G. and Brinson, Gary P., *Global Investing*, McGraw Hill, 1993.

IMF, *World Economic Outlook – Spillovers and Cycles in the Global Economy*, Chapter 3, Exchange Rates and the Adjustment of External Imbalances, April, 2007.

Issak, Robert, *The Globalization Gap*, FT Prentice Hall, New Jersey, 2005.

Jalan, Bimal, *The Future of India: Politics, Economics and Governance*, Viking, Penguin Group, India, 2005.

Jalan, Bimal, *Indian Economy in the New Millennium – Selected Essays*, UBS PD, India. 2002.

Jalan, Bimal, *Exchange Rate Management: An Emerging Consensus?*, Speech delivered by the Former Governor, Reserve Bank of India at National Assembly of Forex Association of India, on August 14, 2003.

Jalan, Bimal, *The Indian Economy – Problems and Prospects*, Penguin Books, India, 2004.

Keynes, John Maynard, *The General Theory of Employment, Interest and Money*, Macmillan & Co Ltd, London (First published in 1936, Reprint 1961).

Klause, L. B., *A passive balance of payments strategy for the US, Brookings Papers on Economic Analysis*, No 2, Washington, 1970.

Krugman, Paul, *The Accidental Theorist: And other Dispatches from the Dismal Science*, W W Norton & Co., New York, 1998.

Lamfalussy, Alexander, *Financial Crisis in Emerging Markets – An Essay on Financial Globalization and Fragility*, Universities Press, 2002.

Lamfalussy, Alexander, *Financial Crisis in Emerging Markets*, Universities Press, 2002.

Lequeux, Pierre, (Ed.), *Financial Markets Tick by Tick-Insight in Financial Markets Microstructure*, John Wiley & Sons, 1999.

Mandelbrot, Benoit, B. and Hudson, Richard, L., *The (mis)Behavior of Markets: A Fractal View of Risk, Ruin and Reward*, Profile Books, Great Britain, 2004.

McElvaine, Robert, S., *The Great Depression: America, 1929–1941*, Times Books, Random House, New York, 1984.

Meade, James, *The Balance of Payments*, Oxford University Press, London, 1951.

Mohan, Rakesh, (Ed.), *Facets of the Indian Economy*, Oxford University Press India 2002.

Myrdal, Gunnar, *Asian Drama – An Inquiry into the Poverty of Nations*, Vintage Books, 1972.

Nayak S. S., *Global Monetary Experience and India*, Kedien, Mumbai, 1991.

Nayak, S. S., *Exchange rate policy under the regime of floating rates – A critique of Indian experience, Economic and Political Weekly*, XII (3), January 1977.

Niederhoffer, Victor, *The Education of a Speculator*, John Wiley & Sons Inc., 1997.

Ohmae, Kenichi, *The Borderless World: Power and Strategy in Interlinked Economy*, Harper Business, 1990.

Phillips, Kevin, *Arrogant Capital: Washington, Wall Street and the Frustration of American Politics*, Little, Brown and Company, 1994.

Rajan, Raghuram G. and Zingales, Luigi, *Saving Capitalism from the Capitalists – Unleashing the Power of Financial markets to Create Wealth and Spread Opportunity*, Crown Business, New York, 2003.

Ranade, M. G., *Present State of Indian Manufacturers and Outlook of the Same*, Thackers & Co., 1898.

Rangrajan, C., *Indian Economy – Essays on Money and Finance*, UBSPD, India 1998.

Reddy, Y. V., *Lectures on Economic and Financial Sector Reforms in India*, Oxford University Press, India, 2002.

Reddy, Y. V., *India's foreign exchange reserves: policy, status and issues, Economic and Political Weekly*, May 18, 2002.

Reserve Bank of India, *Report of the Committee on Fuller Convertibility of Capital Account Convertibility*, July, 2007.

Review of Economic Statistics, LI (2), May 1969.

Sachs, Jeffrey, *Making the Brady Plan work, Foreign Affairs*, 68 (3) (Summer), 1989.

Sachs, Jaffrey, *The End of Poverty: Economic Possibilities of Our Times*, The Penguin Press, New York, 2005.

Schumpeter, Joseph A., *Capitalism, Socialism and Democracy*, Harper, New York, (First published 1942), 1975.

Sen, Amartya, *The Argumentative Indian – Writings on Indian History, Culture and Identity*, Penguin Books, New York, 2005.

Singal, Vijay, *Beyond the Random Walk*, Oxford University Press, New York, 2004.

Skidelsky, Robert, *John Maynard Keynes – Fighting for Freedom – 1937–1946*, Volume Three, Penguin Books, 2000.

Soros, George, *On globalization, Public Affairs*, 2002.

Soros, George, *Alchemy of Finance: Reading the Mind of the Market*, Touchstone, 1987.

Stewart, Michael, *Keynes and After*, Penguin Books, 1967.

Stiglitz, Joseph, *Globalization and its Discontents*, Penguin Books, 2002.

Stiglitz, Joseph, *Making Globalization Work – The Next Step to Global Justice*, Allen Lane, Great Britain, 2006.

Stiglitz, Joseph and Charlton, Andrew, *Fair Trade for All: How Trade Can Promote Development*, Oxford University Press, NY, 2005.

Summers, Lawrence H., *Reflections on Global Account Imbalances and Emerging Markets Reserve Accumulation*, L.K. Jha Memorial Lecture Reserve Bank of India, Mumbai, India, March 24, 2006, The Wall Street Journal, March 25, 2006, p. B5.

Tarapore, S. S. *Capital Account Convertibility – Monetary Policy and Reforms*, UBSPD, India 2004.

Thurow, Lester C., *Fortune Favors The Bold – What We Must Do to Build a New and Lasting Global Prosperity*, Harper Collins, 2003.

Tobin, James, *Global capital flows: should they be regulated?* in *World Finance and Economic Stability – Selected Essays of James Tobin*, Edward Elgar, UK, 2003.

Woodward, Bob, *Maestro – Greenspan's Fed and the American Boom*, Simon & Schuster, New York, 2000.

World Bank, *India's Five Years of Stabilization and Reforms and the Challenges Ahead*, Washington DC, 1996.

World Bank and Oxford University Press, *Globalization, Growth, and Poverty – Building an Inclusive World Economy*, 2002.

Annual reports and surveys

Bank for International Settlements, Annual Report.

Bureau of Economic Analysis, Government of the United States.

Consolidated Gold Fields, UK, Annual Report.

Government of India, Economic Survey.

International Monetary Fund, Annual Report; World Economic Outlook, Survey.

Reserve Bank of India, Annual Report, Report on Currency and Finance.

World Gold Council, Annual Report.

Index

For Product Safety Concerns and Information please contact our EU
representative GPSR@taylorandfrancis.com
Taylor & Francis Verlag GmbH, Kaufingerstraße 24, 80331 München, Germany